Uncle John's
73 Classic Events

Narrated by **John R. Gohmann**

Transcribed by **Patrick Naville**

UNCLE JOHN'S 73 CLASSIC EVENTS

Narrated by: John R. Gohmann
Transcribed by: Patrick Naville

DEDICATION

This book is dedicated to my father, Herbert R. Gohmann, Jr. My favorite names for him were Dad, Father, Grandpa, Bud, Herb, and the Old Man.

Dad attended Christ the King Grade School, Manual High School, and received his Civil Engineering degree from the University of Louisville (U of L) Speed School. He was an officer on a minesweeper in the Navy in WWII.

He was the father of six and founded his own construction business in 1950, the year I was born. He was the owner of two limestone quarries and a trucking company. Dad was a lover of the outdoors, hunting, fishing, boating, barbecuing, woodworking and reading.

My father loved his dogs, Misty, Sugarfoot and Rocky, and they were as much like family to him as his own children.

Dad had a fondness for Hereford cattle, Gilbey's gin, fine scotch, Camel cigarettes and Roi-Tan cigars. He also loved his time at his condo at the Palms in the Florida Keys, at Islamorada, the sportfishing capital of the world.

One of his hobbies was raising flowers and plants in his greenhouse.

He was on the Floyd County Bank Board of Directors, and was also a board member at the Providence Retirement Home in New Albany.

Dad was also very excited and happy to watch two of his sons and one of his daughters take over the business and expand its construction activities by some 100%.

He was a member of the American Legion and strongly believed in God and country, but to me, he will forever be the Commander-in-Chief.

Thanks for everything you did for us, Dad. You might be gone, but you're not forgotten. I love you and miss you.

Your #3 son, John

Also by John R. Gohmann

Paving My Way Through Life . . . With Tenacity!

Table of Contents

Table of Contents, cont.

Table of Contents, cont.

Death leaves a heartache
no one can heal,
love leaves a memory
no one can steal.

From a Headstone in Ireland

Uncle John's
73 *Classic Events*

Many men go fishing
all of their lives without knowing
that it is not fish they're after.

Henry David Thoreau

1

~ Airplane Rides ~

As I recall, it was back in 1964, or thereabout. I had my first opportunity to take a ride on an airplane. It was my father and me, and one or two of my brothers (I don't recall exactly who was along). Thinking back, I can still see the blue, twin-engine DC-3 parked outside the hangar at Stanford Field in Louisville, Kentucky.

The air that morning was damp, cold and very windy as we stepped out of the building. We walked across the tarmac and up the three steps into the side door of the plane.

There weren't many seats on board the small craft, two on each side of the narrow aisle and maybe three to five rows deep. Dad and I were in the third row back and I was given the window seat. I can still recall the nervous excitement that was building in me.

A uniform-clad, female hostess of sorts stood at the head of the rows and instructed us on the safety precautions we were to follow while on the flight. The door to the plane closed with a slam and I heard the loud, metallic click of a heavy bolt as it was locked. We were almost ready for takeoff.

Looking out the tiny window, I watched a man dressed in coveralls walk up to the prop of the engine. He reached up, grabbed the highest blade, gave it a long hard pull down and quickly stepped back from it. The propeller spun, hesitated, then spun again almost as if it was trying to decide whether to come to life or not. I heard the sputter of the engine as it belched and farted, coming to life. The propeller began to rotate and in less than a second, was a blur of movement.

Moments later the plane was rolling. We turned out onto, and taxied down the runway. Looking out the window, I watched the ground flash past faster and faster as the plane picked up speed. It rattled and shook and seemed to take forever when suddenly, the ground fell away as we lifted into the air.

The engine droned loudly as we ascended up at a sharp angle. I felt myself being pushed back in the seat. Within minutes we were in the clouds and unable to see the ground. The engine's noise tapered off to a normal level as the plane reached its cruising altitude.

As the journey continued, I asked Dad about the possibility of what would happen if a wing broke off. He smiled and said, "Son, just sit back and enjoy the ride. It won't be long before we'll be in Marathon in the Florida Keys and doing what we both love—catching fish!"

"Okay," I said. Looking out the window, I asked, "Why is the motor vibrating and shaking so badly? And look," I said, pointing out the window, "there are two bolts out there on the wing rattling and bobbing up and down." I noticed there was also an oil-like substance oozing from the motor cover. It ran down the wing, caught the back draft, and was blowing into the air creating a greasy film on the window I was looking out.

Dad replied with, "Son, pull the shade down and take a nap, or have a look-see at the airline magazine; everything will be just fine."

About that time, the plane lurched up, then dropped down. I felt like I was on a roller-coaster. It shook, groaned and squeaked. The flight lady instructed us to buckle up. She said we were in for a rough ride from here on in.

Feeling nauseated, I looked at Dad and said, "Pop, I think I'm going to puke!"

He said, "Hold it, son," and from the tattered pocket of the seat-back in front of me, he pulled a white paper bag with a draw string. He handed it to me. "If you can't hold it, puke in this bag."

I swallowed hard fighting back the sour taste and lump in the back of my throat. Luckily I managed to avoid filling the bag. It looked like my first flight was turning out to be a good one!

We landed and I commented, "Wow, that was a short flight. Are we in Marathon?"

Dad said, "No, son, we're not even out of Kentucky yet."

Come to find out, we were on the mail-run flight. This up and down scenario would play out no less than eight more times before we actually landed in Florida.

While in the air, the hostess asked if I wanted a drink of water or perhaps a soda. I told her a soda would be nice and was given a glass bottle of Coke and an opener, which I had to return to her.

Dad ordered a few small bottles of Beefeater gin and a bottle of 7-Up. He later requested some cigarettes and was handed some thin packs that held three or four smokes—Camels, as I vividly recall.

Out came Dad's Zippo lighter. He smoked one after another and deposited the butts in the ashtray on the armrest of the seat. When it was full, he passed the butts to me and I'd pack them into the ashtray on the other armrest. The ashes were sprinkled on the floor.

There was no toilet break, no moving around ... no nothing. Finally, after about the fifth stop, we were able to use an outhouse by a hanger while we waited for a load of mail. Soon, a small van arrived and blue-green canvas and leather bags with *US MAIL* printed on them were transferred from the van to our plane. No sooner than the load had been transferred, we were back on board and in the air again.

We did arrive finally in Marathon. We spent too short of a week fishing and having a great time, only to repeat the fine DC-3 plane ride on the return trip home. Man, what a flight to remember!

We repeated this trip once or twice a year for the next few years. Looking back, it sure seems like a long time ago.

As time went on, I took many other prop plane rides, as well as flights on jets (both large and small), private and commercial, intercontinental and even helicopter and military planes of all sorts, makes and models, but those DC-3 flights to Marathon in the Florida Keys will *never* be forgotten. Many times over the years, I've reached back in my file and these good memories from the past have come to life.

2

~ Ice Tea to Ice Cubes ~

Back in the 50s and 60s, cool water and ice tea were the drinks of choice. Water was kept in a glass pitcher in the icebox—the predecessor to the refrigerator, for those of you too young to know what that was.

We were required to use the same glass all day. Later, we were allowed to use a paper cone from the dispenser mounted by the kitchen sink. When the pitcher ran low, we were to fill it with water from the tap, which came from one of the two cisterns where hauled-in water or rainwater was caught and stored.

For the most part, only a grown-up was allowed to open the top freezer door, empty an ice tray and place the cubes in a white porcelain tub kept there for that purpose.

The top shelf in the refrigerator always had a glass gallon jug of milk. We later switched to plastic jugs. We were allowed to drink the cool milk whenever we wanted, and boy, we sure did!

In the door rack of the fridge, a long, tall bottle of Canada Dry Ginger Ale was forever present. This was only to be consumed by the adults. They mixed it with their Yellowstone whiskey. Once in awhile, you might sneak a drink of the ginger ale, but if you got caught, you paid the price.

Drinking directly from the pitcher, milk bottle or ale bottle was strictly forbidden. If you tried it and got caught, the adults made sure you'd never forget it. There were only a few times I ventured to drink from the bottle, but fortunately, I was never caught.

The standard breakfast beverage was percolated coffee with a spoonful of powdered creamer. The kitchen always smelled wonderful when that morning pot of coffee was bubbling and gurgling on the stove and steam drifted from under the lid.

Orange juice was served at every breakfast. The OJ was made from a small, frozen can that claimed it was fresh from Florida. And of course, there was always plenty of cold milk.

Lunchtime came at 12:30 sharp. Our normal drink at that meal was Kool-Aid made in a frosty-cold, aluminum pitcher and served in colorful tall aluminum cups. Nothing tasted better and most times it was green, orange, or grape.

Since sugar was pretty expensive back then, we sweetened the drinks with just a tad of it coupled with the artificial sweetener, saccharin, which came in small pink bags and was on all of the tables in restaurants.

Suppertime usually came between 5:30 and a quarter to six. Ice tea was our favorite beverage of choice for that meal, while water and milk were also available. After dinner, coffee was served. Back then there was no such thing as decaf, cappuccinos or other creamy, frosty, *frou-frou* beverages.

At seven or eight o'clock in the evening, it was hot tea time. A pot of water was boiled on the stove, but later, an electric teapot was used. A little milk in the tea was common along with one square lump of white sugar—but sometimes the cube might be brown in color. Later, we'd get a drink of water and then we were off to bed.

All weekdays were the same as far as our drink choices, but occasionally on Saturdays, we were treated to a Coke, Seven-Up, Pepsi or RC (Royal Crown) Cola—whatever was cheap and on sale at Kroger's.

Later, in my teenage years, we experimented with and refined our sodas by adding peanuts, M&M's, cherries, syrup—usually cherry or chocolate if we could get our hands on some—or whatever else we could find. The soda came in returnable bottles.

Sometimes we had other fruit juices that came in a tall can which was opened with a wedge-shaped, hand-held unit, the same tool the older folks used to open their cans of beer. There always seemed to be a big can of V-8 juice opened in the fridge with a thick tomato crust around the triangle opening.

Once in a while, when visiting my uncle and aunt, we were treated to a small bottle of Welch's Grape Juice. It was dark and sweet and had a wonderful flavor.

Free run of the things to drink back then was not an option. There were no cases of soda pop or other sweet drinks sitting around the house, nor was there money in your pocket to run and purchase a soda or other drinks when the feeling struck you. There were no fast-food places with carry-out to speak of, except for White Castle, and it was too far from home to be practical.

School lunches were pretty much the same every day. We all carried our lunch in a brown paper bag and returned home with the same bag to be used for the week. I remember the lunch milk we got at school was warmer than what we had at home. It came in a small glass bottle with an aluminum cap. The kids who worked the cafeteria lines—"Cook kids" we called them—got to punch holes in the aluminum cap for the straw with a small tool of sorts that fit on two fingers.

The glass bottles were later replaced with paper cartons. Today, most everything is throwaway glass, plastic, or paper. Looking back on it, we were ahead of our time in the recycling game.

Today, whiskey, wine, beer, pop, and beverages of all sorts pretty much come in disposable containers with twist caps. This has essentially eliminated the need for specially designed openers or for corks and other devices to be used for sealing the containers, once opened. Granted, there are a lot of wines that still use corks and the really decent ones will continue to do so. But ease of opening and closing a container is here to stay.

Personally, I'd like to see us go back to a simpler time. A time when life moved at a slower pace; a time when we didn't get so bent out of shape and ready to sue over every little thing ... a more innocent time when people had a lot more respect for each other. A time when I could open the icebox and get that cold glass of water or ice tea!

3

~ Gordon Lodge–Door County, Wisconsin ~

In the mid to late 80s and early 90s, my wife and I started family vacations up to Door County, Wisconsin. These annual trips went on for several years until our daughter and her good friend, Ms. J, grew older and our pace of life seemed too slow, and now boring, to them.

I would borrow an SUV from work, hook up our canoe and trailer, load her to the gills with gear and supplies and off we'd go to a cabin on the lake at the Gordon Lodge. It was about a nine-hour drive, not counting the short stop we always made to visit my sister and brother-in-law at their home on the bluff of Lake Michigan, just south of Waukegan. We'd refuel, eat, visit a while, and then be back on the road heading north.

Two-thirds of the way up the peninsula was Door County. There, nestled in the woods on 130 acres at 1420 Pine Drive in Bailey's Harbor, was a place called the Gordon Lodge. The lodge was named after Dr. A.J. Gordon and his wife. They'd built their first summer home among the evergreens and sparkling waters of North Bay 80 years ago.

The excitement would build as we'd turn off the county highway and head east down a long, winding road. We all had the same feeling … *almost there!* The road stopped at the edge of Lake Michigan on the grounds of Gordon Lodge.

The lodge was located on a heavily wooded, mosquito-infested large tract of land. Strategically placed on the grounds were small, rustic, two-bedroom log cabins. The grounds were immaculate and with beautifully manicured lawns, the atmosphere was most inviting. When we'd arrive, it always felt like *we were home!* We managed to get the same cabin each year and in that regard, we knew what to expect.

The cabins and furnishings, along with the main dinner house and bar set right next to the pristine waters of the lake. Each time we went there, it was like the clock stopped and the place was frozen in time.

We rode bikes, hiked in the woods, drove golf balls into the lake, fished from our canoe and caught many a fine lake perch. It was always so peaceful and relaxing canoeing among the coves and inlets.

A favorite memory of mine was, we would canoe into a cove and would ease our way into an area the size of a football field covered with black diver ducks—cormorants. These long-necked birds had distensible pouches under their bills for catching and holding fish.

We'd sit and listen to the quacking, fussing and frolicking of our feathered friends and after a few minutes or so, I'd say, "Okay, girls, clap your hands!" and all at once, the larger-than-life flock would smartly rise into the air. The sight and sound was truly amazing. To see it and be a part of it always felt like a once-in-a-lifetime event.

The Lodge was a place where you enjoyed your three meals a day, at the same time and in the same building. The Lodge was your only food source for miles, and all of your needs were met which was great because once you were in place—and a beautiful place it was!—you didn't want to leave.

We'd stay two weeks at a time and Friday nights were my favorite. Dinner at the Lodge was served promptly at seven and consisted of all the fried lake perch you could eat along with all the trimmings. Two ice-cold Budweisers were included. I have yet to repeat the taste, the setting, the friendship and camaraderie of being there with family and newly acquired friends on the lake and watching the sunset.

Saturday night was movie night in the local town. It was about a twenty-minute or so drive. The movie house was located in a World War II Quonset hut, which looked like the top half of a very large galvanized pipe sitting on the ground. The price of admission was one dollar per head. All of the snacks, candy, pop, etc. were also one dollar each.

The theater urinals were tall white porcelain units. They ran from the floor up to your shoulder. Two pots sat side by side in an opening along the wall, and a galvanized ten-inch gutter attached to the wall ran at an angle from left to right to maintain a downhill water flow. It was yet another place to relieve one's self. While restrooms don't generally captivate me, this one was truly a step back in time to experience.

As you entered the theater part of the hut, unlike today's super-theaters, there were no raised rows or seats. Everything was on the same level. The wooden chairs had curved backs and were very similar to the rows of old schoolhouse classroom seats.

The show would start with a safety film that was around three minutes long. A *Road Runner* cartoon would follow, then the main attraction was presented. I still remember the movie—it ran two summers in a row. It starred Tom Hanks in *Forrest Gump*, and boy, what a movie it was! After that run, they showed another feature with Tom Hanks, *Apollo 13*. It, too, was an edge-of-your-seat film. The movies they showed were all of the highest caliber and left an everlasting impression on me.

Another memorable event was after lighting a fire in the cabin fireplace. Even in the summer, the air cooled at night and a nice crackling fire was very pleasing. The four of us would sit, sipping our sodas, telling stories and making memories that would last a lifetime.

One night, a large bat flew out of the fireplace. It fluttered and darted about the room. Screams, followed by panic and chaos, erupted from all of us. (Truth be told, I think the bat was more scared than we were!) My wife dove under a table, screaming. My daughter, also screaming, ran into the bedroom and hid in the closet. Ms. J and yours truly, *Old Dad*, quietly walked out the front door of the cabin.

The panic and screams continued inside and tears were flowing. Ms. J calmly walked over to the Lodge and reported what was going on. The bartender rode his golf cart over to the cabin, slowly walked in, and with a water glass in one hand and a square piece of cardboard in the other, captured the bat.

He instructed those who were hiding to come out … the danger was over! He smiled and assured us that this happened all the time, although, to us, it didn't seem all that funny at that point. Looking back on it though, it brings a smile to my face and I have a fond remembrance of a great family moment.

One of the side trips we'd make while on vacation at Gordon Lodge was to drive over to Egg Harbor which was located on the west side of the peninsula. It was roughly a 17-mile drive. I think it got its name because instead of sandy beaches, it had smooth, flat stones that resembled eggs. It was a quaint little town and as of 2010, only boasted a population of approximately 200 residents. On our return trip to Gordon Lodge, we stopped in a small village—the name escapes me at the moment—and there, we enjoyed our first boiled fish dinner. It was excellent!

Those vacations at Gordon Lodge flew by way too quickly, and before we knew it, we'd be on the road heading back to Indiana. There was a lot of silence on those drives home. All of us were lost in our thoughts of the wonderful time we'd just had. On top of that, we were eagerly awaiting our *next* return visit to the Gordon Lodge!

4

~ Virgin Gorda - Paradise Found! ~

It was sometime in the 1990s. Our daughter was now a teenager and it was Spring Break. Our route was American Air—Louisville to Charlotte, NC, then down to Miami, FL. From there we flew to the Virgin Islands and our last stop was at Virgin Gorda.

On this last leg, we were on a small, four-seat, prop plane. Our bags were carefully arranged so as to not overload the plane or cause any weight shifting.

Problems: daughter and wife were in the back seats. I was flying shotgun—also called the navigator seat—and there, behind the controls, was Captain Clutch Cargo! He was a rather short man, had the goggles on along with the leather helmet and a Snoopy scarf like something out of WWI. He looked like he should be climbing into a bi-plane, giving a thumbs-up sign, ready to take on the Red Baron.

I had the feeling that this was going to be the flight from hell. As if to confirm my suspicions and to top off the pilot's appearance, he was perched on two old, thick telephone books complete with yellow pages.

The plane labored and sputtered down the runway, which was a grass strip that ended at the water's edge. Amazingly, we somehow got airborne. We made a circle over the terminal, a concrete block, one-level building with a one-plane garage door and a red windsock flying overhead.

The plane's noise was deafening. We were unable to hear the pilot speak. He just pointed and smiled. The scenery was beautiful though. The water below was a deep indigo blue as far as you could see. After a while, small specks appeared on the horizon and as we got closer, we could make out small islands—rugged terrain, high mountains and thick underbrush.

As we neared our island, "Captain Clutch" killed the motor and glided over it. An eerie quiet came over us. I questioned him as to why we had no power and wondered if we were in trouble.

"No sir," he said, "we're saving fuel." He mentioned something about riding the air currents over the land.

A short time later we were circling what looked like a speck in the water below. All at once the plane started to dive. My wife had her eyes closed and our daughter was screaming and crying.

Out of nowhere, we spotted a red windsock, an outhouse and a building the size of a one-car garage. There, along a narrow strip of sand, was an open slice of beach that was the landing strip and down we went. The plane hit the hard-packed sand and bounced high as the wings dipped side to side. This was followed by another one or two jumps and bounces, then it came to a stop just feet from the garage. Waiting for us was what looked like a 1964 short-bed Ford pickup truck with an old auto seat mounted in the bed facing backwards.

We climbed into the seat and the local native driver loaded up our suitcases, bags and what looked like a trunk on wheels—my wife's suitcase. Off we went again. This part of our journey took us up and over a fairly large mountain pass on a long, windy road and down the other side to a mountain village with very small homes, and a dock on the water's edge. Here, we were loaded onto a small ferryboat for a twenty-minute cruise to our final destination—Virgin Gorda.

We were among the thirty or so guests on the ten-day stay. We were escorted to our rooms on the lee (windy) side of the island. We had our own private cabin on the water's edge with a deck extending out into the water. Because the island was small, we could not only watch the sunrise, but also watch it set. The view was stunning!

Being on the windy side, the music or sound of the waves crashing below the deck was like a mild sedative. Counting the stars, which looked like a million sparkling diamonds scattered on a carpet of black velvet, and with no foreign light to distort the view of the Big and Little Dippers, sleep came easy.

Every morning where the distant water met the sky, we'd watch the sun rise in all its majestic glory. What an everlasting picture in one's mind!

At the highest point on the island, which was within walking distance from our cabin—or a golf cart ride for those who didn't feel like hoofing it—was an oblong-shaped, open-air building—the dinner mount. It was the only place to dine for your three meals a day. Breakfast, lunch and dinner, and each one featured fantastic gourmet food.

Every other night, one of the meal choices was fried flying fish. My beverage of choice with this wonderful dinner was Red Stripe beer. To this day, flying fish rates high in my book for great eating. Its flavor is right up there with Michigan lake perch and yellowtail snapper from down in the Keys.

The evenings dining in the open air to the setting sun was more stunning every night. Dessert was helping yourself to an array of many fine cheeses and olives, sipping Port and watching the fiery ball of the sun slowly sink into the ocean and soon thereafter, watching the millions of stars fill the night sky.

There was a pristine beach on the leeward side of the center high point of the island. There was a small gift shop and activities included shuffleboard, cards and other various game and sports.

My favorite escape, which was included in our package, was the private use anytime I wanted of a 12-foot Boston Whaler with a ten-horse Johnson outboard. It came complete with three life jackets, a paddle, a small cooler of water and juice, and an anchor made of a round granite stone. It had a hole through it with a long thin cord attached.

There were many pools, inlets and small bays, many of which were bare and some with light vegetation, that were all waiting to be explored and enjoyed. My favorite memory for some reason was a lonely out-of-the-way island about the size of a baseball infield. It was in the middle of the open water not often found or visited by the tourists. It was used by the local folks to unload their daily catch. It was also where they'd discard the most beautiful conch shells. These were piled high over the entire small island. Searching for ones without any chips came easy and we filled our duffle bag with every trip out to the island. Many of those conch shells are spread around our house and property back home on Floyd's Knobs.

Another pleasant surprise was snorkeling. You didn't have to go far out, just over and around a bend of the coastline. On one such venture, I saw a beautiful woman, whose body had been blessed by the sun, slowly walking along through the rocks on a winding path to who knows where.

Later that day, I found that path and walked along it for a half-mile or so. Unbeknownst to me up to that point is, it led to a deep water port on the farthest remote point of the island. It was called "The Bitter End," and there wasn't much of anything to speak of there. There was a general store where large sailboats and other watercraft stocked their galleys with food and essentials to continue on their journeys.

There was a waterside open-air bar with tap beers of many kinds, which I sat and enjoyed for the longest time. I felt as if I had discovered paradise! As much as I hated leaving this new gem I'd discovered, I walked back to the VG resort. The family was enjoying some quality time on the beach and lunched on the foods delivered to them there.

While we relaxed on the beach, a warning came for all swimmers to clear the water and move back. To our surprise, off to the left and about 100 yards out in the ocean, a large waterspout had formed and was twisting along the beachfront. It was truly a sight, sound and feeling one will never forget.

Come Sunday morning, we were off to attend Mass, Virgin Gorda style! The priest was a half hour late. He arrived by way of boat from another service on another island somewhere. Mass was held in an open air bar—there were no church buildings.

We had our own bar table. The priest was in front of the bar and used a tall table as his altar. Behind him and over his head, was a very large wood carving of a big-breasted, naked sea woman much like what would be found on a large, old-time, wooden sailing ship

The Hosts were made of some kind of island bread-concoction and had a corn taste. Instead of wine, rum was used which I suppose was traditional for the island

When mass was completed and the services had been rendered there was a mandatory donation amount one must make. I recall it was something like two dollars per head. The congregation all paraded down to the dock and saw the priest off. Once he was out of sight, we all returned to the bar and had rum punch drinks, fruit and cheese. This was one of two Sunday Masses I will never forget, and I long to attend another one … Amen, Brother!

Time flew by and the ten days seemed like only a day or two. Leaving was sad and I think we all were a little misty-eyed. The journey home was a repeat of the flying excitement but on a lower scale. Knowing what awaited us on our return home had a way of bringing you down. It would be back to work, back to school, and back to our normal routine of life in southern Indiana.

My departing memory was of checking through customs—I believe it was in North Carolina—with our many suitcases, a trunk, a duffel bag of swimming gear, and bags of souvenirs. The Customs official commented, "Who in the world taught you and your family how to pack?"

Back at home, our dog was returned by my niece who was babysitting it, groceries were bought from Jay C Market and our bags were deposited in our various rooms. Life went on and it felt as though we had never left our home in Floyd's Knobs, Indiana.

5

~ Borrow Pit - Scottsburg, Indiana ~

It was June in the summer of 1973 on a warm Saturday morning. I had the day off from work—finally. My dad, brother and I had a one-day fishing trip planned. We got an early start and I had the 14-foot Jon boat on the trailer along with an electric motor hitched and ready to roll.

I also had lunches made, drinks in the cooler, including a few pink cans of Tab, Dad's drink now that the hard stuff was behind him. We made a quick stop at the White Castle and we were on our way.

One hour later we're sitting in the middle of a large borrow pit. For those of you who aren't familiar with the term, a borrow pit is a location, usually off-site, but not always, from where a construction project is taking place. A contractor will excavate needed fill material from this site—"borrowing it"—to use in another location on a project he's building. The resulting hole can be used in a variety of ways. It can be used as a depository for other unwanted excavation materials and eventually filled in, it can be used as a detention/retention pond for runoff from the construction site or, in this case, it can be converted into a pond or lake.

The pit, which was now a lake, was located just off I-65 at the Scottsburg exit. The property was owned by a friend and construction competitor of my father's. The pit had various depths of water ranging from a few feet deep to some that exceeded 100 feet at the far west end.

The lake was an open body of water with willows and cattails surrounding a good part of the bank line. I was on the back seat facing the transom. I operated the motor and was casting my favorite plug straight back, catching one big bass after another and quickly filled the fish bag.

Being my normal self and getting excited when I caught something, I was cutting up, carrying on, hooting and hollering after every catch. As I recall, I was six for six (six casts - six fish) with all of them in the box.

Dad sat in the middle seat facing forward and was casting his bait to the right side of the boat. He'd catch a small one every now and then and was in a rather unpleasant mood. Along with me rocking the boat, I'd bother him with, "Hand me a drink from the cooler," or, "Hand me a snack," or I'd be standing with my hand on his shoulder for support as I relieved myself over the edge of the boat. Of course, my good father was downstream.

There in the bow of the boat, was my brother casting to the left and also catching a few keepers. He too was delivering commands to Dad to pass him this, hand him that—"Give me another piece of bait," or, "Put this fish in the bag."

At one point, he said, "Boy, brother, you sure picked a good fishing spot. I never caught so many keepers—just one after another!"

As most fishing buddies know, with three in a Jon boat, the middle seat is a lot like sitting in the middle seat of a three-hole outhouse. The middle man wipes like a girl, keeps his eyes forward and his comments to himself.

This good fortune went on for the better part of the morning on mine and my brother's part. Seeing a likely spot to cast, I held my Lew's Speed Stick, which was equipped with my left-hand crank Garcia 500, open-faced, bait-caster reel along with my favorite lure, my Bayou Buggy which I had been given from my good friend, Jimmy, back in Bastrop, LA.

I gave the fishing rod a real hard double pump and reached back as far as I could in an attempt to cast it into a patch of cattails. My rod came forward but my Bayou Buggy didn't. I then gave her another good pump and that's when Dad came off his seat and onto my back.

I shouted, "Get off of me! I'm trying to fish!"

Dad calmly said, "Son, turn around and get this hook out of me."

To my surprise, one barb of the treble hook on my Bayou Buggy was buried deep in the skin of my father's neck.

Dad had loose skin on his neck, a lot like the skin on an old snapping turtle. My double pump had stretched the hole in Dad's neck to where removing the hook was quite an easy chore. As I laughed, and my brother stared in disbelief, good old Dad quietly sat there while I removed the hook.

I could feel the steam rising though, and once the hook was

removed and my red bandana was tied around Dad's neck to staunch the flow of blood, Dad calmly managed to get himself out of the boat, in three feet of water. He slowly walked his way to the bank, over to the truck and off for home he went.

My brother and I kept fishing. With no cell phones at the time, we debated on who would make the long hike back to the truck stop near the interstate and call for help. To our surprise, my good friend, Nick, drove up with the truck and fished a while from the middle seat. Come sundown, we headed for home.

Monday came and back to work we went. Not a word was mentioned about the great fishing, or the hook in the neck that happened up at George L's borrow pit that past Saturday.

6

~ Elderberries, Green Head Flies ~
and Bees

Down in Harrison County on the banks of Buck Creek, which runs through my friend's father's 15 acres of trees and high weeds, was a deep waterhole full of goggle eyes and red hearts sunfish. A private "Honey Hole" for sure.

Along this stretch of creek, the elderberries grew long, tall and healthy and were heavily loaded with perfect black, round, juicy, ripe berries. This year I was making a 10-gallon crock of elderberry wine. If you know anything about making this fine wine, it takes a lot of berries.

I harvested the berries into large plastic trash bags using pruning shears. I'd snip the berry-laden flowers a few inches below the fruit, and in the bag they'd go.

When I got home, I'd put a few branches of berries in a brown Kroger bag and shake it for a few minutes which dislodged the fruit from the branch. I'd then pour the lush berries into a giant colander which I'd purchased for two dollars at the Mount Saint Francis yard sale at a time when funds were short and my income was rather sparse.

My homemade wine filled the bill! The mighty fine squeezings were a bit tart, but when spiced up with a half-gallon of Christian Brothers Brandy, the wine took on a pleasing taste with a bit more kick than regular store-bought wine.

It never fails that while out on these outdoor adventures, the call of Mother Nature seems to strike me at the oddest moments. It takes a lot of elderberries to make wine, and after a few trash bags full, I'd managed to down quite a few cold, Falls City beers. This was not long after I'd earlier consumed four sliders (White Castle grease bombs, also questionably known as hamburgers) and a black coffee.

It was no wonder that the bowel movement from hell was rapidly approaching. As the urge hit, I dropped the harvest bag, ran a few yards into the tall grass and weeds and stomped down an area about six feet in diameter so as to have a spot for an what was shaping up to be a super morning constitutional!

Squatting, as if perched on a five-gallon bucket, I proceeded to let all hell break loose. The immediate release was heavenly.

Before I could wipe my ass with my blue bandana, wetted from the creek for my equivalent slice of Charmin bath tissue, I was attacked!

I have no idea where the Green Head flies appeared from, and in swarms, but they seemed to attack your ass and your deposit there on the ground. They immediately, and very aggressively, buzzed your face and attempted to land on your nose, lips, head and ears with their now feces-laden bodies.

To make things worse, the excreted pile of digested matter landed squarely on top of a yellow-jacket nest there in the ground. Angrily, they swarmed out and up like a load of buckshot. Needless to say, I was stung multiple times on both cheeks of my ass some six inches down from my tail bone. It amazed me how fast I could run with my pants down around my ankles while the swarm chased me!

In spite of that, there was no way I was going to let this ruin my day of finally fishing in the Honey Hole. I baited my cane pole and braced it in a Y of a willow tree I'd cut and stuck deep in the ground on the shore. My shirt came off which I used as my beach towel. Seeing no one around, I dropped my trousers and shorts.

As I fished, I straddled my bare ass on a cold can of Falls City to relieve the pain and swelling from the bee stings. When the can of beer warmed to less than ice-cold, I'd replace it with another one from the cooler and would consume the one I'd just removed from my butt cheeks.

This played out for the rest of the day. Finally, after a short nap on the creek bank, and with my stringer full, it was now time to gather up my bags of elderberries, my cooler and call it a day. I headed to my home by the tracks back in good old New Albany. A little sore in the ass, but happy with my take for the day!

7

~ An Interesting Experience Shared ~
Only with Me and Bobby L.

I don't tell stories; fabricate places or happenings about people, especially about a dear friend. While every person in this story is real, the names I use for them are false. My following comments are factual and fall into the category: SHIT HAPPENS!

In 1987, Bobby was invited to come along on the Gohmann Company Florida Keys fishing trip, sponsored by RUDD Equipment Company. Rudd picked up the tab for the four-day trip. Dick Morehead, the sales rep for RUDD, carried the credit card, but he was certainly not the group leader.

I, along with Bobby, my brother Jim, my brother-in-law, Roger, and, I might add, Jackass Dick Morehead, made up the fishing party.

We departed Bowman Field in RUDD's company jet. Two hours later we were in Marathon Florida, down in the Florida Keys. My friend Little Sam Snow was there to meet us with a van and packed us up to Islamorada. Big Sam Snow is Little Sam's father and they are good people.

At mile marker 80, my dad had a small condo in The Palms. It was close to Bud & Mary's, the marina we fished out of. Jim, Roger and I, being family, stayed at the condo with my father and stepmom. Bobby and Salesman Dick got a room at the Breezy Palms—a no-tell motel if there ever was one!

We all had dinner at Papa Joes, across Highway One, and afterwards, drove Dad and Mom back to the condo. With the night still young, we boys decided to help bolster the local economy by paying a visit a few miles up the Key to "WOODIES STRIP CLUB" in Islamorada.

We were having a great time, but since it was nearing midnight and we were all pretty well toasted, we decided to head back to the condo. Dick Morehead decided he needed a few more drinks, so we left him at the club and dropped Bobby off at the Breezy Palms on the way home.

Bobby was fast asleep in his double bed when Dick came home at a little after two in the morning. Bobby said he was awoken by someone in his bed, *stroking his backside!*

He said he quickly turned, threw the haymaker of his life and busted Dick's lips wide open. Then he threw him out of the bed. Old Morehead spent the night on the floor and also stayed there most of the next day. He never made it to the dock and was left behind.

Bobby and I were fishing from the same flats boat near Flamingo, Florida. I noticed Bobby acted a little distant and I could tell something was troubling him. I asked him what was bothering him and after some hesitation, he told me about what had happened back at the motel the night before. He made me promise to never talk about that night with anyone.

Well, the two of us passed live shrimp and cold beers back and forth the whole day. We even won the Big Fish and the Big Boat contests —the Big Boat was having your three big fish in the boat.

I'VE KEPT HIS SECRET ALL THESE YEARS!

Since he's departed this world, I'm sure Bobby doesn't care now. Those were the good old days!!! (Well - maybe not *all* of the things that happened were so good).

Keep fishing, Bobby, and I'll see you in my memories the next time I pull into Woodies.

Your FRIEND ... John G.

8

~ The Farm and Finches ~

The story begins sometime around the summer of 1997, give or take a year. A few years prior, my wife and I, along with two other family members, purchased 375 acres down in Harrison County, just two miles north of the Ohio River. Over the years with subsequent purchases of adjoining land, the farm has grown to 1000 acres, plus or minus. It offers prime deer and small game hunting.

Later we added a cabin, and after that, a three-acre fishing lake. Today on this pristine piece of terra firma, gravel roads have replaced the old dirt logging roads; fences have been mended; trash timber has been harvested and the fields are mowed.

Approximately 30% of the land is sharecropped. It might be beans one year and popcorn the next. Occasionally a winter wheat crop is planted and harvested. It's a neat, well-groomed and cared-for piece of land.

From Day One of our new ownership and occupation of this parcel, the property was overgrown with milk and thistle weeds, locust, gum and willows along with just about every other species of trash trees and wildflowers of all kinds.

The property was littered with junk and farming waste. It had two barns (both in a very dilapidated condition), a corncrib, two chicken houses and a burned-out farmhouse.

The first year or two, we explored the property on foot. Weekly trips were the norm. It was usually family, and sometimes a friend of our daughter's would accompany us. Each of us was equipped with boots, insect repellent and tick spray, a water bottle and energy bars of different types, and we always carried a sturdy walking stick too.

On one occasion, we were just 50 yards from the old barn. The weeds were waist high. We were on the path that would take us to the upper, or high land, area of the farm.

I was leading the group through the weeds and sure as shit, I had the misfortune of stepping on a very large snake! When I say large, I mean this sucker was something like ten or twelve feet long and was as big around as a fire hose!

At one point, I was actually balancing myself up off the ground while hanging onto my walking staff, and glad I was a pole vaulter in high school! As I would come down, I'd step on another section of the snake and up on the pole I'd go again. All the while, the three ladies behind me—my wife, daughter and her friend—were laughing their asses off and wondering what was going on.

I took off running through the field and continued pole vaulting myself away from the snake. Stepping on him must have really pissed him off because even though I ran and jumped, he stayed right after me.

After three or four minutes of sheer panic on my part, I guess the snake tired of chasing me and lost interest. I was able to escape his fury without so much as a scratch, although I'm sure the episode did a number on my heart! The snake's make, model and sex are unknown to me even to this day. After things calmed down, we continued on our hiking adventure.

The next summer the clean up was slow but we were making progress. We teamed with a reputable farmer in the area for the sharecropping and went with a mix of corn, beans and winter wheat for the rotation of the crops and mowing program. Our property was really shaping up into a fantastic hunter's and nature lover's paradise.

A John Deere Gator was added to our growing collection of farm tools and machinery. The next season, at the edge of a large planted field some 75 acres in size, we added three acres of wildflowers. It was a square plot of land surrounded on three sides by crops while one side paralleled the main dirt road that ran through the property. The area surrounding this 75 acre-plus field was surrounded by woods, which were also part of the farm property. It was an excellent site for stargazing as there was no artificial light for miles.

It was late in the summer on a cool Saturday afternoon; my wife, our daughter and I were driving the J.D. Gator around the farm. Along the edge of the field approaching the wildflower plot, we flushed a covey of quail. They glided low to the ground and landed just inside the wildflower plot. I vividly remember saying, "Hold on girls, were going after those quail." Into the expansive field of colorful wildflowers we went with the Gator wide open and moving fast.

Just inside the waist-high flowers, we kicked up the covey and again they flushed up in front of us. The brown and white flash of color, accompanied by the loud flutter of wings and that special *CHEEP* sound a quail makes when startled can only be appreciated by the avid hunter, birdwatcher or a lover of nature.

A moment later we flushed a large bunch of bright yellow finches—the technical term for a group of finches this large is a "charm." They exploded into the air from 360 degrees around us on a now-stopped Gator. The sudden burst of hundreds of the beautiful yellow birds and the sound they made as they took flight was beyond belief. It's hard to describe that sound and the only thought I had was that it must have been a gift from God.

We were surrounded by a vortex of yellow that lasted for several minutes. I estimate that the size of the charm was nearly three-quarters of a football field long and about a half a football field wide.

They landed ahead of us just inside the bean field. I said, "Girls, can you believe this!" After our excitement died down, I suggested we hit the bean field in an attempt to induce a command performance like we'd experienced moments before. As we started moving forward, a scout must have warned the massive concentration of birds to take flight and move on. They did, too! Even to this day, my wife and I still ask, "Do you remember when that yellow burst of finches brightened our day down at the farm?" It was a once in a lifetime event that we were fortunate enough to experience!

As time went on, we added a cabin at the farm complete with all of the modern-day conveniences, yet made sure its design maintained a rustic charm. The barn and outhouses were also restored. Respect for nature and the land once more existed on our slice of heaven here on earth.

I mentioned that we added a three-acre lake. We stocked it with trophy fish, and it had an abundance of deep croaking bullfrogs. It was also the perfect place to harvest a jet-fast teal, a green-head or a Suzie, and even a Canadian goose on special occasions.

The farm offered a cornucopia of wild things to feast on. Small game came in the form of rabbits, squirrels, dove, quail, and wild turkeys. From the plant kingdom came persimmons, walnuts, hickory nuts, acorns, a few chestnuts and a buckeye or two. Of course, there were blackberries everywhere, but along with them came chiggers and ticks. Other wildlife included mice, rats, coons, opossums, bobcats, fox and coyotes. Even a black bear was once reported in the area. There was plenty of firewood for all and timber was harvested every ten years or so.

I have many incredible memories of happenings at the farm, almost all of which were made with my family. Some of our wildest dreams have come true. Now it's up to our daughter and our niece to follow in our footsteps and make *their* dreams come true. I can only hope and expect that they'll enjoy the farm and its surroundings as much or more as I have.

But for now, it's time to set these fond memories aside and head out to check our deer stands to ensure they're safe for the upcoming hunting season!

9

~ They Don't Make Men ~
Like My Dad Anymore

Here I am, sitting down here in Islamorada. It's a clear, sunny, rather warm day and the wind is blowing like a bat out of hell, at least 20 MPH out of the east. The ocean is white-capping and way out on that line where the water meets the sky—I love that phrase by the way!—the picture never grows old.

You can see "The Elephants" … trunk-to-tail and marching due west. What a sight, but only if you like sitting and killing time under the boat dock tree, forced to share this time with an Irish-descendant friend who is more used to *eating* fish than *catching* them.

We were admiring the wash job on the boats, the expertly repaired anchor rope and the birds riding the air currents above, while we discussed which spot and what fish we'll pursue come morning. Then down comes another buddy … Mr. G.G. He's a mix of German descent and upper New York State cowboy, a man who's caught more big fish than anything I've ever even dreamed about.

Old G.G. informs us that he's going to have an upcoming procedure on his ticker. "Nothing to worry about," he explains. "Just a mild setback and a few missed days of fishing." We listen as he describes the problem. We discuss the cure and I offer to come to visit him up at Kindle Hospital when the day comes.

"That won't be necessary," he tells me and then adds, "I only plan to spend one night there, then return to my normal duties of fishing and maintaining my boat."

Being of good sport, I offer to come and visit him anyway and promise I'll sneak him in a half-pint of good Kentucky whiskey—Woodford Reserve, his favorite. "No, no, that won't be necessary," was his response. "We can share a drink here, under the tree, upon my return."

This half-pint talk reminded me of a time when I was a young boy, and I asked "Speedo," the guy who was sitting next to me, "You ever heard of Saint Edward's Hospital back in New Albany?"

"Heard of it?" he says, laughing. "Hell, I spent time there." He went on to explain how he'd shared a room with his brother while in an adjoining room, was his mom and dad. After a long, drawn-out story of how the whole family came down with symptoms of the flu and pneumonia, he explained that they were all hospitalized for a week back in the '60s. "Anyway," he says, "why'd you inquire about Saint Edward's?"

I explained. "That half-pint talk reminded me of a time when I was a boy and my father was admitted to Saint Edward's for what was supposed to be a five-day stay, as best as I can recall."

It seems *Old Dad* had developed a pair of hemorrhoids the size of two very swollen Silver Creek leeches, and removal was the cure. After we'd finished visiting Dad, the family had left his room and was headed to the car for the trip home. Dad motioned to me and said, "Son, come here." Back then, you came when called.

"Son," he said. "When you get home, go out to the Buick Wildcat. Under the seat is a half-pint of Black & White scotch whiskey. Fetch it, then get on your green Schwinn bike and bring it back here to me." He added, "And be quick about it."

"No problem, Dad," I said, excited that he chose me to help him out on this covert mission. "I'll be back soon." We arrived home 15 minutes later, and five minutes after that, I found the half-pint and had it tucked away in my pocket. Thirty minutes later, I was walking up the steps of Saint Edward's with a brown paper bag in hand, the scotch inside. Mission accomplished!

Dad smiled as he looked in the bag and said, "Good job, son. Now be on your way so as not to miss supper."

Back home no one had missed me and I was at the dinner table five minutes early. That evening, I slept good knowing I'd helped Dad out. I was up at sunrise and ready to spend the day fishing down at the pond. A short while later my Uncle Jim, Dad's brother, pulled up in his car and said, "Johnny, I need you to come and take a ride with me. I may need a hand with something."

"Sure," I said. "What are we doing and where are we going?"

"Just jump in," he said, "and we'll be on our way."

Well, 15 minutes later we pulled up to Saint Edward's Hospital, and there on the curb, in front of Kraft's Funeral Home which was across the street, stood Dad in his pajamas. He was barefoot and looked rather perturbed, to say the least. Dad decided he'd had enough of the hospital business and was going to recuperate at home.

Now you see why I say, *They don't make men like my Dad anymore!* As we drove home, the conversation quickly turned to bass and crappie fishing and tomorrow's plan. I felt very close to Dad at that moment and I smile as I think back on my memories of him. He was one helluva guy!

10

~ Marble Hill & Frogs ~

I think it was in the winter of 1974, but I could be off a year or two. I was working the winter months and was happy to have a job as that's when a lot of layoffs occurred in the construction trades.

In addition to the hard physical labor outdoors, I was working in that southern Indiana humidity-laden cold that would go right to your bones regardless of how many layers of clothes you wore, and *that* made it a bitch! In spite of that though, it was rewarding. I was working with a great bunch of men—a team—fellas who worked hard and looked out for one another. I was treated as an equal even though I was the company owner's son. I busted my hump every day to prove that I was just as hard a worker as any of them, and they appreciated that.

We labored, froze, shared rides and covered for one another when it was necessary, and we got the job done. Our crew had three laborers: me—they called me "JR," John Dukes and Johnny Johnson. We also had one equipment operator, Donnie Franks.

There was one supervisor, Mr. Kenny Franks, the "Boss Man." I had the highest respect for this man. He was a WWII veteran and a Purple Heart recipient. He'd been wounded in his right arm from hand to biceps. As a result of his injury, there was muscle missing in his arm and he had three fingers permanently curled on his right hand.

Kenny was a good friend of my father's and was a trusted employee who worked well with his crew and peers. I never knew until a few years ago about Kenny and his Purple Heart. His son, Don, and I were lunching at the Cracker Barrel. We were reminiscing about the times and jobs we'd worked on together.

I asked him, "What happened to Kenny's arm?" All he said was that Kenny had been shot and wounded in Germany and that's all knew about it. My Boss Man was truly a hero but kept it to himself all the years I knew him.

On most workdays, Kenny and Donnie drove up from Corydon. They'd swing by the company office and pick me up. We'd share the ride in Boss Man's truck. The three of us sat in the front seat and up to Marble Hill we'd go. Marble Hill was the new power plant that was being built near Madison, Indiana.

There were no places for carry-out food at the job site, so we brought our lunches and snacks for the day. I recall my lunchbox was a metal one with a red and silver thermos tucked securely in the box lid.

This one rather cold morning we were installing cattle crossings on the drives, and laying pipe where drainage channels crossed under the County road. Kenny supervised the whole show. Donnie operated the 680 Case extendahoe, while Charlie ran the other 680 Case.

Johnny was grade-checking for Buster, John and me. We were setting and bolting the sections of the cattle crossings while Don ran the 680 that set the iron pieces in place. Every now and then, Don would re-cut part of the ditch to get it to drain properly and to help keep the icy water from ponding around our feet.

I was in the trench with the grade stick and John was on top standing behind the level shooting elevations for the flow line. On one of the passes with his bucket (some two-feet plus into the wet, mucky and rather disgusting soil in the ditch) Don pulled it forward with a full load and turned the boom to one side to dump the excavation next to the ditch.

I, being a man of detail and keen eye, spotted something rather interesting buried in the muck. "Stop, Donnie! Stop!" I hollered as I waved my arms. He killed the motor thinking something was wrong.

Johnny handed me a *sharp shooter*—a long-nosed spade. From the side of the cut the bucket had just made, I began to gently, and delicately, with the precision of a skilled surgeon, remove these plump, gigantic bullfrogs that had buried themselves in the soil with plans, I'm sure, to spend the winter there, secure in their resting place.

I remember removing the thermos from my lunch box and carefully placing as many bullfrogs as I could neatly fit inside. I filled the box up to the lid, much like sardines in a can. I also twisted off the bottom of my thermos bottle, and after removing the glass bladder from it, I used the cavity to pack another five or six of the big hibernating frogs inside.

We had a good productive day's work. Everyone was exhausted.

It was Friday and it had been a long, cold, 50-hour workweek. We were off on Saturdays through the winter months.

On the ride home, we placed our three lunch boxes on the floor in front of the seat, out of the way of our feet. With the heater turned up and three bodies in the cab, it wasn't long before two of us were sound asleep. We knew the Boss Man would get us home like he'd done so many times before.

Maybe fifteen minutes or so had gone by when I got a nudge to wake up. "What's wrong, Kenny?" I asked.

"JR," he said, without taking his eyes off the road, "Your lunch box moved and sounds are coming from inside."

I picked up my box and set it on my lap. I slowly opened the lid and as soon as I did, out came those frogs like a bunch of bloated old men who'd been crammed in a prison cell and had suddenly been sprung free. They were squirming and stepping all over one another in their efforts to escape.

Kenny slowed the truck while Don and I grabbed jumping frogs. I was trying my damndest to stuff them back into the box and felt like I was fighting a losing battle. I'd get one or two in, and three more would jump out. I got some of them back in the box and more of them into a gunnysack we had in the truck. It was also half-filled with the frozen frogs.

We hadn't considered that the warm air from the truck's heater, which was blowing full out on our feet, had also warmed the box and the sack and brought the frogs out of hibernation. We arrived back at the shop yard where I quickly retrieved a pickup with a camper on the back.

I placed the sack full of frogs in the back and off for home I went. By the time I pulled up the driveway to the Big House, our home, the frogs we hopping all around in the back.

That night, after supper, I went down in the cellar basement and on a white porcelain table with newspaper laid down, I proceeded to skin and clean every frog. I ended up with a good mess too that would feed the six of us who were living at the Big House.

Come morning, my great aunt—"Beanie" is what we called her—who was the Chief Cook and Bottle Washer, declared that come suppertime, from her skillet and fried in bacon grease, we'd be having a frog dinner with all the trimmings.

At 5 p.m., Beanie had the grease hot. I was sitting there on the red metal stool to the right of the stove watching her preparing to work her culinary magic, while a few of the others were sitting on the bench that ran on two sides around the kitchen table.

Well, when my sweet Aunt Beanie dropped the frog legs into the hot grease, out of the skillet they jumped! There was total pandemonium in the kitchen for a moment, accompanied by screams and shouts of the on-lookers. Everyone was scrambling like hell, not certain of what was happening, but trying to make damn sure they weren't going to be a part of it.

Beanie was down and out for the count as she hit the floor. Moments later she was on her feet and scrambling for a skillet lid. She'd fork out one set of legs and toss in another followed by a slamming of the skillet lid. You could hear the thud on the lid from legs as the muscles in the legs made their last twitch.

A short while later, we had a platter full of crispy, brown-crusted, hot-fried frog legs, and the feast began!

We felt we'd hit the jackpot because the way we'd usually harvest frogs was to gig them one at a time while walking along a stream bank or floating on a pond in a canoe or Jon boat while scanning the shore with a spotlight. In lieu of a gig, we'd sometimes use a .22 single-shot, bolt action rifle. We'd often have to wait most of the summer until we had enough frog legs for a full dinner. Now-here we were, enjoying the fruits of one short afternoon of harvesting hibernating amphibians!

11

~ Best Friend, Peas and Corn ~

It's pre-marriage. Courting and love were around. It was a time when things seemed as though they couldn't get any better. I was working for our company down in southwestern Indiana. The project was going as planned, on-schedule and was making some profit as well.

The crews were all good, skilled people. The inspectors were cooperative and it was just one of those construction and paving jobs where almost everything was running smoothly. Because of this, it made getting up in the morning a delight. It was a joy to rise early and head out for the job.

Ten or twelve-hour days were the norm and all was good. The only negative I can think of was Sunday through Thursday nights. My "home" or sleeping quarters was the Drury Hotel some ten miles or so from the project.

Fast-food, more along the lines of rotating hog troughs, was the norm for dinner. The routine was to clean up first, dine out, hit the rack early, then rise and shine at the crack of dawn. Before going to bed, the evenings could be long with plenty of TV being watched.

Wednesday nights were the time to go down to the lobby bar and have a few drinks. Fridays were long days. The anticipation of an eventful weekend lay ahead. It would be a two-hour drive home, clean up and then hit the town for a few hours with my lady friend and future wife, MJB.

We were always eager to see each other and catch up. While I was on the road, MJ would make daily trips from Louisville to my shotgun-style house in New Albany, to walk, water and feed my beloved pet dog, Bearfoot—a pure-bred, Norwegian Elk Hound.

He was black with shades of gray and off-white. He had a tail that curled up onto his back. His coat was very thick; he was bred for cold, windy winters. He had big paws for traction and was a stud dog, but had the temperament of a well-mannered canine. He reminded you of the kind of dog a neighbor might own, but you always envied.

Bearfoot was my first dog that was truly *my* dog ... *my* pet and a friend from birth to the end. He was a once in a lifetime dog. He was raised on dry food, table scraps and left-over carry-outs from every ethnic style and type of restaurant. Nothing went to waste; his appetite was ravenous and his physical manner was one of high energy. He was always ready to play or run.

On one Friday night, after a long week on the road away from home, MJ had a turkey breast dinner awaiting me, complete with all of the trimmings along with a bottle of Portuguese Vin Rose, our favorite at the time. Of course, she also had my most favorite mix of vegetables in life: an oversized bowl of fresh peas and corn.

Dinner was consumed, thoroughly enjoyed, and the dishes were cleaned in time to kick back and catch up with the goings-on in our busy lives and schedules. As the evening progressed, Bearfoot eventually came around. It was feeding time.

His food bucket was nearly empty. We put a cup or so of Purina into the large mixing bowl and gave him all of the leftover peas and corn. His bowl was full. We added a little water and nuked it for a few minutes in the microwave. We now had a meal fit for King ... King Bearfoot!

Saturday morning came early and so did our appointment with Dr. Hollis, the veterinarian over on Charlestown Road. MJ and I both noticed Old Bearfoot was moving a little slower than usual. He seemed to be blue and not quite himself.

Doc Hollis said, "John, see if you can get Bearfoot up on the stainless steel examining table." With the big boy up on the table, his shots were administered and his check-up continued. Next, it was time to check his temperature as well as his privates.

The nurse was taking notes while MJ cradled Bearfoot's neck and head. I also had one arm around his neck and one hand on the base of his tail.

Doc Hollis added a little lubrication to the temperature probe from a tube that looked like Ipana toothpaste. The device looked more like a small torpedo. It was about two inches in diameter and was quite long.

In and up the rectum it went. Bearfoot froze, his body tense. Then he made a slight shiver. His eyes got very large and distended. The look on his face was one of fright and disbelief. All seemed to go as planned until old Doc quickly extracted the thermometer. Bearfoot stood there with a look of relief on his face and in his eyes. I noticed his body relaxed too. All at once, he ripped off a boisterous fart and blew out peas and corn that covered half the table. It was all over the floor even hit the wall six feet away and stuck to it. To top it off, old Doc's hand was also covered. I can see it to this day—the look of shock and surprise on everyone's faces.

Doctor Hollis looked at the thermometer and calmly declared that Bearfoot's temperature was normal. He immediately turned to me and said, "Mr. John, you should probably *not* feed your hound peas and corn in the future.

Bearfoot now had a clean bill of health, his shots were up to date, and *one* of his owners was completely embarrassed. To me, this was all just a normal day. A bill was presented and, possibly due to the circumstances, cash was demanded by Doc.

Since this visit, my significant other refused to accompany me on future vet appointments.

For the rest of his dear life, Bearfoot continued to consume peas and corn along with other food that would have normally gone down the garbage disposal. He lived a good, happy life and was well-cared for. Even though we continued to feed him the peas and corn, we never did it the night before a vet appointment!

Bearfoot lived to be 14 years old and died on the deck at our home awaiting a handout from the grill where I was cooking steaks. My old friend is buried out back behind our home near the edge of the woods by the fence. There's a large piece of limestone from our quarry up in Sellersburg serving as his headstone. He was a great dog for sure.

12

~ Turkey Shoots ~

Back in the 50s, 60s, 70s and early 80s, "Turkey Shoots" were a major fundraiser for all of the Catholic churches in the area. The fundraising was not limited to just the churches though. Other organizations such as the Shriners, the Coon Hunters Club, the VFW and American Legion, private clubs, taverns and just about any other organization looking to raise some quick money also held Turkey Shoots.

There were no real turkeys to shoot at. The target was a 6" x 6" wooden board with an "X" in the center. The center of the cross was formed by the intersection of pencil lines connecting the opposite corners of the board.

The object of the sport was to try and get a piece of buckshot fired from a shotgun closest to the center of the X. Whoever's shot was closest to the X was declared the winner. The gauge of the shotgun was limited to a 12, 20 or 16 gauge, which was the size of the gun's bore.

Barrel modifications were allowed at most shoots as well as poly chokes. Some of the modifications were where the end six inches or so of the gun barrel was heated, then tapered or choked down so as to produce a tighter pattern when the shot left the barrel.

A few of those old boys even mounted scopes on their shotguns. At first, I didn't understand the reasoning for this because a lot of pellets were contained in a shotgun shell, not just a single projectile. As it was explained to me, even a shotgun will tend to shoot a pattern in the same approximate location. You could be aiming dead center, but your tightest grouping of pellets might hit a little to one side or the other, or a little high or low. With the scope, you can sight it in to hit where the most pellets are concentrated.

The matches were varied and the winning pots were of different values or prizes—most often it was cash, but occasionally, it might be something else entirely. Each round was usually limited to 20 shooters or less who stood on a line 40 yards from the targets. The targets were hung on individual posts downrange from each shooter.

You paid a fee to shoot. You only got one shot. You could shoot in as many rounds as you wanted, but you only got one shot at one target per round.

Once the shooters paid their fee and everyone was standing on the firing line, you were given the appropriate size shell for your gun. When the command to fire was given by the range master, you had one minute to load your gun and get the shot off.

Safety was a big concern. The rules were strictly enforced and followed by all. In all of the shoots I attended over the years I don't recall a single accident. The jackpots were made up of cash and the organization sponsoring the event took a cut of the total pot, usually half of what was charged for the shooting fee.

There were various costs to shoot, depending on what the jackpot was for that particular round. The fees ranged from $2 per shot up to $20. Some even had an entry fee as high as $50 to $100 per shot. Those pots obviously got very large and only the private clubs shot rounds for these amounts, never the churches or smaller clubs.

I mentioned some of the different items that might be awarded for the jackpot. At some of the shoots, the winnings might range from poultry, weapons, clothing, maybe a half of a hog or a side of beef, sporting event tickets and at one shoot, a four-foot-long baloney, of which I was the lucky winner! This was down at the Brown Derby Tavern in Schnellville, Indiana.

Through the years I've brought home every kind of prize imaginable. You could eat, drink, ride, toss or shoot the various things I've won.

At one of the matches I attended, a large splatter board held the target. A sheet of paper was attached to the board and a large circle was drawn on it. Lines were drawn to divide the circle into wedges or segments, much like slices of pie. You bought a wedge and put your name on it along with a small X anywhere you wanted in the wedge. The firing line was some 50 yards from the target. One person would be selected to take a shot at it. Sometimes the board would be spun like a Wheel of Fortune game at a carnival.

After the one person shot, whoever had a shot closest to the center of their X was declared the winner. This was pure gambling at its finest and nothing they offered in Vegas could match the excitement or thrill of it!

My gun, I might add, was modified by a gunsmith friend who choked the muzzle end down to the size of a dime. The gun was a 12 gauge, single-shot, Harrington & Richardson, Long Tom goose gun with a hammer and open sights.

I acquired this shotgun back in 1969 while stationed at Altus AFB in Oklahoma. My service buddy, Jimmy, and I were participating in the annual "Rattlesnake Round-up" in Magnum, Oklahoma. I recall trading a snake collector my tote sack containing ten rattlesnakes along with a 12-pack of cold Lone Star beer for the award-winning gun that brought me great luck many years later.

A final thought before I close this story. One Sunday afternoon, my cousin, Jimmy, and I walked down from the Big House and through the woods. We walked across the 4th Dam over Silver Creek there at Blackiston's Mill. This dam got you across the creek and onto the grounds of the Blackiston's Mill Private Park, where you could hear the shooting from the match that had already begun.

Jim and I had a system worked out where we lined up next to each other on the firing line, and unbeknownst to those who were running the shoot, Jim would fire at my target. Then he'd swear up and down that he'd missed his completely.

Jim used my short-barreled, open choke so that when the shot flew it had a very wide, open pattern. Not many of the pellets would hit the board, but a few always did. After we'd managed to win two or three big money rounds, the sponsor of the match became suspicious and knew something was not quite up to par.

The next round we shot in, Jimmy was four positions to my left. Under watchful eyes from management, Jimmy was observed aiming his gun at the 2 o'clock position and not at 12 high noon.

The command came to cease firing and stand back while the judges walked by and inspected the targets. When they came to Jimmy's, it was blank. It didn't have one single shot in it! The judge declared that Jimmy was cheating, and off he ran with a few of the pissed-off judges hot on his ass. Jimmy flew over the dam, up through the woods, through grandma's cow pasture and hid in the barn.

I calmly put my gun over my shoulder and walked away across Blackiston's Mill Road. I went through the woods, crossed the creek in knee-high water and up through some more woods. I crossed the road again and made my way to the house.

Lesson learned: *never* cheat, but especially don't when some or all who are watching you are holding guns! Needless to say, that put an end to Jimmy's turkey-shooting adventures.

As for me, I still attend the shoots when I can find one. Sadly, it's a fading form of fundraising and entertainment that today's generation knows little about, or for that matter … even cares.

13

~ Stingray City ~

The Stingray ... I have a fascination with this fish. I *guess* it's a fish? As unappetizing as they look and strange as their bodies are, you can actually cook and eat them. They clean like a regular fish and they make tasty dinners.

I've actually only caught three through the years—one off the coast of Marathon, Florida; one from the dock at The Palms, our first Keys condo, and one in ten-feet of water due south of Coral Harbours, our current home in the Keys.

They taste like scallops, and I've wondered, are they on the menu? I've never seen them listed or advertised as the "Daily Special." Stingray scallops make for great conversation at dockside and Tiki bars while sipping Budweiser or Pineapple Punches and playing games of Ring Toss for dollars or free rounds.

A few years back, after landing the one at Coral Harbours, I was told about a technique of cleaning and preparing stingray scallops for the table. This required a special cookie-cutter type of utensil, which I didn't have, so I made some of the cutters back home in the company's repair shop.

I took a four-inch length of pipe. The diameter chosen was based on what you wanted the size of your scallops to be, and I used a 2-inch diameter pipe. I then sharpened one end of the pipe as you'd do with a knife blade.

When you pounded this through the wing of your stingray, a very neat plug of meat was produced. You then cut away the skin, and there's your mock scallop. At that point, you would prepare or cook it just as you would with any scallop.

Back at our Florida home in Islamorada, I gave each of my fellow fishing buddies one of my homemade stingray scallop cookie cutters. My own personal cookie cutter was lost at sea when my dock box was swept away during Hurricane Irma. I don't plan to make another cutter, for I have lost my taste for—plus gained a respect and love for—this odd and unusual fish. These days, it's only catch and release for me, not the old catch and filet.

Years prior to the above action and happenings, I recall a spring vacation with the family to the beautiful Cayman Islands. One sunny day we all signed up for a boat ride that would take us out a mile or so from shore to a sandbar. For those of you unfamiliar with the term, a sandbar is a ridge of sand that is built up by currents. They can occur in rivers or in ocean waters. They can range in size from small to very large.

We anchored in about four feet of water and overboard we went, snorkeling and frolicking around in the water. From the advertisement on land and also on the boat, our destination was described as "An excursion to Stingray City."

The boat captain would throw bits of cut-up raw squid into the water and the rays would flock to the area in search of a snack. These daily feeding trips became quite a tourist attraction. At first, swimming with the rays at Stingray City was scary. You could touch them and sometimes grab a wing and off they'd go. It was exciting for children and adults as well.

While standing in about four feet of water, my sister, who is an avid swimmer, took a large squid, jerked open the back of my Speedo swim trunks, stuffed it inside, then swam away. Before I could extract the squid, a giant stingray clung to my backside and proceeded to suck the squid and the red Speedo's off my body!

Lucky for me, the ray spit my out my shorts and I was able to recover them. You've never experienced anything until you have a stingray wrap his wings around you and proceed to vacuum your backside!

Several years after this incident, we heard the news that Steve Irwin, known for his TV show, *The Crocodile Hunter*, was killed in a freak accident while filming a documentary off the coast of Australia when a stingray he was handling nailed him in the chest with its tail. The barbed tail delivers venom that causes excruciating pain but rarely kills.

14

~ Expressions Explained ~

The following old or ancient expressions could tell a good short story in themselves. I've heard all of these many times over the years, and I am sure you have, too. After hearing the meanings of them explained to me, I thought it might be interesting to list some of the sayings and explain their origin or meanings. So, after a considerable amount of research, here we go!

HOGWASH - Steamboats were a popular way to transport both people and animals many years ago when this country was young, roads were scarce and 18-wheelers were still a hundred years in the future. The rivers in this country were the equivalent of the present-day Interstates.

The pigs and hogs were incredibly dirty and smelled worse than an outhouse on a hot August day when the swine were brought in fresh off the farm. The muck, dirt, grime and excrement they wallowed in was washed off before they were loaded onto the boat. It was horrible stuff, considered as nothing good and was viewed as "hogwash." That's why this expression still stands today and is used when someone is trying to convince you that something they're telling you is good or valid. Don't fall for it. It's crap folks—plain and simple!

BUYING THE FARM - In WWI, soldiers were issued life insurance policies worth $5,000.

This was approximately the cost of a small farm back home, so, if you were killed, you essentially "bought the farm" for your survivors.

SHOWBOAT - Years ago there were floating theaters built on barge frames that were pushed upriver by a steam-powered, paddlewheel boat. The floating theaters played to towns up and down the mighty Mississippi River and were generally the only source of entertainment for the folks in the lonely pioneer towns. The boats were tacky-looking and had bright paint with attention-grabbing lettering and graphics on the side. This is why we say someone who is being the life of the party, show or event is "showboating."

OVER A BARREL - Before CPR, a drowning person would be placed face-down over a barrel and rolled back and forth in hopes of emptying their lungs of water. Although the idea behind this maneuver sounded good, the technique was not very successful. So when you're "over a barrel," you are in some deep trouble!

RIFF-RAFF - The rivers were the main mode of travel in the early days of this country. The riverboats carried people and freight and the cost was expensive, so wealthy people were the primary users of the glamorous boats. The majority of everyday river travelers used rafts. Most all of the large boats on the river had right-of-way over the rafts. The steering oar on the small rafts was called a "rift," and so these small vessels were known as "rift rafts."

That term was associated with poor people and later, the kind of people you didn't want to associate with. The term morphed into "riff-raff," and is still used today to describe the more unsavory or low-life elements in society.

BARRELS OF OIL - When the early oil wells were drilled, no one had a plan to store the oil, so they used water barrels. And that, my friends, is why we refer to the quantity as barrels of oil and not gallons!

IRONCLAD CONTRACT - This term originated from the ironclad ships of the Civil War. Its meaning is something so strong, it could not be broken.

And these, my readers, are but a few of the many expressions we Americans still use today, yet many don't know their true meaning or the origin of the terms.

15

~ Yellowtail Fishing ~

Yellowtails are the best eating and are also one of the hardest hitting and running fish of their size here on the reef fishing off of Upper Matecumbe, also known as Islamorada. Personally, they are my favorite eating fish followed by mangrove snappers. But then, grunts, grits and eggs down at Robbie's is also pretty damn tasty!

For larger fish 18 inches and up, you want to fish in depths of 65 to 105 feet of water. Using your fish finder, look for them on the depth-finder between the 50 and 70-foot range. Once you locate a good mass of fish, you have to determine the drift required to get your chum and bait to the spot where the fish are.

It does no good to anchor in 90 feet of water and have your chum and bait running offshore 125 feet away from the fish. When chumming, you don't need to find the right anchor point to hit your targeted fish spot. The fish will come into the chum, but it helps to get the flow correct. A nice current helps the cause!

Once anchored and you're sure the anchor is holding, begin chumming. When you start chumming, don't start fishing right away. Start getting your lines and reels set up and ready to go. Toss a handful of thawed glass minnows into the chum line. It usually takes about 15 minutes, depending on the current, to get things started.

Continue to toss in a handful of glass minnows every once in a while, or toss in a bean can full of oats, cat litter, sand or some birdseed.

At this point, you're ready to fish. You can use Silverside minnows, small slices of ballyhoo cut in a triangle shape, or my favorite: fish hearts found in the chum bag. You have to feel for them amongst the stinking, ground-up mess though.

You can make an easy cast or just let the bait drop in water. If the current is good, the bait will be carried away in the chum line. Leave the bail open and continue to feed out the line. The line should never stop peeling off the spool. Sometimes the fish will hit in close in just a few minutes, other times they'll bite when the line is further out. The important thing is, just keep feeding or letting line out and be alert for the strike.

When the line does rip off the spool, drop or flip the bail down and reel. Do not jerk or try to set the hook; you'll miss them every time if you do.

The fish down here are much different from the bass and other freshwater fish. If your fish is small or just a borderline keeper, bring it aboard in one pull of the rod and swing it into the boat. If he's a big fish, have your buddy man the net and bring him aboard. If it's a *really big* fish, have your buddy use the gaff. In one continuous motion, the gaff goes in the water and up into the fish. With two hands, bring him aboard. All of this takes practice and over time, you'll master the art rather quickly.

It's always wise to be careful so as not to get bit. Use a gloved hand to pick up the fish. I like a microfiber towel to grab the fish and then into the box he goes. It's also imperative to have a bag or two of ice in the fish box to keep your catch cold until you return to the dock.

Once on the dock and your fish are piled in five-gallon buckets or in your dock cooler, drag it over to the cleaning table. Here's where the fun begins—I love to clean fish! I pull up my old high stool and get positioned. I personally use an electric knife which I find works best, or I'll use my filet knife for touch up or special trimmings.

I toss the filets in a plastic colander … they cost a buck at the Dollar General Store. I tend to roll and rinse the filets only once in the colander. The carcasses or bones and guts go into my dock freezer to be used later as bait for my crab traps—crab traps is another story in itself.

After I clean up the table and area around the dock, I place the filets in a plastic baggie and keep them iccd while I head for home. As soon as I walk in the door, I get the cutting board out and sit at the counter to trim up the fish. Don't be afraid to waste some of the filets. You want to remove all of the bones, gristle and blood veins. There's nothing as bad that will turn you off quicker than to find a bone or other strange hunk of something in with your dinner filets when you pop them into your mouth.

With a portable Weight Watchers scale, measure out the amount of fish you wish to eat. Eight ounces seems to be about the right portion. I'll put twice that amount in the Ziploc baggie—it feeds two. You're almost done. Be sure to label the bag with the date and list the type of fish. We keep two bags out of the freezer for eating over a three day period. The frozen fish is good for consumption up until the time you begin to see some frost starting to form on the filets.

Why yellowtail? Because I think it's the best eating fish in the sea. They're very sporty to catch and there are plenty of them. The legal size limit is within reason and there's no limit on numbers that I know of.

When you hook a yellowtail, though, hang on because you're in for a damn good fight. They're like little torpedoes. Just about the time you think you have one worn out and get him close to the boat, BAM— off he goes with a renewed burst of energy!

16

~ Captain Kenny ~

Islamorada, the Florida Keys: the year is 1988, my father has passed away. The next year we would sell the Rita-Sus-Ann, Dad's Grady White boat. After that, we sold the condo at The Palms at MM80 in Islamorada. Before the "Old Man" died, he was the glue that held the family together and often united us in doing things together. It was a tight-knit circle, indeed.

After Dad's death, things and people just seemed to slowly slide, shift positions and go their own way. There were no more extended family vacations, cookouts, and a general coming together. With no Keys condo to go to, no boat and no family patriarch, my family, being lovers of the Keys and all there is to offer, eventually purchased our own condo in Islamorada.

Up until that time, however, we spent our vacation time in the intervening years at the Cheeca Lodge in Islamorada and we were having the time of our lives. It was a great place to stay and had lots to offer in the wonderful tradition of the Keys.

We managed to stay in the same suite each time over by the Camp Cheeca area, a camp on the site for our daughter. Then as everyone knows—and in the category of, "crap happens"—while playing golf one day on the 9-hole, par-three course, I twisted my back and in the process, cracked something. It was a pinched nerve and took me to the ground. My wife talked with the front desk and set up an appointment with the in-house massage master—"The Masseuse."

He arrived precisely on time and was a very interesting man. He brought along his massage table and set it up outside on the screened-in porch. I asked the fellow his name, and he identified himself as Mr. Art Cohen.

He was originally from out west but now made his home and living here in Islamorada. As he worked on my back, which gave me the relief I enjoyed, we talked and the conversation turned to Keys fishing.

I told Art the story of my father, the condo, the boat and how all had been sold and that I was in dire need of finding a fish boat captain, one specializing in backcountry fishing. Someone knowledgeable of fishing in the coves among the mangroves but was also knowledgeable of the reef fishing as well.

Mr. Art made the comment that his son was the best fishing captain in the Keys and specialized in back-country fishing. Two days later, my wife, daughter and I were down at Bud and Mary's Marina in Captain Kenny Cohen's 18-foot, Action Craft flats boat powered with 150 Yamaha.

From that day until November 2014, for some 24 years, we grew close to Captain Kenny and became great friends. We fished with Kenny every time we were in the Keys (some two or three weeks a year). We also ran all company outings and company vendors who provided fishing trips to Islamorada through Captain Kenny. He was the lead man for all of our outings, including both personal and work-related events. Kenny was truly the Captain of the Keys.

As life would have it, and too often it seems to happen to the truly good people, Kenny and his wife lost their lives unexpectedly, and way too early. Their ashes were disbursed in the water in the backcountry by a no-named Key that was known as a "Kenny's Honey Hole" (more on the story will follow). The following news clip pretty much summed things up about Captain Kenny and his wife:

May the two rest in peace. Both will never be forgotten. The Keys are Kenny!

One last thought about Captain Kenny: about the third time my wife, daughter and I went fishing with him—he only liked to fish two in the boat but, with his permission, I tagged along as the photo man—I sat perched upon the trolling platform, out of the way. I asked Kenny if he would take the time to hone my daughter's fishing skills and arrange for the wife to catch a few for some family pictures.

Joanna was using a redhead jig with a live shrimp as bait. Kenny, being a much more patient man than myself, was giving her instructions on how to cast and fish. And I might add, my daughter and wife *listened* to him as opposed to me when the three of us are out alone on the water.

They were flipping jigs just to the edge of the mangroves when I see the current rippling around the end of the mangrove island. Joanna makes a perfect cast, just inches under a low-lying branch and into the current. With her bail open and feeding line, Kenny tells Joanna, "Get ready and when I say *now,* close the bail with your rod out straight, jerk it and then start cranking fast."

As if the fish was programmed to what Kenny had just said, the line shot out and daughter followed his instructions to a tee. The fish left the mangroves and headed for deep water. Kenny knew it was a big one. He hollered, "Keep cranking!"

When I saw the dip net come out, I knew for sure it was a big fish. It was reeled in, netted, and into the boat she came. Daughter had just landed a five-pound gray (a Mangrove Snapper).

Kenny proclaimed that it was the largest Mangrove Snapper ever in his boat. Our daughter was riding between her mother, Kenny and me, and she was proud as could be about her catch. When we were almost back to the dock, Kenny said, "I've never asked anyone in my boat who I took fishing if I could have a fish to take home but ..."

Before he could finish, our daughter replied, "I would love for you to have my big fish!"

In large print, one newspaper headline read:
Long Key couple killed in Ocala highway crash

Ken and Jay Anna Cohan were well known in the Keys fishing community, Village of Islamorada.

Another article read:

A Florida Keys couple, long familiar to the local sporting community, died Thursday after a head-on crash on 75 south of Ocala. Long Key resident Ken Cohan, 53, and his wife, Jay Anna Cohan, 63, we're headed south around 9:30 a.m. when a tractor-trailer going north blew a front tire. The massive 1986 International truck veered across the median and into the southbound lanes per the report. The semi slammed into the Cohan's white pickup truck destroying the 2010 Sierra. The couple, who were both wearing their seat belts, died at the scene.

Ken Cohan was a South Florida native who worked as an

Islamorada charter captain for nearly 30 years. Cohan ran an 18-foot flats boat out of Bud and Mary's Marina after working a decade as an offshore captain.

Jay Anna Cohan worked at the Key Colony Inn on Key Colony Beach. Jay Anna was a fixture on committee boats for several Islamorada fishing tournaments.

The couple was well-loved in the fishing community of Islamorada and will be missed.

Services will be at Bud and Mary's Marina and at 4 p.m., a flotilla of boats will motor out to Indian Key for the burial at sea.

It was a very sad day. I miss Captain Kenny and thoughts of him cross my mind every time I fish in the Keys.

17

~ Cards ~

From weddings, birthdays, graduations and every special occasion in between, cards are the most special way to spread some joy. Cards are also a more subtle way of spreading love and happiness. They can express your feelings or understanding of one's special event, be it one of sorrow, happiness, a remembrance or to express any feeling one may have for another.

In almost all cases of cards received, the recipient feels some cheer or happiness from being on the receiving end. Sure, you can send an email or a text message, but that's rather impersonal. This form of expression (a card) is truly better for remembering a loved one or a friend.

It's not much effort. It's the remembering that counts. A kind word or gesture never hurt anyone and besides, the sender, in most cases, feels good about it, too.

Stop and think about the gift of receiving a card. The sender has to first remember your special occasion, he/she then makes the effort to drive, walk, bike, etc. to a place where cards are sold, and then spends the time to choose the card that fits the event and the feelings of both the sender and the recipient.

Then there's the time spent waiting in line to purchase the card, the spending of your hard-earned money, driving home, taking the time to address the envelope and compose a special note. The sender then realizes that another trip to the post office is necessary for stamps. And of course, there's the time spent on a trip to the drug store to get something to help mend the cut on your tongue you got from licking the envelope. Your card is now ready to send! There's also the trip out to your mailbox by the road, and, by the way, it's raining so you get sopping wet.

Finally, the card is on its way to the special event celebrator. You discover, though, that the card has returned to your mailbox four days later because you apparently wrote the wrong address, zip code or something else incorrectly.

More time is spent on a new envelope, another 50-cent stamp—in order to impress, you bought an over-sized card that required additional postage—and another hike to the mailbox. Most cards are mailed out within three days of an event so as to time its arrival on the exact day or a day or two *before* the special event.

Now the card arrives late and you look like a fool. Or perhaps the card was an afterthought and one that was chosen without a lot of sincerity behind it. In most cases though, an enclosure of some kind, a few written words perhaps, can sure change the receiver's thoughts and feelings about the intentions of the sender.

If there's an enclosure, then for sure, a thank-you note of some sort will be in order—through snail mail, a phone call, an email or text message—as an acknowledgment of the gift received. It's rewarding and *both* parties feel nothing was taken for granted.

For everyone, and especially my family members and friends, acknowledged gifts and disclosure of personal information, especially pictures of the celebrator that are posted on social media sites such Facebook, Instagram or any other public site, is very disturbing and most unwanted. I find it insulting. It downright stinks and I don't appreciate it.

As for me, the receiving of cards is most appreciated and enjoyed. Nothing means more to me. Someone—a family member or friend—has taken the time to remind me that they're glad to help make my special day a bit better. In regards to the enclosure, it makes no difference and I really prefer there not be one. The card itself is plenty and they are very much appreciated. If it contains an enclosure, then in those cases, I feel a thank-you note is appropriate.

Having just celebrated my 69th birthday, I was very thankful to be here another day. Having been blessed to have survived two years more than my father, my outlook on life is one of gratitude. Live today and be thankful and happy that family and friends thought enough of me to take the time to send a card and well wishes. I might add that the calls, emails and texts were all appreciated too.

The day is over and gone, and now I move forward into the new year. I sit here and take one final review of my birthday cards. I have orders, "Clear the table of your cards; be thankful and move on." The cards range from funny to serious.

I now wish to share a few of the cards with you. They are from my wife, daughter, brother, sister, niece, nephews, great-nephews, in-laws and friends.

At 69, nostalgia can tend to set in. My cards cover everything from great memories to best wishes. I place this first group into the *Remember when?* category.

Remember when grown-ups seemed glamorous? When people said "please" and "thank you"—and were sincere? When moms called their kids in for dinner at dusk? When you played tug-a-war and climbed trees? When downtown seemed so far away? When you caught lightning bugs in a jar? When you tied a thread to a junebug's leg like a leash and let it fly around? When you and your buddies all drank from the same hose and never worried about catching a fatal disease? When drugstores had soda fountains? When all kids had a bike—and some clothes-pinned trading cards to the frame so the spokes would sound like a motorbike? And who remembers when no one had a pedigreed dog? When you read comic books daily? When you could buy candy for a penny? When you drank chocolate milk? When you knew each day was going to be fun? If these simple things brought a smile to your face, it means you were lucky enough to have lived in such good times! It also means that at 69, you're *kind of OLD!*

Here are some of the things that were in my birthday cards:

Happy 69th Birthday.
Love always,
MJ, Puppy Toes
XXXOOXOXOXO

There are all kinds of Grandpas ... funny, smart, sweet, cool, loving, and then there's my Grandpa!

Dear Papa/Dad, John, who's all that and more–happy birthday. Buy some bait on us, have a fantastic fishing trip out on the Joanna-Marie and enjoy the snacks.
We love you,
J & J & A

75 % OFF? I know how much you love a bargain, so I got you this cheap-ass card!

(Pretty sweet deal, A?). Happy birthday and enjoy the sun. We're getting ready for snow … finally!

M&N

Because you're my brother, we share so much … memories, family, love… and every year, I appreciate you even more and how much you mean to me.

Happy birthday! We hope your year is off to a good start. You're another year older and wiser. Come visit us in SB. We LOVE seeing your "Papa John" pictures on Instagram.

You're a natural!

XOXOXOXXO,

A&D

Handmade card and note:

T W IN. THANKS

XOXOXO … C & B

Family is the gift of Christmas handprints from B, and print from C

Happy birthday

Every year is a new adventure … discover yours. There is a whole world to explore.

Happy birthday!

I'm wishing you a very Happy Birthday, a year chock-full of love and good health.

Enjoy your day!

Love "K"

Got wind it's your birthday … did you fart? Cake and ice cream?

Happy birthday!

Keep your wind down there in Florida.

All the best

"P"

It's your birthday. Happy birthday to a guy who's a rare breed of wonderful. How's the fishing down there?

Miss you guys. Have fun!

PC

There's only one word for someone like you … Amazing, thoughtful, unique, kind, generous, wonderful …. (Okay, so apparently there's more than just one word) - Happy Birthday!

Wishing you an awesome birthday. Enjoy the warm Florida sunshine doing all your favorite things.

Love you.

S&B

XOXOXOX

Birthday paradise? I thought two weeks in Hawaii would be nice for your birthday.

I'll give you a call when I get back!

Enjoy your birthday in your paradise, Islamorada.

Sincerely,

B & R

A WIS HFORT HEBESTD AYEV ER

If you can read this, you're having a birthday (Hope it's great!)

Love,

B & G

And finally, the best for last …

My doctor said I have "reptile dysfunction"

The wife said, "I didn't even know you had a snake!

Don't let another birthday keep you down

Happy birthday!!

D & R

So now you see, cards do make you smile, and life is too short not to smile. Relax, ease up, let the stress go, go fishing, hunting, walking … whatever moment you enjoy. Let the good times roll! In my case, my special day was my 69th birthday.

Again—thank all of you for making my day special. I'm working on #70—one day at a time. I only hope I'm around to enjoy it ... and to walk down the driveway to check the mailbox for some cards.

Hakuna Matata, my friends!

18

~ Coons, Skunks, Groundhogs and Possums ~

It seems that raccoons or coons as they're also called—"Boone Coon" was a family pet—are pesky varmints, and seem to hang around the property, the house and garden in general, just doing their thing, but always getting in the way.

It all started with my compost bin back at the edge of the woods behind the house. Into it went the table scraps, leftovers, expired food from the fridge, stale bread, chicken bones, you name it … it went into the compost bin.

The box, made of plastic, was a three-foot cube. It had a lid and holes to let water in as well as to let water drain out. The holes also provided air which was essential to composting the materials we placed inside.

It seems that with the scents coming from this big black box, it was just too much for old Mr. Bandit and his buddies to pass up. I'd put the lid on; the coons would take it off. The dexterity these animals showed with their paws—which resembled human hands—was amazing. They could figure out to open just about anything if they thought there was a tasty morsel inside. They could be safe-crackers if they were human!

I'd put a stretcher strap/bungee cord over the lid and they'd chew it off. Finally, using wire and a large stone I was able to outsmart the old boys and found a way to keep them out.

We next noticed that our bird feeder, the corn feeder we had for squirrels, the finch feeder and our suet cake feeder were all being picked clean day after day and wondered why.

One night I turned the backyard spotlights on and there were two coons on one of the feeders, and two on the ground. They were working in tandem to consume all of the dropped seed and suet.

After some deep thought and planning, I managed to come up with a bird feeder that was squirrel, coon and possum proof. It consisted of a two-inch pipe in the ground some ten feet tall. It had two round metal discs about 16 inches in diameter spaced approximately two-feet apart affixed halfway up the pole. There was no way those critters could climb the pole and maneuver their way out and over the disc.

Not to be deterred, Mr. Coon and his associates then moved their operations over to the garden and proceeded to eat the tomatoes, sample the squash, steal the sweet corn and in general, just about wrecked the garden completely. I fenced in the area, put up whirly-birds and a plastic owl on a post, but they had little effect in scaring the bandits away and they still managed to reap my harvest before it was ready.

As the summer went on, I was going on twice-a-week fishing trips. After cleaning the fish, I'd walk back in the woods to dispose of the guts, heads, and other non-edible parts. The next day, I'd notice the fish waste was gone and there'd be tracks all over the place. Over by the deer feeder, I'd also see tracks everywhere and noticed that most all of the shelled corn was eaten.

I'd had enough! I broke out the humane, catch 'em alive, metal wire, box traps. I started catching one coon a night—every night. It was a never-ending harvest of coons.

Our stone quarries salesman's father had a small landscape business in Louisville and an old gentleman, Fred, who worked for him and cleaned up and maintained the grounds. He was the outlet for my trapped friends.

I'd put the cage in my pickup and take it to work with me. The salesman would come by the office, take the cage over to his father's place and give it to the old gent. That old boy loved coon! He declared that it was his favorite and most-consumed meat of choice.

This worked well for a month until one old raccoon relieved himself in the backseat of the salesman's car. He emptied his bowels of seed, tomatoes, suet, fish heads, guts, dog food and other foods he'd managed to consume. In addition to the obvious mess, the smell was horrendous. That put an end to the hauling of the animals in his car. It took some major cleaning and riding with the trunk lid open until the disgusting odor wore off. From that point on, he only hauled the trapped coons in the trunk.

Fred would come by my office and retrieve the critters out of my truck. One day I said, "Fred, I'd sure like to taste some of that coon meat."

"No problem," he said. "I'll barbeque one tonight and drop you off a hind leg tomorrow."

True to his word, Fred came in the next day and we traded one live coon in a trap for a hind quarter of a big, fat, mean, male buck, right off the grill along with sauce and potatoes all wrapped up in foil. I put the leg in the microwave and warmed her up. The office personnel started to complain of the smell.

I would describe the smell as being a mixture of grilled shit and the burning of an old outhouse, complete with gum tree chips and Sweet Baby James BBQ sauce. I apologized to the folks in the office and opened the windows and doors to air things out. I then headed to my office for my lunch of hot BBQ coon, potatoes, white bread and a cold bottle of Mountain Dew.

That old coon leg lay on the foil in some kind of weird-colored juice. There were short, stubby hairs on it that resembled the bristles on a hog's leg. I managed to eat the potatoes, bread and drink the soda, but the big bite I managed to pull off the top part of the leg had my stomach gurgling, my eyes watering and my nose running. I felt that sour taste in the back of my throat and leaned over the wastepaper basket just in time to blow my morning breakfast—two egg sandwiches and a coffee from White Castle, along with the potatoes, white bread and half of the 16-ounce Mountain Dew.

I threw open the window and tossed out the remainder of the coon leg. Off I went to Burger King and ordered a quarter-pounder with double onions and extra sauce. I liberally sprinkled Tabasco on my fries along with lots of catsup to kill the flavor of the coon and rid the nasty-as-hell, lingering taste from my mouth.

I chewed a whole pack of Juicy Fruit gum on my drive back to the office. Old Fred came by the next day to retrieve the latest coon I'd caught. He asked how I liked it. I commented that it was the best coon I'd ever eaten, and since it was the *only* coon I'd ever eaten, that wasn't a lie! I begged him for more and I believe I sounded sincere, but I also suggested that maybe that treat could wait for another time.

I eventually grew tired of this program so it was time to put up the traps. Then Saturday morning I caught another. My daughter and I drove him down past Corydon, Indiana, and let him go at Hayswood Park.

We put the traps up for the season and decided we'd just live with the never-ending parade of the illegal aliens as they tracked through my property and on their way down to the creek. Early the next summer, I got the traps back out and on the first night, I caught a pair—two coons in one trap.

My friend, Jason, an avid hunter, begged me to let him take the coons home so he could use them to train his Mountain Cur dogs. He bought me lunch, and he got the coons. Again the traps went back to hang on the barn wall.

Next, my neighbor, Jim, had a family of coons move in under his hot tub. He borrowed one of my traps and the next day I received a phone call asking me if I would stop by and take this big old boar coon into the office for Fred.

"Sure thing," I said. "I'll be there in the morning at six a.m." Jim lived on the left on the way out of the development. His driveway had a pretty good slope to it. I'd say it was maybe 30 yards down to where his mailbox was at the curb. Jim was a retired car salesman from the old Bales Auto Sales up in Jeffersonville. He could sell a car to a monkey! Jim also had a gimp leg which he'd acquired from a terrible car accident years ago and walked with a severe limp.

Jim came out of his garage and was walking down the sloped driveway carrying the cage with the monster boar coon he'd caught from under his hot tub. Me, being a good sport, sat in my truck down on the road giving him a friendly toot of the horn.

About halfway down his drive, that old boar ran his right arm out the side of the cage, took a swipe at Jimbo's leg, and tore a hole in his khakis. He then went after Jim's bare leg. The coon drew blood and down Jimmy went. He first rolled left, then right, then down the drive with the cage on top of him. The boar ran his arm out again and made a grab for Jim's privates. Jim backed away from the cage keeping his legs spread and trying to keep his cojones out of harm's way. The coon missed but continued taking swipes at Jim's jewels.

Well here's Jim, lying with his head downhill; his legs are spread apart and the trap is between them and upside down. Jim has his head up like an old turtle and I'm in the truck watching the show and laughing my head off. It was unbelievable!

The trap was upside down. The problem with this was, to open

71

the door normally when it's right-side-up, you slid two rings up on each side which allows the door to open. Now that the cage was upside down the rings dropped into a position that allowed the door to open. There lay Jim, eyes wide with panic, scared stiff. He decided to lay flat and remain still.

The old coon looked at the opening, paused, then slowly walked out. He sat there studying Jim's privates again but apparently decided he wasn't hungry this morning. He scrambled up Jim's body, jumped over his head, shot down the driveway and ran under my truck. The last I saw of him he was going through the field headed for the woods.

Jim rolled over, got up and composed himself, then walked calmly back to his garage. He didn't speak to me for three weeks. Later we laughed about the incident on the many fishing trips we took, but that put an end to the coon trapping. Jim told that story many times before he passed away. In honor of my deceased friend, I decided to write his story down and add it to my book.

The next year I had a garden out back under the power lines in full sun. The soil was very fertile; the plants thrived and produced a great bounty. One morning as I was walking back the trail to the garden, I paused at the gate and observed a big healthy groundhog helping himself to my lush green plants. That night I had my box trap out and was going after Mr. Hog.

The next morning when I checked the trap, there he was. Being the true sportsman I am, I took him down to the farm to turn him loose. When I opened the cage on the tailgate of my truck, out he ran.

He was hauling it as fast and his big chubby body would allow through one of our large, open grain fields when, about halfway out into the field, out of nowhere comes a gray and white coyote. He nailed that hog and ran off with the big creature hanging from his mouth. I then retired from trapping for another period of time.

As time went on, I decided to trap squirrels—"tree rats"—who were taking over the bird feeder in the yard. I'd catch a few here and there and often, I'd manage to catch two at once. I took them out to Dad's house and when I'd open the cage to let them go, they'd always head for the woods. It made for some good hunting later on.

Now come the skunks–one day while trapping squirrels, two black and white skunks decided they'd try the cage, and sure enough I caught both of them. Not being familiar with how to deal with these stinky-but-beautiful creatures, I called a friend who was an expert trapper and he showed me a way to get them out of the trap without getting doused with their odiferous perfume.

My other run-in with the black and white varmints, sometimes called a "woods pussy," was back in 1970 while stationed at Altus AF Base. The skunks took over that town like a bunch of thieving outlaws in a spaghetti western.

There were no fences in or around Altus at that time and the skunks came from everywhere, spreading rabies to dogs and people alike. Back then, firing a gun within the town limits was not against the law. You were not only allowed to blast any skunk that came into your sights, but you were encouraged to do so, and I sure did. I took out over 100 skunks just by myself during that open season. That's how badly they'd overrun the town.

Now about opossums, or as they're more commonly called, possums. They look like giant rats and when they feel threatened, they lie still with their eyes closed and look dead. There've been a lot of phrases and songs using the word possum over the years.

A few samples are: *He's just playing possum – "I've eaten possum, and it's no good,"* George Jones sang. *– You can't put this possum in a bag* or, *Hey, Mick Flynn, is that your face or a possum in your shirt collar?– I could not give a possum fart. – Dead possum in the middle of the road along with the skunk and stinking to high heaven.*

Back in the 1970s, our company erected a portable Aztec asphalt drum-mix plant down in western Indiana where two county roads crossed a state highway. We had a large paving contract there. Across the road from the plant's property gate was an old general store. We all bought gas there along with gum, candy, aspirin, chewing tobacco and other various sundries. They made a great SPAM sandwich and also offered pickle loaf as well as most all other lunch meats. The sandwiches came fully dressed and most all of the workers got lunch there.

Friday finally came around and, as usual, I was the last one to leave the plant site. I gathered up the timesheets, cash from the week's cash sales, truck tickets and what have you. I locked the gate and decided to stop by the store for a bag of BBQ pork rinds and a quart of A&W root-beer for the long drive home. By the way, the name of the store was *Possum Junction General Store*, at, of course, Possum Junction, Indiana.

Over in the corner of the store was a rack of tee-shirts. They carried small, medium, large and extra-large. It was early December; Christmas was close by but it was cold out and the owner said the shirts were not selling well since winter had set in. He said he'd make me a deal if I bought one.

"How much?" I asked. He thought about it a moment, working the numbers in his head, then gave me a price. Always one who loved to bargain, I countered with, "Take another 50 cents off each one and I'll buy them all."

He did, and I did. On the front of the shirts was a picture of a large possum and the words, *Possum ... the other white meat.* On the back was the location–Possum Junction, Indiana.

Come Christmas, everyone in the family, along with neighbors and friends received a Possum Junction tee-shirt. Everyone laughed at my generous gift and not one person complained. I'm convinced that they all wore their possum tee-shirts with pride!

19

~ The Eiffel Tower ~

Back in the late 1980s, my family and I took a two-week vacation to Paris, France, on an art and sightseeing tour. It was a long flight, but it went well. While the food was good, the wine was better, and it was free and flowing. I stayed up all night, instead of sleeping. I was drinking no-nitrates red wine. Getting off the plane I had a pretty good buzz and a headache going.

The currency used in France was not the Euro, but the franc. My bank at home had ordered some of the French money for me and I was advised to carry some for taxis, tipping, etc. until I got settled in at the hotel. Then I was to use my Visa card for most everything.

The accommodations were great. We were all in the same room. It had a double bed and a foldaway, one bathtub, one commode and a towel-warmer. I'd never seen one of these, but was duly impressed! When I got home, I had towel-warmers installed in both of our upstairs bathrooms. Now back to the story.

Our plan was we'd spend two nights in one location, then move on to another place closer to the events we had planned for the next day. The first day we were up and out early. We had breakfast at the hotel and the breakfasts were always very good. The typical fare was thick-sliced bacon, French cheese, baguettes along with some excellent butter and jelly, nasty plain yogurt, and a small cup of strong Mississippi mud coffee.

We took a cab to the Louvre Art Museum. The cabs in France were very different from those in the States. All of them were black and they had what are known as "suicide" doors that opened from the front to the rear like my old 1950 Dodge. They were nothing like the American cabs or the Ubers, Lyfts, etc.

If you've never been to France, the roads don't follow a grid pattern like a lot of them do here in the states. If you look at a road map of Paris, you'd think you were looking at a drawing of a plate of spaghetti! Consequently, the rides were always an adventure. The drivers were a hoot and coming up with the correct fare was a challenge for me. It seems that all of the French people have their hand out for a tip of some sort.

At the Louvre, the girls spent a full day touring and took in every painting, rug and art artifact there was in the famous museum and we even had lunch in the basement.

I'm not a great fan of the French people in general. If it was not for the American soldiers liberating France during WWII, the French people would all be speaking German today. Courtesy and respect for the American tourist, and for the USA in general, was very much lacking, in my opinion. This was very disheartening when you think that the American taxpayers footed most of the bill to rebuild France, as well as most of Europe for that matter.

We had perfect timing arriving at the Louvre. There was hardly a crowd. My personal mission was to get eye-to-eye with the Mona Lisa. I did for quite a while and it was an awesome experience, to say the least. That was what I came for. My walkthrough took 30 minutes after visiting my famous lady. My wife and daughter spent the rest of the day touring, studying, comparing notes on things and discussing all the museum had to offer.

I found my perch in a chair near the front door and here I took up residency doing what I do best—watching people. It was kind of like going to your local zoo. I met the ladies for lunch in the basement and then returned to my chosen seat.

You can't imagine what types of people—I think they were people?—that came walking and crawling through the front door. On the cab ride home, we stopped for a late afternoon tea or wine and cheese. The TV in France was really a bummer and BC TV is next to nothing, as in, it was no good. Then it was time for a shower and off to dinner.

We wined and dined in many different restaurants and they were nice. In one restaurant, the people seated next to us had a big dog sitting in the chair at the table. They were feeding him niblets of whatever they were having. Dogs eating at the table was a new one for me!

The duck I ordered was covered in thick gravy and the plate had strange-looking grains and other mystery foods. To me it was nasty. I thought the only thing good was the bread and wine—they *do* make excellent bread and wine in France. It was not the best dining experience for me. The dessert I had was not much better.

On the following nights, the food got somewhat better. I had pigeon that was good and dove that was also tasty. The horsemeat was a hoot, but only the wine and bread were consistently good with every meal.

The many other sights we saw were interesting. The Cathedral of Notre-Dame de Paris was most beautiful and was well worth the tour and visit. On each side of the front of the church were tall towers that extended up higher than the roof. There were doors on the front of each tower. Curious, I walked over to one and when I pulled on the handle, the door opened. We proceeded up the narrow old stone steps in a constant spiral. The steps had depressions in the middle from the countless footsteps that had worn them down over many hundreds of years. They were so narrow that two people could not pass.

We finally came to the top of the stone tower and out onto a small flat roof area. You could touch the copper gutters of the main roof and here is where I found a six-inch piece of a copper gutter-tie, which became my favorite souvenir from the trip.

I noticed there were two big ladder-type steps up to a 2 1/2 foot x 3 foot solid wooden door. Being of a curious nature, I pushed on the door and to my surprise, it opened. We crawled through the small opening and up a few more steps to a wood landing. Just below us was one of the bigger-than-life, Notre-Dame bells. We were at the top of the bell tower and no one knew we were there! In my mind, the image of Charles Laughton as Quasimodo in the 1939 movie, *The Hunchback of Notre Dame*, swinging on the bells came to mind. My wife nudged me and I awoke from my daydream.

We took pictures and admired the bell. What personally interested me the most was the four-foot square timbers that were crisscrossed for the support and cradle of the bell. The girls grew tired of looking at the bell and timbers and we made our way back down the winding staircase to the street level.

When we got there, there was a group of six tourists and one tour guide giving them a lecture of what they were about to do—climb the steps up into the tower, gaze at the bell and the Paris surroundings—the same adventure we'd just finished with me as the guide, and all on a free-of-charge tour.

We tagged along as the guide went on to explain all about the tower, the bell and the history of the church. Then he came to the wood timbers which cradled the bell. They were chestnut, from virgin trees, and they had an unbelievable history. Bugs, termites, rot and decay do not affect the timbers. This was definitely one of the highlights of the trip for me.

From there, it was the same—the cab ride, afternoon tea, rest up, dinner and get ready for tomorrow's exploration.

The next day's adventures consisted of museums along with a visit to the Arc de Triomphe. There were so many other places and so many stops that I draw a blank on them, but I know that I had a blast.

The day after that was more of the same, except this time, after dinner, we got the opportunity to climb the Eiffel Tower for views, sights and pictures of Paris.

It was a peaceful night and the tower was beautifully lit, as it is every night. We walked up several flights of stairs until we got to a platform about a third of the way up. From there the stairs were closed, but you could take an elevator to the top, which we did.

At the top, there was an area where you could walk around and gaze out over the city. Only a set number of people allowed there at any one time. You could feel the structure swaying to and fro. I noticed there was a line of people standing in front of a door, and there was a very stout woman of French or German descent who was standing guard there. She had a large, oversized church-key of sorts, and she was the matron of the only toilet at the top of the tower.

My stomach was churning from the combination of the swaying, my fear of heights, fear of being packed in the cramped elevator with no room to move while my face was pressed to the glass watching the land drop away and disappear before me.

Added to this was the grumbling and gurgling of my stomach from the rich, dark, gravy I'd had for supper that covered more of the mystery meat, plus the fact that my guts were about to explode and knowing what a mess it would be at the top of the Eiffel Tower.

Me, being in the back of the line and not wanting to cause a scene, I walked up to the guard-woman with the key, reached into my pocket and came out with a fistful of French francs and said, "Ma'am, I need to use the toilet—and I mean *right now!* I don't feel so good."

She accepted the cash, opened the door, grabbed a young man who was seated on the commode, by his long hair and proceeded to jerk him off the toilet. She then flushed it and wiped down the seat. She checked to make sure there was toilet paper and gave the place a once-over. She then stepped out and said, "Sir, it's all yours. Take your time." And take time I did!

I left the room in a better mood and felt very much-relieved at having averted what could have been a very nasty gastrointestinal explosion at the top of one of the most famous towers in the world. I gave the lady another wad of French coins and paper currency and said, "Thank you, ma'am."

"My pleasure," she replied.

We finished our sight-seeing and called it a night.

When we were on the plane ride home, the wife inquired, "How much did that toilet break at the top of the Eiffel Tower cost you?"

After a few minutes of thought, I replied, "I am sure it was $100 or more, and it was worth every penny!"

Soon, we were home and back to our normal way of life. That trip seems like it happened so long ago, yet I'll have memories from it that will last a lifetime.

As an aside, here's a little something I saw at the tomb of the great artist, Leonardo da Vinci.

Leonardo da Vinci's Tomb

The great Italian Renaissance painter was laid to rest here in the Chapel of Saint-Hubert.

In the gardens of the Château d'Amboise overlooking the Loire, a small, intricate chapel houses the tomb of the "Renaissance Man," Leonardo da Vinci.

In Leonardo's final years, the Italian painter, inventor, intellectual and all-around genius spent his time working for the French rulers controlling Milan. In 1515, King Francis I offered Leonardo the title of Premier Painter and Engineer and Architect to the King. Leonardo then moved to France to work for the French monarchy, never to return to Italy. He lived in the Chateau du Clos Lucé in the town of Amboise near the summer palace of the king. Here he focused on scientific studies until his death on May 2, 1519.

Leonardo's wish was to be buried in the church of St. Florentin in Amboise, which took place on August 12, 1519. However, the church was demolished during the French Revolution in the late 18th century (and later by Napoleon I). The alleged bones of Leonardo da Vinci were discovered in 1863 and moved to the Chapel of Saint-Hubert in the gardens of the Château d'Amboise. Today, the tomb can be visited on the left side of the tiny chapel, where two epitaphs (in French and Italian) hang on the wall describing his birth, death, and how he came to rest in the Chapel of Saint-Hubert.

20

~ My Friend - Pat ~

It was February 1975. I was attending IUS taking evening classes and I'd also just gotten hired to work at the Floyd County Surveyor's office. The first day I walked in, I saw a somewhat familiar face talking to the old boy (Walter S.) who was the County Surveyor. I say "somewhat familiar" because that face belonged to Pat Naville, a guy who also attended Providence High School, but was two years behind me.

I knew Pat through his family but didn't know him real well personally. He was just one of those guys I knew at arm's-length, saw in the halls of OLPH occasionally and knew he played sports, but that was about it.

I discovered that Pat, who'd just graduated from Purdue with his degree in Land Surveying, was going to be the survey crew party chief and my immediate supervisor. I wondered what it would be like working together. I had my answer a few hours later as we headed out to the field for our first day of work. It was like Pat and I had known each other all of our lives, and were damn good buddies.

We discovered that we had a lot in common, aside from the obvious of growing up in the same hometown and attending the same high school. We both loved the outdoors, fishing, hunting and knocking back a few cold beers.

On weekends during the winter months when it was hunting season, we could be found in the woods hunting squirrels or deer. In the summer months, we'd be on my boat fishing up at Hardy Lake or on the Ohio River. If fishing wasn't good, we'd just cruise and enjoy some beer and conversation. I had a strict rule while fishing though—you weren't allowed to open that first beer until someone in the boat caught a fish. Talk about incentive!

In addition to the hunting and fishing, we'd sometimes just take my canoe and go for a float trip down Silver Creek. I remember on one such trip, we saw a groundhog on the bank. Pat, who had his shotgun along, managed to shoot the animal and was pretty excited to take it home and cook it on the grill. Neither of us had eaten groundhog before but reasoned that if it was properly prepared, it had to be pretty good. Wrong! Pat told me that he'd cooked the meat slowly over the grill and had basted it with barbecue sauce the whole time. He said it was like eating shoe leather!

Our jobs at the County Surveyor's Office were CETA funded by the federal government in six-month allotments. In addition to our first six months, we received funding for two more blocks which essentially gave us a year and a half of employment. Knowing that we were going to be out of a job at the end of that last allotment, we opted to look for work elsewhere. I went to work for my dad's company, Stumler-Gohmann Asphalt.

Pat, who'd always wanted to see the west, packed a tent, a cooler, a few changes of clothes and took off in his old '66 Chevy Impala, "The Tank," on a road journey. He spent three months exploring the back roads of the just about every state west of the Mississippi River and fell in love with that part of the country. When he returned from his trip, he stopped by my office to chat. He told me he'd found a job and was moving to Denver. We shook hands as I wished him luck. I wondered how long it would be before he'd be ready to return to his hometown. That was in 1977.

Pat never returned to live in southern Indiana. When he'd be back in town for a visit, he'd swing by and say hello. As with all things like this, we kind of fell out of contact. In spite of that, I still felt a kinship with Pat. We'd had too many good times together to let 1700 miles come between our friendship.

I hadn't heard a word from Pat for a few years, then in July 2004, I received a postcard in the mail. On the front of the postcard was an image of a book cover. The title of the book was *Echo Whispers*. The author was none other than my friend, Pat Naville. I was both surprised, yet happy. Pat had always enjoyed telling, or listening, to a good story and I knew he'd talked about wanting to write when we'd worked together, but chalked it off as just one of those dreams we all seem to have when we're young. But here it was, right in front of me … a book written by Patrick Naville! I purchased a copy of the book and truly enjoyed the story. I could easily hear Pat's voice in the dialogue.

Flash forward—roughly a year ago, we had our first grandchild, a boy. Before that, I'd faced some serious health issues and wasn't sure how long I'd be around. My dad died at the young age of 67. I didn't know if I was going to follow in his footsteps. I wanted to get my "life story" down in print for our grandson—as well as future grandchildren—while I could.

I contacted Pat and asked him if he would be willing to assist in the technical aspects of the writing of my autobiography. Pat enthusiastically said he'd be happy to help in any way he could. Together, we fine-tuned and honed my story. My book, *Paving My Way Through Life – With Tenacity,* has received eleven five-star reviews on Amazon.

I discovered while working on my book that one goes through many highs and lows. You relieve the good times, and that makes you smile. But you also recall the bad times and that often will bring you to tears. I shed both tears of sadness and tears of happiness. But, as Pat pointed out, this is what it takes to make a story good. You have to draw the reader into every emotion you're feeling.

Pat has gone on to write and publish five more novels, all of which I found enjoyable. He was nominated to the New York Times Bestsellers List for his first book. His second book made the Amazon Top 100 Best Sellers List for westerns. His most recent book, a crime novel titled *Ripper* came out earlier this year.

After 45 years, Pat and I are still good friends to this day. He worked with me on this book of short stories you're currently reading!

21

~ PETA ~

"PETA" is the acronym for, *People for the Ethical Treatment of Animals.*

When I was a kid, I grew up eating meat—wild game meat, farm-raised meat and fowl of all kinds. Meat was meat and how it was prepared made all the difference.

I never really thought of, or for that matter, really cared about the impact of my actions on wild and domesticated animals. Here are some of my thoughts on the subject.

Become a PETA member? *I don't think so!*

Become a vegan? *Not a chance.*

For those vegans out there: *Personally, I'm rather fond of the old saying, "I killed this cow because he was eating your food!"*

T-bone steak: *$1.89 a pound—bring it on!*

Help the lowly Gorilla Foundation? *Nope.*

Lobsters do feel pain and must be protected. *I don't think so.*

No hunting ducks and geese: *Naw.*

Let's ban mice and rats from experiments. *Not a good idea.*

PETA says animals are not ours. *Wild animals I agree, but domesticated animals are.*

Outlaw deer hunting. *What a joke.*

Commercial breeding of all animals: *Do you want to starve?*

Halt muskrat killing? *Not me. The five ponds on my properties all have dams. Muskrats do tremendous damage to these and to protect them from degradation, a few of the critters have to go.*

Ban the selling and manufacturing of RED RYDER BB GUNS! *Funny, very funny!*

Animals' rights? *What about the rights of the American people?*

Save the seas—fishing should be banned. That's cruelty to fish. *Get a life!*

This list could and does go on and on.

Real men do not live on seeds and organic foods.

"Make America Great Again" should be the new slogan of PETA.

Animal testing? Why not look at all of the positives of this—the advances in health, medicine and science that has improved our lives, instead of the negatives.

I have enjoyed, and still do enjoy a good circus, a visit to the San Diego Zoo or the Louisville Zoo.

As you've probably gathered, I'm not a big PETA fan.

If we follow the rules in the book, enforce the rules in the book, limit the new rules, and remember that the percentage of Americans who are members of PETA represent a true minority of people. It is a well-founded principle, and one I strongly believe in, that a minority does not rule. A minority should be heard, but as far as making policy, that's strictly the job of the majority.

Since I'm probably considered by PETA to be an animal hater, I'm likely also considered to be a racist, homophobic, gun-toting, Bible-thumping Midwesterner, as well as a pickup truck driving, tobacco-chewing, whiskey or beer-drinking (and not wine or tokay), sports-loving, animal hunting, fish-catching redneck!

I mentioned in one of my short stories about Possum Junction General Store and the tee-shirts I bought that read, "Possum ... the other white meat." There, during the next construction season, was a new supply of shirts. I purchased many for gifts. On the front of the shirt in big, bold letters was the word—PETA. Below that it read, *People Eating Tasty Animals.*

I rest my case. *Have gun–will travel.* If my hat's missing, I've gone fishing. I think I'll have the special: *Surf and Turf!*

22

~ The Baker ~

We had the opportunity to travel to France another time. We flew into Paris, spent the night in a nice, private hotel not far from Heathrow Airport. For dinner, the girls had fish of some sort with a foreign-sounding name, of which, they claimed they loved. Myself—I dined on a bottle of Beaujolais wine (free of nitrates), a baguette, warm olives and a variety of French cheeses. Come morning our rental car was delivered and we were ready to roll.

What a surprise our car was. It was a black shining beauty—an Italian Alpha Romero sports car. The rental quote was for a sedan. They bumped up the class for the same price and my guess was it was the only one left on the lot.

It was a four-door and it was beautiful. It boasted a lot of horsepower under the hood. And true to the European tradition, the steering wheel was on the wrong side, compared to what we were used to in the States.

Shifting gears with your left hand takes some getting used to, and it had many gears. I never really knew what gear I was in after the first few. I shifted by the whine of the engine or the movement of the tach gauge.

After we loaded the car, the small trunk was full and two-thirds of the back seat was full to the sunroof. My wife, the navigator, with her American AAA road map and TripTik, was in the front seat. There was just enough room for our daughter in the back seat. Off we went.

The first stop and a two-day stay was south of Paris at Le Mans. We saw the sights, then the girls did some serious shopping. I spent time in the two local hardware stores working on my used pocket knife collection. While visiting the equivalent of True Value Hardware stores of France—one can only spend so much time there—the owner noticed my car and suggested I go to the world-famous race track there in town to take it for a spin and see how fast she would go.

You could buy thirty minutes of track time for $100, which I thought was a great investment. I'd never run a car as fast as it would go. I had her up to 100 MPH, then backed off from fright. I still had more gears to shift through and plenty more horsepower to go, but this was fast enough.

Back to town I went. I sat in an open-air bistro. It was like sitting at a table out on the sidewalk. I enjoyed some red wine, cheese, bread and crackers while watching for my lady shoppers to come by at any time.

Some three hours later, they showed up with bags in hand. We enjoyed lunch and the price was reasonable. The wine was outstanding as always. The bottle on the table was a large, clear glass type with a stopper. It was maybe a gallon or so in size. When I sat down and before my first glass, my waiter marked the bottle with a crayon at the pre-consumed level. When we left, he marked the bottle at its current level, then charged us accordingly for what we'd consumed.

I found this concept very interesting. With one look at the bottle, you could see what had been consumed. We walked away and I was thinking, *what a deal!* With the post-consumption mark on the bottle, the next customer could easily see where he/she started.

The next leg of the journey we took a half-day drive north and west through the countryside and passed through many small towns. We stayed at a nice bed and breakfast and it was very accommodating.

The food, shopping and sight-seeing was enjoyed by all. We also noticed how nice, friendly and extremely welcoming the locals were compared to the people of Paris. In Paris, the majority of people we encountered were rude, had body odor, hairy legs and armpits—just as I expected, the impression was to get out of Paris and never look back. The countrymen of France were a different breed and it was one that agreed with me.

The town we stayed in was Tours. We visited castles, chateaus and even visited the grave of Leonardo da Vinci. I believe he's a distant relative of mine. I make my claim of this based on the fact no one has ever disputed it!

As a lasting memory: I left a pair of dirty shorts hanging on a blade of the lazily circling ceiling fan in our room.

The next leg of our journey was to the home of Pierre and Marie

LaBoulanger. Their name translates to "The Baker" in English. They lived in the farm country outside of the town of Tours. They were distant relatives and we were in France to attend the wedding of their son. It was indeed a grand affair. With all of the church festivities, along with the wining, dining and dancing, the party stretched over two days.

We stayed up all night celebrating and had a party breakfast the next morning. We dined on wedding leftovers for lunch and kept the soirée going until 5 p.m. that evening. I'll say this for the French people, they *do* know how to throw a wedding!

At the farm, which was substantial in size, their living quarters was a stone house with a stone wall fence around it. When we first arrived, two mean dogs had me pinned at the front door archway. The groom walked up, snapped his fingers and the two dogs calmed down immediately. They walked up to me, licked my hand, sniffed my crotch and began wagging their tails. They were my good buddies from then on. Come to find out they only knew, or responded to, French ... no English.

As a kid, I learned how to milk a cow over in my neighbor's (the Paynes) barn. The next morning I lent a hand with the milking. There was no electric milker. The five cows were milked daily by hand. I was seated on a short stool giving those big swollen teats the push up and finger roll, pull-down, and the milk came a-squirting. I even placed a perfectly aimed squirt of the juice squarely on the forehead of my daughter, some 15 feet across the barn stall.

We toured and visited Normandy Beach and what a feeling it brought, thinking of the famous D-Day invasion. It literally gave me cold chills to stand on the same beach where so many American soldiers, along with our allies, had died. To see the landing irons still visible in the water, the German bunkers on the hill, the berms 80 yards from the water with nothing between but open space between the two was a somber feeling that really can't be described—it must be experienced.

Of course, this part of the story would not be complete if I didn't mention the Normandy American Cemetery. The cemetery site sits at the north end of its half-mile access road on the bluffs overlooking the ocean. It covers a little over 172 acres and contains the graves of 9,380 of our military dead, most of whom lost their lives in the D-Day landings and ensuing operations.

To walk that site and see all of the white crosses marking the graves is something would move even the strongest man to tears. You know you're on hallowed ground when you stand there and you can feel the presence of those brave soldiers. To know that they died to protect our freedom is even more moving. It will definitely choke you up.

The next day we explored Utah beach and the surrounding area, then headed over to the small village of Sainte Mere-Eglise. This is the place where, on June 6th, 1944, an American soldier, John Steele, along with his division, parachuted behind the German lines. Unfortunately, when Steele was dropping in for a landing, his chute got stuck on a church steeple high above the town and an encampment of German soldiers. He hung there for days and played possum to make the Germans think he was dead. He was later brought down by the advancing allied armies led by the Americans, and he was still alive. He recovered in England and lived to tell his story. There is a celebration in the town every year honoring this brave American soldier. Red Buttons played the role of John Steele in the movie, "The Longest Day."

During this time, the groom's grandfather, Jean-Paul, and I became friends and hung out. We drank wine and reminisced about the war. He was a great patriot. The family farmhouse was about forty miles from Normandy beach. The Germans had used his house to set up a base camp. Jean-Paul was taken as a prisoner of war and had to march/walk across France to Germany.

When the war ended Jean-Paul then walked back across France to his farm home only to find all the surrounding neighbors' homes, barns and outbuildings had been destroyed by the Germans. Only his stately home, which was hundreds of years old, was standing and in a livable condition.

The Germans apparently left in a hurry when they heard the allies were rapidly advancing on them. Years later I was informed that my friend Jean-Paul died of old age. He was buried on the farm.

As fate would have it, the groom eventually divorced the American woman and I have lost all contact with my wonderful French country friends. They are always in my thoughts and prayers.

A few days passed and we were on our way to Brussels, Belgium. With another day's drive across northern France, my pocket knives now filled my pockets and a satchel.

In Brussels, we stayed in a clean bed and breakfast, dined on rabbit, mussels, waffles, visited the Peeing Boy statue, the battlegrounds at Waterloo and other war memorials, and then we were off to Gosselies, Belgium.

Gosselies is the home of the largest Caterpillar Tractor plant outside the USA. We took a tour of the plant in a golf cart and had lunch in the Cat cafeteria. We were furnished with an English-speaking lady to show us around—she was a most beautiful woman I might add! She chauffeured us in a company car and fed us for two days and nights all at Caterpillar's expense.

We departed with smiles and wonderful memories. Outside of Brussels was an autobahn to Paris, where we were to make our flight connection to return home. While on this road, as the girls slept, I pushed the Alpha Romero to 105 MPH with a lot more peddle to go. As a warning to those who've never driven on one of these ultra, high-speed highways, stay out of the left lane!

If you're in the left lane and someone coming up behind you flashes their lights, get over into the right as fast as possible because you're about to be quickly passed. The left lane always has the right-of-way. With me driving a sluggish 105 MPH, I was passed by a *lot* of cars. There is no speed limit on this autobahn.

We went from Paris to New York to Atlanta to Louisville to Floyd's Knobs and back to work one day later at the office in Clarksville, Indiana.

The following Wednesday we purchased a CAT 990, a pit loader for our quarry in Sellersburg, along with three big 50-ton CAT quarry trucks—a purchase worth well over two million dollars.

Our European trip had been arranged by our local CAT dealer and proved to pay dividends for the company and the local distributor here in Louisville.

A little back-scratching goes a long way!

23

~ Mahi-Mahi ~

The year is 2018, Coral Harbours Club Marina, Islamorada, The Florida Keys. The Joanna Marie, my 27-foot Grady White, is safely docked in her slip. We returned from a very successful fishing trip some 7 miles offshore at the edge of the reef.

My fishing buddy, "Speedo," had just finished cleaning the boat and preparing her for the next trip out to sea. I finished cleaning a fine catch of yellowtails, porgies, a nice mutton snapper and a bunch of trash fish that we put in the freezer as crab-trap bait.

The dock was backed up by a four-foot-high, coral stone wall and on top of it was a small tree, the only shade around. We had three deck chairs set up where we could sit and relax and watch the dock, the boats, the dock-box freezers and the fish-cleaning table.

Speedo and I sat in two of the chairs admiring our clean-up work, discussing the big one that got away, the ones I'd cleaned, the mating sea turtles, the flying fish, the hooked shark, the ballyhoo running across the water surface and the birds flying above against the backdrop of the deep-blue sky.

On the water about two miles out, we spotted our dock neighbor and friend, Captain TDGP. We called him Captain TD after an old woman resident whose old hound dog was named "TibbaDo." She was a Cajun from Monroe, Louisiana. She was a great woman and that was a super dog.

Old TD had his 30-foot, center-console boat wide open and was on course for the inlet to our marina basin. The hull of his boat lowered as he approached the first piling while the stern simultaneously lifted on the wake as the boat was carried a few feet forward like a sluggish surfboard.

TD brought her in at a no-wake speed, took a left and then a big wide right and straight into his slip. We heard him shift to reverse and the boat come to a dead stop. For some reason, it reminded me of a hungry cow heading for the barn.

I was told that his mate, Mr. Fritz, a Brooklyn man, had been a medical student many years ago. He'd come down this way to observe surgeries that Captain TD performed. TD had lost contact with Fritz for over 40 years but then bumped into him while on the internet.

Fritz got off the boat and prepared to bring ashore the catch. First, he set out two five-gallon buckets with fish of no substantial size, i.e. none stuck out over the top of the five-gallon buckets.

Then, stepping off the deck came the captain with a monster grin. He knew Speedo and I were watching. He hefts up a huge 40-pound mahi-mahi and holds it chest high while Speedo and I snapped pictures from the finger pier.

Pictures taken, Old Fritz walks out on the finger pier. Captain TD goes to hand him the fish but it slips through his hands and he drops it into the water. As the fish darts off, glad to have escaped, a five-foot barracuda from hell comes out of nowhere, hit the mahi-mahi and cut him in two.

Luckily, I had a throw-line with an alligator treble-hook used for snagging big fish, alligators, floating debris, and in this case, mahi-mahi from under the boat that have been bitten in half by cudas or sharks.

One throw and Old Fritz had half of the giant fish hooked again. Up and out of the water and onto the dock he came. He immediately went to the cleaning table. We watched as Fritz skinned and filleted the fish. He put the meat in a zip-lock and on ice while Captain bought us a round of Budweisers in aluminum, long-neck cans.

Speedo and I sipped our beer and discussed what we'd just witnessed. I got an elbow from Speedo and a whisper, "Let's cut Captain TD and Old Fritz a break and not tell anyone what had just taken place."

"10-4, Speedo," I said. "Sounds like a good plan!"

24

~ Bee Stings and Stones ~

Quite a few years back, the wife would follow my lead, and the daughter was always one step behind *old Dad*—those days when the daughter had to sit between her mom and me, and in her innocent young eyes, her dad could do no wrong!

One sunny Saturday in July, the three of us planned for a day trip to our 1000-acre farm where we could ride the John Deere Gator, snap pictures, picnic up on Hayes Hill, the highest point on the farm, ride the log roads, check the deer stands and game cameras, load the deer feeders, ride the fence rows and look for deer, rabbits, squirrels, turkeys and other wildlife.

At our home, we were building an addition to the house. It was going to be one very large room across the back of the house that overlooked the woods behind us. The back wall was going to be all windows and in the center was to be a fireplace made of sandstones, which we'd planned to pick up at the farm.

There were a lot of sandstones around the outskirts of the open fields at the farm and on the log roads that ran through the property. As we moved around on the Gator, we would load a stone or two until we had a full load, and then we'd transfer them to our pickup truck to be taken home.

We explored the farm until mid-afternoon and had a pretty full load of handpicked stones. It was, as I recall, a rather warm July day—sunny and quite hot. Off we went for home. We locked the gate and up Highway 135 we went.

As we approached the south side of Corydon—Indiana's first state capital—we all wanted an ice cream cone to help us cool off, and to also fill a craving for a dessert to hold us over on our forty-minute drive home.

We took a right-hand turn and down the hill we went. We crossed the Indian Creek bridge and on the right, just inside the city limits, was an ice cream and soda shop called "Emory's."

The shop, which was an extension of her home, was originally started by Mrs. Emory in New Albany, and for as long as I could remember, was located on Beharrel Avenue. All of the ice cream was handmade by Mrs. Emory and you never tasted anything finer. When Mrs. Emory passed away, her house, along with the ice cream shop, was bought by a Corydon couple. They moved the operation to West Walnut Street in Corydon on the banks of Indian Creek.

We pulled off and parked across the road from the shop, eager for a cold tasty treat. We all ordered triple-dipped cones covered with chocolate. We were three happy campers as we licked away on our frosty delights, and across the road we went back to our truck. There was no traffic coming and, at the centerline, the wife, never missing a lick, went to catch a big drip that had melted down the side of her cone. In doing so, she licked a good-sized bumble bee who had apparently decided it wanted some of the ice cream too. The bee nailed her on the tongue. The wife screamed and went ballistic! She threw the four-dollar cone on the pavement and screamed, *"John—get me some Benadryl, get me some Benadryl!"*

I obviously had none on me and was thinking, *Where am I going to find this?* I looked down and saw the cone lying on the pavement, and not wanting to see her ice cream go to waste, I bent over and picked it up. Bad move on my part. Now the wife was not only in tremendous pain, but she had to deal with my insensitivity to the situation. To be honest, I wasn't trying to be uncaring; I was just thinking of that ice cream cone. The wife tore into me and was letting me have it. All the while her tongue was starting to swell. I quickly tossed the cone back onto the pavement.

We were all hot and tired and in a slight state of shock at what had just happened. We hurried to the truck and off we went to the old Corydon Hospital located about a mile away in town. As I drove, I could feel the wife seething. I knew it was best to keep my mouth shut.

We were in the ER for three hours while a nurse held ice on the wife's tongue. She was given a shot of something about every hour until she was declared safe to go home. We were told to keep ice on her tongue and that she'd be fine in the morning.

Home again, the wife tried to rest as comfortably as possible, being in our cool home. She had a bag of ice on her tongue to help alleviate the swelling. My daughter and I unloaded the stones from the truck and it was back to life as usual. The whole thing was just another one of those bumps on the road of life. There was no way I was going to downplay or make light of the situation to my wife, though. There are times when a husband just knows instinctively that if he opens his mouth, it might be the last time he does so.

My wife, quite understandably, was extremely irritated with me over the whole incident, and to be honest, how I handled it was very stupid. I came across as showing a total lack of compassion and sympathy. It's not that I truly felt that way, but I'd never dealt with anyone getting stung on the tongue before. I wasn't sure how I was supposed to react, but if it ever happens again, I'll for damn sure know better the next time!

Come the next Saturday, we were off again for another load of stones. In all, we made 12 trips to gather the decorative rock. We have an amazingly beautiful fireplace to show for our efforts. I think what makes something like this even more special is when you have sweat and skin in the game, or in my wife's case, a bee sting to the tongue. It was definitely a memorable family event.

25

~ Two Bucks ~

One morning a few years back, while going through the company mail at my office desk, one of our asphalt paving foremen walked in and asked if I had a minute. I, always trying to be prepared and one-up on the employees, asked if this was business or personal.

For the record, I will refer to the foreman as "Silas." Silas hesitated a minute then replied, "It's personal."

"Okay, man," I said. "Close the door and have a seat. What's on your mind?"

Heartbroken, Silas explained, "The wife and me are splitting up, divorcing."

"Are you sure?" I asked. "You've been together a good while. You have two grown kids. How can I help?"

He tells me, "You know my farm up at Salem where you deer hunt with me and the boy?"

"Yes," I said.

"Well, I need to sell the property. I need the money to give the ex her half of everything. I can't buy her out because I just don't have the funds."

"Well, Silas," I said. "Tell me what I do to help? You want me to buy the farm? If that's the case, then tell me the particulars of the farm— the ins and outs."

"You've been there hunting," he said, "So you know what it looks like." He further explained, "It's 127 acres, 87 of which are tillable. It's good, fertile land and the yield per acre is excellent. It has 39 acres of woods, a one-acre pond, it's fenced, has good neighbors and a county road all along the west side of the property. There's one old dairy barn falling in and one cattle and hay barn in need of repair. It has an old, two-bedroom house that I rent out, and a two-car garage. It also has three sheds and an outhouse."

"It sounds good," I said. "Let me run it by my home boss ... hang on." I called my wife who was in the laundry room at home. I ran it by her, along with all of the details.

"Can we afford it with no strings attached?" she asked. I said yes to all.

"Then do what you want," she said. "I trust you know what you're doing."

"Silas," I said. "No problem. The boss is good with it and I am too, and I want to buy it. How much?"

Silas spit out a number. I asked, "What does that come out to per acre? What does a Washington County acre in the vicinity of this farm go for?"

He wrote a number of the cost per acre on a sheet of paper and slid it over in front of me.

"That's a little steep, Silas," I said. Not wanting to make him mad, but also not wanting him to say "No," I countered with an offer. He accepted it.

"Boss man?" he asked, "Can it be a cash deal?"

"That's a lot of money all at once, Silas." I knew I could swing it, but needed him to sweeten the deal a little. I said, "I'll need a little off the acre price, a clear deed and title, and the property corners located by a good survey."

Silas scribbled a revised number on the paper and agreed to the other demands. With a handshake, I was the new property owner.

Today, the house is gone, the sheds are gone, the old dairy barn is gone, the hay barn is repaired, the pond dam is fixed and the pond is stocked with big fish; the fences are mended, the fields are planted, a timber harvest is set up and lots of blackberries, chestnuts and a few buckeyes are harvested each year. The three wooden deer stands that were there are now replaced with one Texas-style hunt box complete with a chair and space heater. The property is now my personal hunting, fishing and ATV-riding piece of heaven here on earth. It was definitely a good investment.

Speaking of hunting, some five years back, my dear friend, Albert, asked if he could go deer hunting with me that season. "Sure," I said. "Let's you and me go up to the Salem property on opening day."

The day came and Albert was at my house two hours before dawn.

We loaded my Toyota pickup and off we went for the farm. Once there, I put Albert at the top of the small hill by the pond dam, an L-shaped area. There was corn along one side, woods on the backside and thirty yards of open grass between the corn and pond. Even though there was a tree-stand in the corner, Albert decided he'd feel better if he sat on the ground below the stand.

I went down the hill about a hundred yards, and then over about another two hundred yards from where Albert was and climbed into my tree stand. It was almost daylight and we were settled in. There was no wind; it was very cool, but not cold and was very cloudy. About eight a.m., I get a text from Albert. *See anything?*

I texted back, *No, how about you?*

No, he responded.

I texted him back. *Let's stay till ten, then I'll meet you at the truck.*

At 8:30, off to my left and about 35 yards on the other side of a thicket, I could hear the rubbing of a buck. I could see the four-inch sassafras tree top shaking and through a small opening, I could see a big-racked buck tearing this rub tree apart. I could see his huge rack as he rubbed his antlers up and down.

About two minutes later, the action started. *BAM-BAM!* went two shots from over in Albert's direction. In a split second, my buck stopped his rubbing. He froze, his head cocked in the direction of the two shots fired from Albert's location.

Up went my 44-magnum, Marlin lever-action, and with one shot, the big boy was on the ground. It was a perfect neck shot.

Fifteen minutes passed, then down the tree I came. I walked slowly over and around the thicket and there lay my 10-point buck. He had a perfect rack and was a good size, maybe 180 pounds.

I walked over to Albert's stand and there he sat, sipping coffee with a huge grin on his face. A big buck was lying on the ground about thirty yards from the edge of the corn.

Albert's buck had 11 points and was about the same size as mine. The eleventh point on Albert's buck could just barely hold his wedding band. But with our method of scoring racks, this counted as a point. Due to that, I lost a two-dollar bet and lunch on the way home.

The problem with this was, Albert had no license and lived in Kentucky. I was sure he would harvest a doe and never a buck. The limit was one buck per hunter and up to six does. I thought, *No problem—he gets a doe and I'll check him in on my lifetime license.* Now we had a serious issue—two bucks and one legal hunter.

We opted to leave my buck until I could figure something out. We field-dressed Albert's deer, tagged his ear as required, then loaded him up and drove to the nearest check-in station down at Corydon. While eating breakfast at the WC Lounge, I figured out a solution to our problem.

We'd go home, get the wife and have her tag and check-in my buck. I placed a call to the check-in station in Salem, which was close to the farm and was told, there was no need for your wife to come in. Just tag the deer properly and you're good. Bring it by, or go on the internet under Indiana DNR deer, fill out the online form and your wife is good to go.

That's what we did and things were fine. By this time, the weather had turned cold and the wind was blowing. We headed back to the farm to retrieve my buck and were able to get the truck to within 50 yards of where he lay. The plan was to string him up, field-dress him on the spot, then drag him out and over to the truck.

We came in by my stand and around the thicket and when we got to within about twenty yards of the downed buck, we saw five or six giant Turkey buzzards pecking and pulling, jumping around flapping their wings and having a big old feast on my deer. With one loud clap of my hands, the buzzards were up and away.

We inspected the deer and took some photos. To our surprise, the buzzards had pecked out and ate the eyes, and also removed the side of his ears. Half his privates were gone and his butthole or anus was pecked out to about the size of a grapefruit. His tongue was half gone and his nose was missing.

We field-dressed him, dragged him out and took him down to Webb's processing General Store where we left him to be ground into burger. Albert kept the back straps, and off we went for home, discussing, bragging and sipping blackberry brandy all the way. One week later Webb's called and said the processed deer was ready to pick up.

The next Saturday we headed to Webb's and filled our coolers with venison burger. That year we donated all of the meat—except the back straps—to the soup kitchen in Jeffersonville. We both felt good about the hunt and the camaraderie between us.

The takeaway was people in need were served; nothing was wasted and we had a great tale to tell for many years to come. We were both able to deduct the cost of our hunting trip off of our taxes. We've hunted many times since that cold Saturday morning in November and have never repeated the two bucks and buzzards hunt scenario.

"Hey, Albert? Do you remember that Saturday with the bucks and the buzzards? I sure do!"

We were two hunting fools!

26

~ Frigate ~

The Man O' War bird is also known as the frigate bird; I'll use these two terms interchangeably in this story. These birds are about the size of a laying hen. They have long, thin wings that measure nearly eight feet from tip to tip. They have an extremely long, forked tail which gives them great stability as well as maneuverability while flying. While males and females of the species all have predominately black plumage, the male birds are typically coal-black, while the female frigates have white markings on their undersides.

The male frigate has a distinctive red gular pouch—no feathers—which they inflate during the breeding season to attract females. When the males are on the prowl, this pouch expands and turns bright red which is assured to attract the eye of a female.

The bird has very small feet, with four webbed toes, and sports a long, hooked bill. The bill is used when the bird is engaged in combat, or robbing other seabirds of their dinner consisting of fish.

The Man O' War bird is the most aerial prolific bird in the sky and only lands to sleep, or to tend to its nest. The bird hardly ever lands on the water, as most pelicans and gulls do. The bird is unbelievably fast and skillful in the air at soaring, gliding, riding the air currents, and diving often to recover fish dropped by other frightened and panicky birds. The birds also glide low over the water to catch fish.

Frigates favor tropical sea coasts and islands. They will keep to within 100 miles of land, where they must return to roost. When breeding, there will typically be a single egg in the nest. Both the male and female will take turns sitting on it. I have seen these birds on the east and west coasts, as well as down in the Caribbean.

The seagull is best known as being a scavenger. It's often seen in large, noisy flocks anywhere food is available. They prefer to be around fishing boats, the docks, picnic grounds and garbage dumps—just about anywhere where they might snag some discarded food scraps. Most all seagulls are considered to be a nuisance. They are known as "garbage men with wings." They scavenge dead fish, animals and edible litter of all sorts which could pose potential health threats to humans.

Most folks, who live in the northern regions away from the ocean, would not believe the following story. Just yesterday, January 27, 2019, at 7:30 a.m., the wife and I were sitting on the porch sipping our coffee and enjoying the sunrise. Our porch faces south and sits some fifty yards from the water's edge.

Off the water and straight out ahead of us came an all-white seagull carrying an eight-inch long fish that looked to be a small mangrove snapper. The gull gained height in the sky and was about three palm trees high. He was moving east to the north when, from high above, coming in fast and hard on a direct nose dive like an F-14 Tomcat fighter jet engaged in aerial combat, a frigate closed in on the squeaking, frightened gull. In a matter of seconds, the gull dropped the fish, banked off and away from the dive-bombing Man O' War, quite grateful, I'm sure, to have made its escape.

As the gull flapped frantically away, the fish it dropped seemed to be floating in the air. The Man O' War turned his attention to the falling delicacy and in an unbelievable burst of speed, dove and snatched the fish in mid-air, then disappeared over the horizon.

It was, without a doubt, a once in a lifetime, eye-witnessing, National Geographic moment in nature, which one can only imagine. I was most fortunate to see it acted out in real life with my own eyes from the comforts of my porch.

Later that day, while at the swimming pool, which was just a short distance north of our porch, a friend was telling us of an unusual scene she'd had observed this morning. Ms. Reba Lou, our friend, also saw this event between the Man O' War and seagull play out. She is my eye-witness and could verify our sighting of this spectacular event of nature.

There is a law in nature that has played out since this world began. *The strong prey on the weak or disadvantaged.* This holds true for the animal kingdom as well as the human population. It has always been this way, and always will be.

In the Gospel of Matthew 5:5 in the New Testament, in the King

James Version of the Bible, it reads: "Blessed are the meek: for they shall inherit the earth."

I don't believe the seagull we saw getting attacked by the Man O' War is aware of, or believes in that passage!

27

~ Seenagers - 70 Plus ~

Today, I received a note from my good friend and retired company employee, Tom T. Tom managed our trucking companies for twenty-plus years. He was also an Army-retired, Purple Heart recipient from Vietnam.

My friend has passed the magic number, "70." Knowing that I'm not far behind him, we talk a lot about, *What if you were retired between the ages of say 20 and 60 +/-?*

I don't know for sure if Tom composed the following, or if someone shared this with him, but I found it most interesting, full of good thoughts, and an amazing list of accomplishments.

Tom says he's discovered the name for our age group. We are "Seenagers"—Senior teenagers. Here's our philosophy.

I have all that I wanted as a teenager, only some 60 years later.

I don't have to go to school or work anymore.

I get an allowance each month … Social Security.

I have my own pad.

I have no curfews.

I have a valid driver's license and my own car.

I have an ID that gets me into bars, strip clubs and liquor stores—legally.

The women that I run with these days are not scared of getting pregnant.

We don't have pimples or acne.

LIFE is truly good.

You also feel more intelligent after reading this, but only if you are a Seenager.

Brains of older people are slow because they know so much.

People don't decline mentally with age, it just takes longer to recall facts because they have more information stored in their brains.

Doctors and scientists believe this also makes you hard of hearing as it puts pressure on your inner ear.

Seenagers often go into another room to get something, and when they get there, they stand there wondering what they came for. It's not a memory problem—it's nature's way of making older people do more exercise.

I have friends and family I should send this to, but right now, I can't remember their names.

Thank you, Tom. I really needed this. It was good hearing from you and I'll add a page or two with more memories from the past ... *if* I can remember!

Keep the faith, Chief Master Sergeant Tom. You're drawing three retirements now. Hope your health is good and you live long enough to add to the above, your list of accomplishments.

28

~ Mother's Milk ~

My great-niece, who is a graduate student at the University of Kentucky, and my nephew, had a swim party and cookout last summer. While there, my niece's next-door neighbor was telling a group of us "Old Farts" who were stationed by the pony keg of Budweiser, about a test he'd taken in his advanced biology class. He said the last question on the test was: "Name seven advantages of Mother's Milk."

He explained that the question was worth a hefty 70 points and you either got it all correct, or you got a zero.

He said that one student, who was hard-pressed to think of all of the correct answers he'd been taught in class, came up with this response. He wrote:

1) It is the perfect formula for the child.

2) It provides immunity against several diseases.

3) It is always the right temperature.

4) It is inexpensive.

5) It bonds the child to mother and vice versa.

6) It is always available as needed.

And then he was stuck. Finally, in desperation, just before the bell rang indicating the end of the test he wrote:

7) It comes in two attractive containers and it's high enough off the ground where the cat can't get it.

He got an A+ … only at U of K!

29

~ Abortion ~

Abortion is definitely a hot-button issue. Yes, women should have control over their own bodies. This is the United States—home of the brave and free.

Hard work, honesty, prayer of some sort, as well as a belief in God, are all principles on which America was founded.

For many years, these values were honored, but somewhere along the line, there's been a sad loss of family values and togetherness. It drives home the point of the old saying: "You get nothing for nothing, and damn little for two cents."

The exception nowadays is, you can be whatever you wish to be—unemployed, down-and-out, live in your parents' basement, be an illegal alien, a drug addict, you name it. Only in the USA can you, as a non-productive person, sign up for a variety of "FREE" so-called benefits, and manage to live a suitable lifestyle of choice on the backs of the 48% tax-paying public.

It's hard to understand why the majority of American citizens let the *minority* rule the social programs. A big player in this fiasco is politics and the "power" that the politicians hold, once elected. Why would *anyone* choose to keep electing politicians that cater to the minority?

It is the *majority* who voted for the folks we send to Washington to fill the Senate and House seats, and who are supposed represent said majority and get things done according to the majority's wishes. Sadly though, more often than not, this doesn't seem to be the case.

This brings me back to the issue of abortion—the ending of a pregnancy, an unborn life. If you research the matter online, you'll find statistics that show a vast number of pregnancies are unplanned and are not uncommon at all. In a lot of these cases, many people decide to have an abortion.

The abortion debate is an on-going controversy surrounding the moral, legal and religious issues/aspects on the subject. It plays out in national politics and often, regardless of how a politician might truly feel about the subject, they'll vote whichever way they think will get them re-elected. National politics, in my opinion, is not the place for such debate.

The right to life is a moral principle based on the belief that a human being has the right to life. Article 2 of the Human Rights Act, in a nutshell, states:

"... nobody, including the government, can try to end your life. It also means the Government should take appropriate measures to safeguard life by making laws to protect you and, in some circumstances, by taking steps to protect you if your life is at risk."

Therefore, by law, no one shall be deprived of his or her life intentionally. However, there are some exceptions to this:

For example, a person's right to life is not breached if they die when a public authority (such as the police) uses necessary force to:

- stop them from carrying out unlawful violence
- make a lawful arrest
- stop them escaping lawful detainment
- stop a riot or uprising.
- in the execution of a court sentence following a person's conviction

No state shall make or enforce any law which shall abridge the privileges or immunities of citizens of the USA, nor shall any state deprive any person of life, liberty, or property without due process of law.

With this being said, the issue of abortion is clearly defined as being the law in the Constitution. If it's not liked by a few, then those few should pack up and move to Europe. But, if by chance, the Constitution is changed according to law, then each state shall decide what is legal and what is not with absolutely *no* federal money being spent on any abortion, and no monies being spent on abortions by any state government.

If one does choose to have an abortion, then the costs and consequences are assumed by the individual, and *not* by the state or federal government.

It is truly a sad state of affairs when a person can decide the fate, or make the decision on the taking of a life of another human being. I believe that unplanned pregnancies and the destruction of life by abortion could be resolved and prevented with the return of solid core beliefs and respect and love of family.

In reference to these issues, can you imagine working for a company that has a little more than 500 employees and has the following statistics:

* 29 have been accused of spousal abuse
* 7 have been arrested for fraud
* 19 have been accused of writing bad checks
* 117 have directly or indirectly bankrupted at least 2 businesses
* 3 have done time for assault
* 71 cannot get a credit card due to bad credit
* 14 have been arrested on drug-related charges
* 8 have been arrested for shoplifting
* 21 are currently defendants in lawsuits
* 84 have been arrested for drunk driving in the last year

Believe or not, folks, it's the 535 members of the United States Congress—the same group that cranks out hundreds of new laws each year designed to keep the rest of us in line. And yet, we choose to let this group decide if abortion should be the law of the land?

I don't think so!

30

~ Liberals ~

In my opinion, all legal citizens of the United States of America should know that our great country was founded on sound, conservative principles. The following conversation between a father and a daughter— it could be *my* daughter or son, or yours—explains the difference in thinking between people with opposite outlooks on things.

A young woman was about to finish her first year of college. Like so many others her age, she considered herself to be very liberal, and among other liberal ideals, was very much in favor of higher taxes to support more government programs—in other words, a redistribution of wealth.

She was deeply ashamed that her father was a rather staunch conservative, a feeling she openly expressed. Based on the lectures that she had participated in, and the occasional chat with a professor, she felt that her father had for years, harbored an evil, selfish desire to keep what he thought should be his.

One day she was challenging her father on his opposition to higher taxes on the rich and the need for more government programs. The self-professed objectivity proclaimed by her professors had to be the truth and she indicated this to be so to her father.

He responded by asking how she was doing in school. She answered rather haughtily, that she had a 4.0 GPA. She let him know that it was tough to maintain, insisted that she was taking a very difficult course load and that she was constantly studying, which left her no time to go out and party like other people she knew.

She didn't even have time for a boyfriend and didn't really have many college friends because she spent all her time studying.

Her father listened, and then asked, "How is your friend Betty doing?"

She replied, "Betty is barely getting by. All she takes are easy classes; she never studies and she barely has a 2.0 GPA. She's very popular on campus and college for her is a blast. She's invited to all the parties and a lot of the time she doesn't even show up for classes because she's too hungover."

Her father suggested, "Why don't you go to the Dean's office and ask him to deduct 1.0 off your GPA and give it to your friend who only has a 2.0. That way you'll both have a 3.0 GPA. That would certainly be a fair and equitable distribution the GPA."

The daughter, visibly shocked by her father's suggestion, angrily fired back, "That's a crazy idea. How would that be fair? I've worked really hard for my grades. I've invested a lot of time, and a lot of hard work. Betty has done next to nothing toward her degree. She played while I worked my tail off!"

The father slowly smiled, winked and said gently, "Welcome to the conservative side of the fence."

31

~ Outhouse Bottles ~

In 1960, I was ten years old and was living with my grandmother and grandfather on their small, country-gentleman type of farm. As was the custom, after supper once the dishes were washed and put away, and the sun was setting over Floyd's Knobs, most every night, the grown-ups would sit out back of the house under a large stately maple tree.

There were lots of sitting options that ranged from the old, green, metal chairs, canvas-covered butterfly type chairs, the picnic table or the long swing where they would relax while sipping their cold, adult beverages or the ice-cold sweet tea. This scene played out almost every evening and would last until the sun set and darkness set in.

One rather warm evening, a strange car came driving slowly up the drive. The vehicle stopped about twenty feet from where we were all sitting. There were two men in the car.

"Good evening," the driver said, then asked permission to get out of his car saying he wanted to talk to the lady of the house.

My grandfather, in a commanding voice, instructed the driver to back his car down the drive to the old oak tree some fifty yards away, and then come to talk about whatever was on his mind.

The stranger replied, "Much obliged," and did as he was instructed. The two, well-dressed strangers approached and inquired who was the owner of the place?

He was greeted with, "Who wants to know and what do you want? It better be good."

The driver asked, "May we have a seat?"

"Sure," my grandfather said. "Sit over at the picnic table." It was some distance from all of us, but still within talking range.

"Sir and ma'am," the man said. "We'd like your permission to come in and dig up your outhouse. We'll move it to a new location of your choosing. In return, we'd like the old bottles and what-not that we find in the hole."

Well, that brought a big, long laugh from all of the family members sitting there. My grandparents agreed to the deal, with one exception. That being—my grandparents would get a week's notice of the planned excavation, and they would approve of the clean-up of the area to their satisfaction.

The man agreed to our terms and asked, "How does next Saturday sound? We can start at seven a.m. We'll be able to start and finish in one day."

We said the next Saturday would be fine and off the strangers went. We all enjoyed a good round of cheers and speculation on what the men would find.

I'd never heard of such a request, or even had a clue as to what would happen. In my young mind, I knew of only one thing they might find below an outhouse, and it wasn't pleasant!

My uncle spoke up and said a thing like this happens about every ten years or so. I wondered why *anyone* would want to dig through the foul-smelling, human waste just to *maybe* find some old bottles. But, as the saying goes, one man's trash is another man's treasure.

Come next Saturday at seven sharp, the men arrived in their work clothes and boots. They had a washtub, a few large buckets, shovels, a grubbing hoe, a tamp and other miscellaneous tools. The men spray-painted a circle on the ground to where the outhouse was to be relocated.

A level trench was dug and the concrete-block foundation the relocated house was to sit on was laid, along with the tie-down rebar that were driven deep in the earth to secure the outhouse in windy weather.

The excavation went well as planned. We all came and went during the day to observe the spectacle. As the digging continued, small buckets were pushed into the mess and were used to scoop out the top few feet or so. The thicker solids below the top layer were extracted with post-hole diggers and also long poles with pots wired to the ends. It was quite an organized show.

As the dig went on, bottles of all sorts–whiskey, baby food, wine bottles, medicine and just about every kind of other old bottle imaginable were found. The bottles filled two good-sized washtubs.

Once the bottom of the hole was found, back in went the waste. The dirt from the new pothole was deposited in the old hole and compacted. Any extra dirt was raked neatly around. A handful of seed and straw covered the location of the original hole and the job was just about completed.

The men asked to use the water hose up by the house to clean up and wash off the bottles so as not to stink up their car too much. Grandpa denied them the use due to the fact that water was scarce and costly to be hauled in. We only had two cisterns that caught rainwater off of the outbuildings and house. This was supplemented with paid for, hauled-in water that was delivered in a truck by a very nice and kind old man, Mr. Prather.

But, on the property, not too far away, was a red-handled, manual pump on our well. It was full of cold, clear water. Grandpa told them they were welcome to help themselves to it.

After the clean-up was accomplished, the two strangers drove off, never to be seen again that I can recall.

It seems that the empty liquor bottles were tossed in the outhouse so that no one, outside of the immediate family, would ever see the volume that was being consumed.

Behind the outhouse was a burn-barrel where all the household trash was burnt and the ashes were put in tubs and set out by the garage. A garbage truck would come by every few weeks and haul the stuff off.

If one was to inspect the tubs, all you'd ever find was paper ash, burnt tin cans and some broken glass. Back in that time, it was the custom that what went on at your home or property was no one else's business. Some things were private and were kept that way!

32

~ 1969 Indianapolis 500 ~

The 53rd International 500 Mile race was held on Memorial Day at the Indianapolis Motor Speedway. Mario Andretti was the winner of the race in a car owned by Andy Granatelli. With Andretti's finish time of 3:11:14.71, it was the fastest run Indianapolis 500 up to that date, breaking the previous record by nearly five minutes. *I was there to witness the event.*

In 1969, I was stationed at Scott AFB in Illinois. I was 19 years old and a two-striper in the United States Air Force.

I, along with five fellow airmen, had a three-day pass, so we decided to drive over to Indy for the famous 500 race. None of us had ever attended one of the races before. With nothing but the clothes on my back, a hundred bucks in my pocket and more than one ice chest full of cold Bud, off we went in my friend Mickey's car for a fun weekend.

The drive went well and was filled with lots of BS amongst us, chased with plenty of cold beer. Suffice it to say, upon arrival, we could feel no pain.

It being rather warm out, and our pockets not overly-full of cash, we spent the night before the race in the parking lot with two of us sleeping in the car and the other three in sleeping bags on the grass next to the paved lot. Morning came way too early, as is usually the case after a night of beer-drinking.

After an All-American power-breakfast of Beanie-Weenies with chips and white bread, we were at the front of the line waiting for the infield gate to open. As best as I can recall, the entrance fee was ten dollars. The food was cheap and the beer was free. We had three coolers and back then, you were encouraged to bring your own—which we certainly did!

We might get hungry, but no way were we going to go thirsty. When the gates opened, we managed to outrun the crowd and secured a nice grassy spot by the fence on the first turn, a short distance from a row of port-a-potties and a nearby hotdog stand.

We were set. I believe the unwritten rule back then was to drink till you dropped, and one at a time, we dropped, only to rest up and get back to the party. It was wilder than any Kentucky Derby infield party I'd ever attended in my short life.

We heard the order of, *"Gentlemen, start your engines,"* and the race began. You'd see a flash of color shoot by; you'd hear the tight, high-pitched roar of the engines; you smelled the fuel and the tires burning, and all of this was mixed with the odor wafting over from the port-a-pots. That crap and urine odor grew riper as the day went on.

Halfway through the race, a short shower came and went causing a delay of the race. It also created a muddy, wet infield. With it being hot, humid and wet, coupled with fatigue and the smell of the port-a-potties hanging thick and heavy in the air, the conditions were right for a fight.

I don't recall how it started, but fight we did. It was a hundred-man-plus fistfight. There was a lot of wallowing in the mud and puke, dodging blows and delivering a select few of our own, but, man—what a time! We never thought life could be so good and we were making memories!

Besides fists, the blows were delivered using elbows, feet, coolers, bottles and just about anything else one could lay his hands on. The police and National Guard pretty much let us go at it until someone drew blood with a cut that needed stitches, then they moved in and the crowd dispersed.

Around twenty-five or so continued the brawl and were fighting for keeps. Mickey, the guy whose car we came in, picked up an ice chest and busted another drunk's head open. With that, the police singled him out and off Mickey went to a line of old yellow school buses with bars over the windows. There were no seats—just an open wagon on wheels. The buses were lined up over behind the port-a-pots and out of the way. All the time the race was going strong. Before long, all of the buses were filled with unruly spectators.

The infield crowd continued to party, eat, sleep, carry on and enjoy the flash of color and the sound of jet fuel being burnt. The race finally ended but the celebration went on until the whistles blew and all the stragglers were shuffled out of the gate.

My group approached the infield police chief and declared our status as airmen needing to get back to our base. We explained that our driver friend was in one of the jail buses. An hour or two later, the authorities began opening one bus at a time using the back emergency door. Out they staggered—the captured and guilty! On the third bus, out came old Mickey.

The Fire Department was there with hoses in hand, and five steps out of the door, they proceeded to hose down each departing individual. I suppose this was their way of telling the offenders to sober up.

We left the coolers, the sleeping bags and other personal items behind and carried Mickey back to the car. Mick slept on the back floorboard of the car all the way back home to the airbase. All of us, except Mick, managed to make the reveille call the next day and reported to work on time.

Mick spent half a day at the base first-aid station and was given the day off. He was sequestered to his room in the barracks and was given a letter of reprimand, which was a negative report that stayed in your personnel file for up to a year.

I can't speak for the others, but I learned my lesson. No more infield 500 trips for me. As a matter of fact, I've declined numerous offers to attend the big race for years since that day in 1969. I now prefer to watch the race at home on TV or to listen to it on my headset while cutting the grass.

With age ... comes wisdom!

33

~ Mumblety-Peg ~

Years ago, my Uncle Warren was the Boy Scout Master for the troop my brothers and cousins belonged to. I was too young to be a Boy Scout, and was, therefore, in the Cub Scouts. By the time I came of age to join the Boy Scouts, the older boys had moved on to other interests, and so had I, but I'll share some stories of those early days before my uncle got out of scouting and I lost interest.

Uncle Warren's troop would camp out back in the woods along Silver Creek. They'd hunt, fish, canoe, bike and volunteer for community service, host cook-outs and numerous other activities earning their merit badges along the way. In addition, they earned patches, decorative ropes—"aiguillette." An aiguillette is an ornamental braided cord with decorative tips which some of the scouts wore on their uniforms.

Being at an impressionable age, I thought all of this was very cool and it was something to look forward to. Even though I never made it to the Boy Scouts, I was allowed to tag along on some of the outings. I got to enjoy the fun and made some lasting memories along the way. Back then, most all boys, scouts or not, carried a pocket knife of some sort every place they went. The knife was just part of your blue jeans.

We even carried our pocket knife to church on Sundays, and in my case, I slept with it under my pillow. Most of the grown-up men around us at home carried a knife of some sort. It was just a way of life at that time. Even my Grandpa Gohmann carried a knife. His doubled as his folding money clip which we all thought was very cool. He never played the game of mumblety-peg—which I will describe shortly—with the kids or displayed his knife in public that I recall.

No one thought of the pocket knife as a weapon, or as a danger to anyone. On the school playground out back on the grass, you could always find the boys (never any girls), playing the game of mumblety-peg. I learned this game by watching my older brothers and cousins when they were in Boy Scouts. They, in turn, had learned the game from Uncle Warren.

To this day, I carry a pocket knife of some sort depending on the occasion. I have a knife money clip like my grandpa which I also carry my folding cash in, a knife I carry while fishing, another style I carry while doing "play" things or to work. I carry a longer blade when I'm hunting and the length of it varies depending on what I'm hunting for.

Back in my younger days, there was no cause for concern with carrying a knife. There was no TSA, no police checks and no knife fights—unless maybe you found yourself in the bad end of Louisville, which none of us did. We just showed good common sense taught to us by caring, loving parents, relatives and friends.

The knife was part of who you were. This practice and tradition doesn't translate the same today. While a lot of folks still carry a knife, for most of them, the innocence of doing that has been lost. It's now done for protection, or for some misguided minds because they think it makes them "bad."

But back to mumblety-peg, I taught my daughter how to play at a young age even though I was discouraged by my wife. She said that being a "city" girl, she was unfamiliar with the ways of the Scouts and country boys' ways of thinking. To this day I continue to play the game with myself. It brings back many good memories from the past. A pocket knife and I go together like peas and corn—read that short story earlier in the book! This is one tradition that no one can take away, yet most young men don't even understand.

There are numerous versions of the game. Mark Twain's book, *Tom Sawyer,* describes mumblety-peg as one of the boys' favorite outdoor games.

Here's a brief description of how the game is played. While these rules are based on my recollection, I also had some help from Alexa, Siri, the internet and numerous books.

One version is, the game is generally played between two people with a pocket knife. One contestant throws a knife end over end sticking it as deeply as possible into the ground, after which another player tries to extract it with his or her teeth. In early versions of the game, a "peg" was driven into the ground and that's what the losing contestant tried to extract with their teeth.

In another common version of the game, two opponents stand opposite one another with their feet shoulder-width apart. The first player then takes his knife and throws it to stick in the ground as near as possible to his own foot. The second player, using his own knife, then repeats the process. Whoever sticks the knife closest to their own foot wins the game.

If a player sticks the knife in his own foot, he wins the game by default. The game combines not only precision in the knife-throwing, but also bravado and the proper assessment of one's own knife skills.

There are many variants of the basic game. For example, the first player attempts to stick his knife in the ground using some unusual technique such as behind the back, or off his knee. If successful, the second player must duplicate the feat. In some cases, just getting the knife to stick at all can be the objective, but in others, the players attempt to stick their knives into a peg or as close to it as possible.

In the variant known as "Stretch," the object of the game is to make the other player fall over from having to spread his legs too far apart. To explain, the players begin facing each other with their toes touching. They take turns attempting to stick their knives in the ground as far away as possible from the other player's feet. If the knife sticks, the other player must move his foot out and touch where the knife stuck while keeping his other foot in place, provided the distance between foot and knife is about twelve inches or less. The play continues until one player falls or is unable to make the required stretch. I've seen guys almost doing the splits before they'd concede defeat. Winning the game, after all, was a matter of honor!

Along these lines, there was another highly dangerous game involving the knife throwing, "Chicken." Here, one player bets the other how many "sticks" with his knife he will allow the other to make at his feet. The betting player then stands with his feet as far apart as possible and the other player throws his knife into the gap between them. If the knife sticks, the betting player then moves his foot, whichever one is closer, to the point where the knife is.

Therefore, hitting as close to the center as possible is desirable to make your opponent's feet come close to each other with the least number of throws. The process repeats until either the agreed-upon number of sticks has been accomplished (betting player wins), or one player or the other refuses to go any further. Whoever did not "chicken out" wins. If the knife hits the betting player, he wins.

How the knife is thrown in these games varies. It might start with the knife's tip on a player's body part—elbow, wrist, shoulder, etc. The knife's handle is pushed so it rotates end over end to hopefully stick into the ground. If the first player succeeds, then that player will then decide on the next "trick." The other player is sometimes given more than one try. The game repeats going back and forth until one player cannot duplicate the "trick." If there are multiple players then play continues with each participant trying to "knock out" the others until only one player remains.

As you can see, from the description of the games—it's not for sissies or careless people of any age. It's just good old clean fun taught to me by a great family of which I was afforded the honor to be a part of.

Yes, growing up had its challenges, but looking back on it, the things I encountered gave me a great respect for that time, and also taught me to have great respect for people, animals, the fish in the seas, traditions and customs, our flag, and the Constitution of the United States of America.

I hope you've enjoyed this story from my heart as much as I've enjoyed telling and writing about a time, and a game, which I truly enjoy.

34

~ Dandelions ~

Gardening was, and still is, a favorite pastime and entertainment which I enjoyed while growing up and now, as a senior citizen. We lived in the country and it really didn't make a difference what the neighbors liked. Our home was a quarter-mile off the road and the closest neighbor was a relative, so not much attention was paid to the yellow yard flowers.

Some fifty yards from our house lived my Great Aunt Aggie. She was a master gardener, a super cook—her cookies were out of this world, handmade from scratch for every special occasion. She also believed in eating your greens and vegetables daily, and she practiced what she preached in this regard.

Aggie was from the old school and lived to be in her late 80s. Her flower gardens were always perfectly cared for. There were no weeds, just incredible beauty. Butterflies, bees and hummingbirds hung around in abundance.

Aggie's yard was also like a lush green carpet; closely manicured and cared for with loving hands. Her one big "enemy" was the dandelion. She didn't believe in weed killers, just the natural way of removing them from her yard.

Aggie said you could make wine from them—but she preferred Mr. Kentucky whiskey. The flowers could be dried and made into dandelion coffee. She also braided them into beautiful door hangings and floral arrangements. But her favorite way to eradicate them was: she loved them in making salads. And to her, they were exotic greens.

The internet says dandelions are an excellent source of potassium, calcium, and vitamin-A. She would dig them with a long, wooden-handled tool with a V-fork on the end. According to her, a dandelion had a two-year life cycle—the first year as green foliage. She'd dig them up and would fill brown paper Kroger bags.

If you let them go to seed, the flower end would turn into a white, round puffy ball of fuzz. The next season, you'd have to start the process of digging them up all over again.

Aggie worked hard though and she'd finally get the best of the dandelions. Her lawn was thick, healthy and green for the late summer and fall months. To this day, I feel she always left a few to hide in the grass only so they would come back the following year and give her a reason to dig, harvest and complain, and then admire her beautiful, lush, green yard. I can't imagine that the Emerald Isle of Ireland looked any better. Compliments, of course, were always appreciated!

Aggie was a great lover of the outdoors and it seemed that she was always in a happy mood whenever she was weeding and watering—her most favorite pastime!

35

~ A Short Love Story ~

A man and a woman who'd never met before, each married to other people, were both on the same transcontinental train ride and found themselves assigned to the same sleeping quarters.

Though initially embarrassed and uneasy over sharing a room, they were both very tired and fell asleep quickly, he on the upper berth, she on the lower.

At 1:00 a.m., the man leaned down and gently woke the woman saying, "Ma'am, I'm sorry to bother you, but would you be willing to reach into the closet to get me a second blanket? I'm awfully cold."

"I have a better idea," she replied. "Just for tonight, let's pretend we're married."

"Wow! That's a great idea," he exclaimed.

"Good," she replied. "Get your own damn blanket."

After a minute of silence … he farted.

End of Story

The above story was told to me by my brother-in-law. He swears it's true, but I'll leave it up to the reader to decide!

36

~ The Bike ~

A few years ago, in the fall of 1987, a friend of mine, Bob, owned a bike shop in Clarksville. I had purchased more than a few bikes from him over the years—Schwinns, usually. The quality of his products, along with his professional attitude and friendly service was always top of the line. His prices were a tad more than other places, but friendship and loyalty are worth more than money.

At the time, we were living in town on Elm Street. Our daughter was three years old and we thought if we had a bicycle built for two, we could add to our quality family time. So off to Bobby's store we went, and there in the window was a Schwinn bicycle built for two. It was a tandem, ten-speed bike, red in color with a large front basket and had a passenger or book platform behind the rear seat where a good-sized infant seat could be strapped on.

With the size of our daughter, we figured we could get a few years of riding comfortably. The bike was equipped with front and rear lights, and later on, we added a bell that sounded like the ice cream truck that came through the neighborhood. We also added a Howdy-Doody, bulb-squeeze horn.

Up till then, the wife and I had never bothered to wear helmets. It was never a requirement or even an after-thought on our part. But with our daughter now on board, helmets became a must and all three of us were custom-fitted with Bell helmets.

For years we rode to town. We'd go to Zesto's, the swimming pool, the bakery, the hardware store and just about everywhere else, and most of it was on rather flat terrain.

Then came the building of our new home and the move to Floyd's Knobs. There were very few flat areas or roads to navigate in the Knobs. I was typically on the front seat while the wife took the back seat which is the not-so-good seat on a tandem bike. She, by the way, did most of the peddling. Our daughter was on the back seat smiling, singing, eating snacks and having the time of her life!

With the dangerous potential of the narrow country roads plus our daughter out-growing the child seat, the tandem got parked in the garage and was taking up space. It seems that it got buried with household stuff that piled up high in half of the garage. One cold winter weekend, I decided to clean out the garage and turn it back into a two-car affair so I could park my Toyota there, out of the weather.

Load after load went out and the Schwinn went up. By that I mean, I installed three red hooks in the ceiling and up hung the bike just above head height so you wouldn't knock yourself out on it. The bike hung there until about ten years ago. It was somewhere around 1999, and we'd bought a new condo in Islamorada, a gated community where a walk or a ride around the grounds was flat and over a mile plus. It was a great place to bike. The Florida Keys are flat. There are no hills and it was perfect for a tandem bike, so on the truck it went and off to the Keys we hauled it.

The Keys traffic began to grow over the years and the wife gave up riding with me. For years I rode the bike by myself most everywhere I went. I could hear the locals saying, *"There he goes again. That obnoxious, horn-blowing, one-man tandem rider with an oversized basket always full of something or another."*

The chrome fenders were now rusty from sitting outside in the salt air, but she was dependable and everyone knew it was me on my red tandem bike, now built for one, two years ago.

I noticed the rims were rusty, the gears were slow to react, the horn stopped blowing, the basket was now rusty in color, the cables were close to breaking, and in all, my Cadillac red tandem bike was a sight for sore eyes. Along with that, the hand-pumping of the tires was a daily chore.

My condo fishing buddy, Little Tony, a year-round resident of Islamorada, who scuba dives, boats, bikes, follows all sports and takes his two kids around to every school sporting event there is, expressed an interest in *Old Red.*

We loaded the bike into his new Toyota truck and off we went up to Tavernier, where Tony had a nice home on a canal. I was introduced to *Old Bob*, the used bicycle man. There, under part of the house, were many bikes and a small outdoor, covered repair shop. We unloaded my tandem and as soon as the 82-year-old Bobby saw the bike, his only words were, and I quote, "I don't want it. It's a piece of s**t. I never did like those and still don't!"

After a long discussion and I demo-rode some 15 bikes or so, I took a fancy to a Huffy bike that was designed for both genders to ride. We agreed on a price of $100 and I could leave my tandem there for whatever he got for it. I suggested that he give it to the Montessori school, some five-mile markers down the Key. We shook hands and a deal was cut.

The other part of the deal was, old Bob had to switch the big basket from the Schwinn to the Huffy. This caused a big argument because he felt he'd already lost money on the deal.

"Okay," I said. "No problem. You can keep your Huffy and I'll ride my red bike home."

"No, no, no," he said. "That won't be necessary." I guess the crisp Franklin in my hand and his empty beer can got the best of him.

With all of that going on, sweating, joking around, working, selling and giving old Bob a hard time, a car pulled up to the curb out front. A big-breasted woman with legs on her *like you like them* got out. She smelled of coconut oil and Meyer's rum. Two grown men were following her. She asked old Bob, "Is that red bicycle built for two for sale?"

All of us went quiet. Old Bob smiled, pointed to me and calmly said, "You'll have to talk to that gentleman."

Miss Coconut Oil and Rum proceeded to tell all the story of growing up in north Florida somewhere around the town of Waldo. Her father made a living with the family bike shop, sales and service, and he did pretty well with it. She went on to say that her family all rode tandem bikes like that red two-seater there under the carport, where Bob was working on my basket.

The next words out of her mouth—and all went silent—was, "Sir?"

I replied, "My name is John. Bob there," I pointed to him, "is addressed as 'Sir.'"

She followed with, "John? Is that bike for sale?"

Choking back smiles, tears and shouts of joy, I replied, "Sure! Are you interested?"

"What would like to have for it?" she asked. "I mean, how much?"

There, on the picnic table, was a box and a sign requesting donations and advertising the upcoming yard sale to benefit the Montessori School. I replied, "See that collection box on the table? Whatever you think the bike is worth, put it in there and I'll donate it all to the cause."

Miss Coconut Oil and Rum dug in her purse, pulled a wrinkled up old Franklin and asked if a hundred would cover it?

I looked at Bob as I held back a grin. He looked at me and my three buddies and said, "John, it's *your* bike."

I told the lady I thought a hundred would be fair. She handed me the wrinkled-up bill and instructed her two friends to get on the bike. They did and down the street they went. I got a big hug from the lady and the deal was done. She got in her car and drove off.

By the time all of this was over, Bob had the basket mounted on my bike and it was ready to go.

Old Bob got the wrinkled-up Franklin, and I shoved a fresh, crisp one in the box. With a handshake and a thank you, my three buddies and I loaded the yellow Huffy in the back of the truck and off we went.

Our next stop was at a little hole-in-the-wall bar and grill called "Meat," where they served big, thick juicy burgers. We each had a few cold brews and exchanged lots of laughter with each retelling the two-hour event we all experienced with Old Bob, the used-bike man, up in Tavernier on Tavernier Creek, and the show and smell that Miss Coconut Oil and Rum gave us.

Little Tony asked, "John? What did you mean by, *She has legs on her like you like them.?*"

I replied, "They had feet on one end!"

37

~ Fly Fishing ~

Back in the 1950s within a short walk from home were three ponds and the once-clean-running Silver Creek. Everyone in the family enjoyed fishing and we managed to go a few times each week.

My Uncle Warren lived about a hundred yards from our house. You just followed the path through the side yard and after going under the maple trees, you were at his back door. Most evenings after supper, as the sun was making its slow, sleepy descent in the western sky, Uncle Warren, with a fishing rod in hand, would walk by our back door on his way to the pond or creek.

My father and brothers all had one-piece cane poles that varied between ten and twelve feet in length. For the ponds and open area fishing spots, the cane poles were perfect. If we were going to the creek or a pond where you'd have to cross a fence or two, then three-section cane poles seemed to be the best. On some of the ponds, if the owner spotted you, he'd attempt to run you off. The shorter three-piece cane poles were much easier to run with as you hurdled the fences while the owner chased after you. (I honestly don't think any of the owners were intent on actually catching us, but they had fun scaring us and watching us run. It was a ritual we both enjoyed!)

Uncle Warren was an open-face, bait caster, Shakespeare reel type of fisherman. He preferred topwater plugs, with a large black Jitterbug being his favorite. He always seemed to catch big fish and truly enjoyed cranking them in and holding them up by their bottom lip to admire their beauty, Then he'd calmly bend down and release the fish back into its habitat. Warren was a catch-and-release fisherman. I only recall him cleaning fish the few times he would go down to Herrington Lake in Kentucky. With most of his catches being smallmouth bass, he'd keep and clean them as he was quite fond of the taste of that particular fish.

My uncle's other form of fishing excitement came from fly fishing.

At one time he even tied his own flies. His gear consisted of a silver fly box, a brown and tan tackle bag, a trout bag and a net.

In the early days, Uncle Warren was an appliance salesman in Louisville—for whom, I can't remember. As time went on, Warren eventually opened and owned a very successful Kelvinator appliance distributorship and warehouse over in Clarksville. One year as a promotional deal, he gave away a rod and reel and a small tackle box with each new appliance sold.

One evening on his walk past the house as he headed for the pond, I noticed he had two bait caster reels and two rods. As always, out the door I'd run and would accompany him on these evening fish trips. To my surprise and delight, one of the rod and reels he had was for me. It was one of the promotional rigs from the Kelvinator giveaway program.

Over time, he taught me how to use the reel and I learned the ins and outs of avoiding backlashes and birds' nests. I also learned how to cast overhead, sidearm, the underhand/underarm flip. But probably the most important thing of all that I learned was how to pick the exact spot to cast the plug to.

Uncle Warren taught me about the speed, the jerk and the twist that was to be applied when cranking in the plug, how to reach down and grab the fish by the bottom lip and how to release the fish so that he survived.

From that summer on I carried two poles—my bait caster and my cane pole. Warren also taught me the art of fly fishing, only my pole was a one-piece cane pole. With this cane pole, the movements became natural and my accuracy skills were honed.

Uncle had a beautiful, split-bamboo fly rod and a Shakespeare reel, and he knew how to operate it. He had the patience of Job when it came to teaching me the methods of fly fishing, the tricks and techniques of which, I still use today.

One day, later on in his life, Warren gave up fly fishing. He gave me his hand-tied flies and equipment and I was set for a life of many good times fishing.

I have fond memories of him every time I hit a pond, lake, stream, river or creek. Of all the men in my life, my uncle whet my appetite for fresh-water fishing more than anyone. As life moved on for me, I collected boats, motors, reels, gear, tackle of all kinds for the numerous species of fish.

Some twelve years ago, I gave up fly fishing myself for the most part. I now only use a bait known as a "cork popper." I'll also still use the few hand-tied flies that I have left from Uncle Warren and, unlike him, I practice the art of *catch and eat!* I also only use my split bamboo rod when fly fishing, which is very similar to my uncle's.

All of the books, magazines and catalogs on the *how to* of fly fishing now belong to others. I told my Florida Keys fly fishing friend— *no more wading or boating to go fly fishing.* My fly fishing trips these days are in conjunction with my bass, bluegill and crappie trips. There in the boat, lying idle, is my trusty fly pole. When the bass aren't hungry, out comes the pole with the cork popper on, and I stalk the shallows, lily pads and cattails for big old Mr. Carp. They fight long and hard and are a blast to hook on a fly pole. When I hook up with a carp, I pretend he is my freshwater bonefish. If the carp is *really* big, in my eyes, I'm battling Mr. Tarpon.

Fishing has been an important element in my life for as long as I can remember. It brought my uncle and me closer than anything I can imagine. And, even though he's no longer with us, I still have so much love and respect for the man.

On a summer or fall evening, when the crickets are chirping and you hear that deep, low-throated croak of the bullfrogs, there's nothing more peaceful and relaxing to me than to grab my pole and walk down to one of the ponds on our farm for a little fishing.

It's said that a fragrance or a smell from a long time past can bring back memories of where you were when you first caught scent of it, and I agree, but when I'm standing at the edge of a pond or creek and toss that line out, I'm immediately taken back to many wonderful childhood memories of sharing time with my Uncle Warren.

38

~ Red Ryder BB Gun ~

It was a warm summer evening back in 1958 and I was just eight years old at the time. I was sporting my first brand-new Daisy Red Ryder BB gun, which, by the way, was the *most* popular BB gun ever manufactured by the Daisy company. I thought I was a real cowboy and an expert shot. Many a bird and small critter had fallen to my trusty Red Ryder.

After dinner on that warm summer day, I was stalking prey with my Red Ryder around the wooded yard and ended up in Aunt Aggie's apple tree, which was behind her house over in the side yard of the Big House. I was taking aim at the green apples high up in the tree and was also popping a few BBs at her back window just to hear the ping of the glass. I also let a few fly to rattle the house gutters, and with a well-placed shot, I could make her outside thermometer on the corner of her house by the back door, spin.

From my perch up in the tree, I was watching her large butterfly bush that was over by the lower end of the family garden plot. The butterflies were fluttering all over the purple-blue flowers. My hunter instincts kicked in. I descended from the tree and made my zigzag, crawling approach to the bush without being seen or detected by the butterflies, which were all busy doing their thing.

I'd take a careful, close aim and was desperately trying to knock them off the flower buds in the same manner as a TV sheriff would in blowing a bank robber off his horse.

Well ... if you've never tried, it's hard to shoot a butterfly. The wings are so thin and their movements are so fast that the many angles of fire I attempted never resulted in the "bad guys" going to the mortician's table.

Then, very intent on bagging one of the winged beauties, I took a real close aim. The BB must have gone astray. There was my dad, bent over in the garden, weeding around the tomatoes and the other vegetables when, sure enough, the BB found dad's left arm. I never realized I'd scored a hit till good old Dad called out, "Son–where are you hiding?"

"Over here, Dad," I said, sheepishly, "By the butterfly bush."

Dad slowly walked over to me, lowered his arm and said, "Son, you see this here BB?" It was just under the skin on his forearm.

"Well, yes, Dad, I do."

"Son, take it out."

I hesitated, then squeezed his skin and dug at the BB with my fingernail. After a minute, out came the BB. His arm was dripping some blood, but nothing looked too serious to me.

Dad never flinched or made a fuss. After I had the BB out, he very calmly said, "Son, give me your Red Ryder."

I did as I was told. Over at the other side of the garden was the cow pasture and fence. Dad walked over and sized up a good, stout, fence post, and then with one mighty swing, broke my Daisy in half. He left the broken gun lying there on the ground and then proceeded to go back to his garden weeding.

I cried and ran and hid in the garage thinking I was next in line for a lecture or a whipping, maybe both. But that never happened and not a word was said about the incident. As the sun set, we were in the house and in front of the TV. Dad sat back in his favorite recliner and again, there was no mention of my errant shot hitting him.

I was really mad at Dad for breaking the Red Ryder in half and didn't speak to him for a day or two. The week went by slowly and on Friday, up the drive came the Buick Wildcat with Dad behind the wheel.

"Son," he said. "Come over here."

Oh, no, I thought. I was getting ready for a beating of some sort when the trunk lid flew up and Dad pulled out a new Red Ryder. It had a saddle ring on the side with a long, leather strip tied to it. He handed it to me along with a six-pack of ammo—long tubes of BBs—and some other packs of BBs that came in clear plastic bags, much like what carryout food catsup came in.

I was in shock … his only words were, "Son, here's your Red Ryder replacement. Sorry for last week." Then Dad proceeded to walk over to the sidewalk and up to the house. I think I learned my first valuable lesson about shooting: Be more careful to shoot only at targets and always check your line of fire so you know what, or who, is downrange.

From that day forward, no bird or varmint shed his life-blood again on account of me and my Daisy Red Ryder. To this day, I *still* live by that life lesson I learned all those years ago.

You often don't appreciate the things your parents do for you until you are older. You might think some of the things they tell you, or require of you, are stupid, and as a young child, they often don't make sense. It's not until you come of age, so to speak, that you can fully appreciate those lessons.

As I think back on it though, boy, what a great *Pop* and father he was! I sure miss him some 32 years later.

39

~ Hurricane Irma ~

Hurricane Irma: September of 2017. This massive storm was tracking north and northwest. The weather station was giving early warnings to brace for the worst and be prepared to evacuate the Keys. We had been down at our condos at Coral Harbors MM88; however, we headed back north on the first of May. All we could do is watch the news coverage of the storm from our home in Floyd's Knobs.

Irma was the strongest storm on record to exist in the open Atlantic region and our two condos were in the direct path of the beast at Ground Zero.

I was told by the manager of the condos that the wind blew over 100 MPH for hours; the rainfall was unbelievable, and the waves of water washing over our seawall were also something to behold. Islamorada took a direct hit and one of the condos faced in the direction the storm when it hit landfall.

The asphalt pavement road on the east side of the marina that runs out to the point where my boat slip is, was washed away. Even the sub-base stone beneath the pavement was gone. All but two boats in the marina were gone before the storm.

The surge came over the road with such force that my dock box and freezer were washed away. The marina was full of human debris and non-human junk, trash and everything imaginable. The marina was closed for two months after the storm while awaiting a large excavator on a barge to come, dip out the junk and load it on another barge to be towed away.

The refuse would then be off-loaded and hauled by truck to a dump up on the mainland around Miami somewhere. A few docks were destroyed and some dock lights were gone. The wave of water crossed the other part of the road between the marina and the swimming pool.

The pool was also filled with everything imaginable. The clubhouse roof was damaged but the building itself was spared. The two boats in the marina were unscratched and tied in their slip as though nothing had happened … also unbelievable!

Some condo roofs were damaged, trees were uprooted and gone, and on what trees remained, all of the leaves were gone. All of the tree limbs and weak branches were on the ground. The power was off; the water was off and on and had to be boiled. It took seven days, but the power was finally restored.

On our condo closest to the water, the wind was so strong that four panels of our hurricane shutters were blown off and never found. The wicker couch on the porch was found around on the side of our building sitting up in a tree. The porch railing was gone, all the screens were gone, three ceiling fans were gone, the tile floor on the porch was all buckled up, and two of the sliding glass doors were somehow knocked open.

We then checked out the damage on the inside. There was water on the floor; our large Oriental rug and mat were destroyed and some legs on the furniture were damaged. When the electricity came back on, the power surge caused the furnace/air conditioner and refrigerator to short out. All of the food and drinks went bad. The management went around cleaning out everyone's refrigerators and freezers.

Now the big problems set in. With the power being out for seven days and the outside temperatures well over 100 degrees the entire week, you can imagine what the temperature was like inside of a closed-up condo.

Mold started to grow. The furnace ducts were scrubbed and cleaned and the mold inspector made three visits. Electric service needed repairs and the drywall was removed four feet up and replaced after the mold was removed. We had the entire inside painted throughout. Another kicker was, the mold inspector required that all clothes, linens and bed covers be sent out and cleaned.

All in all, some $50,000 worth of damages were sustained to the unit. The insurance company presented roadblocks, as usual, and communication problems throughout the repair. They finally paid 80% of my costs all because the storm had removed the hurricane shutters. Our Ford Explorer was spared from any damage and still operates as usual.

My boats were stored in Caribee's hurricane-proof boat barn and were just fine. The first thing the insurance company asked was, "How are the boats?" I'd forgotten that they were insured for replacement cost.

A friend who'd I known for years, and overall handyman, started his own LLC and went into doing home repairs after the storm. I was first on his list. He completed my project and did a great job, but I guess the pressure of all his other on-going projects, along with additional stress factors led to the poor guy getting arrested for possession of cocaine. He was busted by the local authorities. He is currently out on bail while the court case is pending. I'd had no contact with him for a long time, then last month, he "butt-dialed" me. I returned his call and left a message, but never heard back from him. He's a good man and has many skills. He made some unwise choices, but I wish him the very best in his recovery efforts.

My other condo which sits further back from the water's edge, sustained water damage, mold problems and electric issues. The power surges destroyed the refrigerator and other electrical appliances.

To date, I'm out $40,000 in repairs. The insurance company is refusing to pay because of, get this—*WIND BLOWN RAIN!* As I write, my claim is in the hands of a local attorney who'll get 40% of any monies that are recovered. How an insurance company can get away without paying honest storm claims is beyond imaginable. They emailed me saying all claims were denied and the claim was closed. This was the ultimate insult after all the money I'd paid those crooks over the years.

There was a $10,000 special assessment levied by the condo association. I must say that the management and Board of Directors of the Coral Harbours Condo Association were prepared as best they could be. All road repairs, landscaping and repairs to the club buildings were made in a reasonable timeframe and come January, some three months later, most all of the Association work was completed and the residents were back enjoying the Keys life.

In 2005, we were at the Palms at MM80 when Hurricane Rita hit and took its toll, but that was nothing compared to Irma. Then twelve years later, Irma slammed ashore. If you can't stand the heat in the kitchen (the Keys), you'd best stay north of the Mason-Dixon Line.

We hope and pray that it's another twenty years before a hurricane makes landfall in the Keys. I will be 89 years young and still playing pickleball and fishing with no time to dwell on when is the next hurricane coming!

40

~ Three Acre Lake ~

I get asked a lot: *How much fun can you have on a three-acre lake down there in the Florida Keys?* You have the ocean on the east side, which is visible from the porch, and from up on the roof, you see the Gulf, the backwater, the mangroves, boats, fish jumping and birds of every species. We even had a 20-ton whale wash ashore.

Our winter home, a condo in Coral Harbours, in Islamorada (which translates to the Purple Island) sits within a 14-acre gated community. A private road circles the property. The condo units are clustered on the inside and a lush hammock of trees, plantings and tropical flowers line the road on both sides of the property. Along the front of the development, there's a fence and greenery to protect and buffer the residents from the noise and dust from the old highway, which runs parallel to US # 1.

On the east side is the private marina. There's a road out to the point, and some fifty feet more to the east is the waterline of the sea. Ten miles out you can see where the water meets the sky. In olden days, man thought that line is where the earth drops off into the gates of hell—it doesn't, by the way! Now, back to my story.

At the very center of the property is a three-acre lake or lagoon that the locals call a smaller body of water locked by land. Buildings A, B, C, the clubhouse and E, F, G and H surround the lake.

Buildings A, C, E and G are four-stories, and B, F and H are the one-story, two-bedroom units. One hundred feet of lush green grass surrounds the lake. On the east side is the brick deck of the clubhouse overlooking the lake. There's a railing around the deck to protect one from falling some 25 feet, give or take, down to the water.

On the west side is the sandy beach for swimming and access to the water. On the north and south sides are large coral stones stacked three rows high. In the center of the lake, there's a floating platform you can swim out to and climb up on to relax or catch some sun. There are also three aerators spread across the deep end to help keep the algae down.

At the deep end on the east side are two large pipes with an iron mesh screen over the ends. The pipes run under the clubhouse and allow the water in the lake to rise and fall with the ocean tide. The screens keep the fish in the lake.

The lake becomes my playground when the wind is high and it's too rough to venture out in my boat to go fishing or crab-trap checking. On one occasion when our daughter was in high school, it was too windy to go out in the boat, so we decided to fish off of the deck overlooking the lake by the clubhouse.

For twenty minutes I was hauling up five to eight pound mangrove snappers, and releasing them just as fast. The lake fishing was strictly catch and release. I'd just put a live pinfish on my daughter's hook when BOOM—the action was on! Daughter had hooked up with a giant, four-foot tarpon.

She cranked and reeled like a seasoned veteran, but for every foot of line she gained, it seemed like she lost two. The big fish jumped out of the water three or four times. I did manage to get a picture of him in the air.

This dance went on for what seemed like the longest time. Then the like broke and the fish darted off. One condo owner who was watching us stated that no one knew there were tarpon in the lake. Another owner from the second floor who witnessed the event proclaimed, "I've been fishing here for years. I've hunted a big tarpon for a long time, and I've *yet* to score. Now here, off of my porch, I've witnessed the unbelievable—a teenage girl hooks up with a big tarpon right here in the lake!"

Not long ago while fishing, both old JS and I hooked up with some big fish. There were some large snappers and a grouper or two. One we hooked was a particularly strong fighter and he was ready to run. With our rods in one hand and a cold Bud in the other—and us acting like two kids on a fun ride at Disneyland!—the fish literally pulled the boat from one end of the lake to the other. If we both weren't in need of another cold beer, we'd likely still be on the lake enjoying the ride.

The following year, in the month of January, a friend of mine, DF, and I were fishing off of the same deck high up above the water. We were catching some big snappers, reeling them in, and then releasing them back into the lake. One of the condo residents, "Old Doc," and his grandson walked up and watched us catching—not fishing.

The grandson was enjoying watching the fun when I handed him my pole. He was rather stunned and not really sure what to do, I said, "Hey, Doc, teach your grandson how to catch the big ones."

After a short lesson from his grandpa, the young boy was catching a fish with every bait he tossed out in the water until his arm began to hurt from the strain of the work.

"Boy, Grandpa," the young man said. "This fishing is easy!"

As they walked away, I heard old Doc say, "Son … it's not always this easy. That's why it's called *fishing* and not *catching.*"

There was, and still is, many a good time to be had here at the lake. Just this past January 2019, I was fishing off the deck with chunks of ballyhoo. The wind was blowing around 25 MPH, the skies were cloudy and we had light sprinkles. It was just another slow, but great day. With all the boats at the dock, I retrieved a big heavy-duty rod from my boat; I had a large hook and a whole dead pinfish for bait. I pulled up a chair to the railing off the deck behind the clubhouse.

After I baited the hook, I took a short cast out with the bail open, then waited for the big strike. Soon, the hit came. The line shot off the reel and then went limp. I thought, *Oh no, he dropped the bait.* Then I felt a slow steady pull on the line.

I would pump the rod and take in line on the way down. I cranked the reel slowly and as I went down with the rod I could feel him pulling away. I set the drag heavier and continued to reel the fish up from the depths.

Old DF and Jimmy P we're cheering me on and talking excitedly about a legendary 50-pound, black grouper that stalked the bottom of the lake. We were all certain that I had Mr. Big Grouper on the line.

As I cranked and played the fish, quite a large group of spectators had gathered around me. They cheered me on expecting to see a record fish hauled from the lake. As the fish came to the surface, the cameras clicked and then laughter erupted. My "big fish" turned out to be a poolside lawn chair that was most likely washed into the lake by Hurricane Irma!

The three-acre lake continues to provide fun and entertainment. Mid-mornings when the sun is up and things are starting to warm up and mid-afternoons when it's rather hot, another pastime on windy days is to walk the parameter of the lake about ten feet from the water's edge looking for long, sneaky, sleeping iguanas.

They range anywhere from ten inches to over two feet long. It's amazing how they blend in and change colors to match their surroundings. If you approach them slowly and then snap your fingers, they run full speed ahead and dive into the water. Iguanas, by the way, are natural-born swimmers. You'd think the large fish would feed on them, but they never seem to bother the big lizards. I have spooked many of them and watched them run to hit the water, but I've yet to see one surface or crawl back out along the bank. Who knows where they go? But come back later and there they are, sunning in the grass.

Just when you think it's time to take in a movie, hit the couch for a nap or just sit under the tree by the boat and hope and pray the wind lays down, no: it's time for some bird watching. Morning, noon and just before dark, anyone who hangs out around the lake is treated to some of the most beautiful and exotic birds anywhere in the world—the Keys' fabulous water birds.

The birds are plentiful and the species are numerous. It seems that every day brings a sighting of a new feathered friend. One can expect to see something different and more beautiful each day. From pink flamingos to brown and white pelicans, long-necked anhingas, cormorants, egrets, gray and white frigate birds, gulls, limpkins, ospreys, sandpipers, skimmers, spoonbills, herons and my most favorite of all birds, the Kingfisher. Even buzzards are known to land at the water's edge.

Then there are the songbirds, many of which are from the north. They hang out in the hammocks around the lake. There aren't as many of them and you hear them sing more than you actually see them.

Occasionally you will see a lone possum scamper through the grass, and here of late, a gray squirrel will come in for a drink. I once spotted a raccoon having dinner on the sandy beach enjoying a nice-sized fish.

Then, out come the children and the sun worshipers and the birds are gone. Early morning and late afternoon seems to be the best for sightings and the most activity.

As you can see, there's a lot more to offer a nature lover, fisherman and hunter than sitting in your boat some distance from the line on the horizon where the water meets the sky. The lake activity goes on every day regardless of the wind, rain or shine.

41

~ Fathers and Sons ~

Mark Twain said, *"When I was a boy of 14, my father was so ignorant I could hardly stand to have the old man around. But when I got to be 21, I was astonished at how much the old man had learned in seven years."*

When we're young, we obviously view the world much differently than adults do, and often, this seems to be even more so when we're talking about how our *parents* look at things. For this story though, I'm going to focus on the Father-Son aspect of it.

I was fortunate enough to have a dad who knew how boys were. I think most dads are like this because, after all, they were boys once themselves.

Dad knew there were going to be times when his patience would be tested to the limit, and times when he probably felt like killing us or at the very least, maybe considered shipping us off to a different state or country.

But the times when his anger flared were like a sine wave. They would come and go and there was never a regular pattern to it. Of course, I, or my brothers, were usually responsible for the flare-ups. I might go weeks without screwing something up, and then I might mess things up several days in a row.

Through it all though, Dad remained reasonably calm and laid-back, and I think he was trying to teach me life lessons by his example.

It's rare that I ever heard Dad raise his voice when he was mad at me or one of my brothers, but there was never any doubt in your mind when he was. You knew it … you sensed it, and you for damn sure knew when to keep your mouth shut!

Case in point: earlier in this book I included a story about me and my Red Ryder BB Gun. The day I accidentally shot Dad in the arm, he remained very calm. But after he had me hand over the air rifle, he casually walked over to a fence post, drew the gun back and smashed it into two pieces. He walked away without saying another word and resumed his gardening. Looking back on it, I think he took his anger out on the BB gun instead of my hide, which was probably a good thing.

At the time I was 8 years old, and I thought Dad was being unreasonable and mean. After all, the shooting was an accident and I meant no harm. Nowadays when I think back on it, I totally get where Dad was coming from. What if that BB had hit him, or someone else, in the eye? It still would have been an accident, but I would have carried it with me the rest of my life knowing I blinded someone.

Dad, in his way of "teaching," made a powerful impact on me when he smashed my gun. He definitely got my attention and in a way that was much more effective than if he had sat me down and gave me a lecture on the rules of gun safety.

No sir, as an 8-year-old watching your dad smash your prized BB gun across a fence post, I clearly knew I'd messed up and that Dad was upset! At the time though, I just wasn't sure why. The lesson I learned that day stuck with me the rest of my life and safe shooting practices are things I still employ to this day.

On a similar note about fathers and sons and lessons learned, a friend of mine, Ned, told me a story about an incident that happened when he was 15 years old. Ned had gotten a "recipe" for how to make smoke bombs from a friend of his. I won't divulge the recipe lest some young kid reads this and decides to try it.

Ned said they had just moved into a brand new house two months prior. It was the *dream* home his folks had always wanted. Ned's parents were bowling on that particular night, so he figured it would be a good time to make the bombs. He knew his dad would have never allowed it if he'd been home.

So old Ned mixes up the first batch in the family kitchen while his little brother (5 years old) and his little sister (11 years old) watched with interest. The smoke bombs were round and about the diameter of a quarter, but Ned said once you lit them, they glowed brightly like a flare and put out a ton of smoke that rivaled anything a chopper pilot in 'Nam might have seen.

Ned said that the small smoke bombs were so impressive that he was curious as to what a large would look like once lit. He returned to the kitchen to start another batch, except this time, instead of making 8 or 10 small bombs, it was going to be one huge bomb about the size of a baseball. He had the pot on the stove and was slowly stirring the mixture as his siblings watched.

Ned said he noticed that the mixture did something he'd never seen before ... a slow curl of smoke drifted from it. About ten seconds later, he learned the meaning of the term "flashpoint."

The mixture exploded in the pan and Ned said it looked like Mount Vesuvius had erupted right there on the stove! He shoved his brother and sister back out of harm's way while smoke and flames jumped several feet in the air and spewed out of the pan. In a panic, Ned grabbed a pan of water and threw it at the flaming, molten mass, which was now bubbling out and over the edge of the pot.

All the water did was carry the flaming mass across the stove where it then flowed down over the edge, catching the cabinets on fire in the process. When the lava hit the linoleum, it ran across it like a slow-moving river and melted into the floor itself.

Ned finally beat the flames out using kitchen towels. The entire house was full of smoke and the kitchen was destroyed. Fortunately, though, no one was injured. Ned ran from room to room and opened all the windows to try and get the smoke out.

About that time, Ned's parents returned from bowling. Ned walked out and met them in the driveway. He said, "Mom and Dad, I kind of messed something up in the kitchen a short while ago and it's not good."

Seeing the smoke still billowing out of the house, Ned's mom ran into the kitchen, saw the massive destruction, and then rushed upstairs to her room crying. Her dream house and her dream kitchen were destroyed after only two months.

Ned's dad walked in and studied everything. Ned said his dad's jaw muscles were twitching, which they did when he was really mad. After a moment, his dad asked, "Was anyone hurt?"

Ned told him no, no one had been injured. He said his dad, in a very calm voice said, "Well, get everything cleaned up as best as you can," and with that, he started to walk out of the room.

Ned said, "Dad, I feel horrible. I mean, this is your new house and I just ruined it. I'd feel better if you'd at least *hit me* or something."

Ned said his dad turned slowly to him, stared him hard in the eye, and in a soft voice, said, "Son, if I was to touch you right now, I'd kill you. Now get this mess cleaned up. I'm going upstairs to comfort your mother."

Just like me when Dad smashed my BB gun, no other words were necessary. Ned knew he'd messed up, same as I did, but in the process, we learned valuable lessons from our fathers on how to handle things.

The following are things my dad said to me many times over the years. The older I get, the more I realize just how smart he was. I guess Mark Twain was right!

- Live beneath your means.
- Return everything you borrow.
- Stop blaming other people.
- Admit it when you made a mistake.
- Give clothes not worn to charity.
- Do something nice and try not to get caught.
- Listen more; talk less.
- Everyday take a 30 minute walk.
- Strive for excellence, not perfection.
- Be on time. Don't make excuses.
- Don't argue. Get organized.
- Be kind to unkind people.
- Let someone cut ahead of you in line.
- Take time to be alone.
- Cultivate good manners.
- Be humble.
- Realize and accept that life isn't fair.
- Know when to keep your mouth shut.
- Go an entire day without criticizing anyone.
- Learn from the past. Plan for the future. Live in the present.
- Don't sweat the small stuff ... it's all small stuff.

42

~ Theatair X ~

Back in high school, around the years of 1966, '67, '68 and even into the 1970s, after I returned from the service, drive-in theaters were a favorite spot for entertainment for family and friends, young and old. The cost of admission was reasonable and the popcorn, Cokes, hotdogs and candy were priced so that the everyday working man could afford a trip to the concession stand if he had his family along. There was none of the gouging like you see in every movie house today.

Even though the restrooms were clean, the boys' toilet was out back behind the car you came in. When you were finished, a good rub of your hands on your pants and you were clean enough to stick your hand back in the sack of popcorn that was usually shared with everyone in the car.

Every weekend there was a "Family Night" where you paid one price for the whole carload, regardless of how many people were in it. You'd bring your own cooler of drinks and your own large Kroger bag of popcorn. Some would sit on the hood and lean back on the front windshield to watch the movie; others would sit next to the car in lawn chairs—you had to be close enough to hear the sound coming from the little silver steel speakers that hung from your window, though.

There was even a pickup truck night where you backed into your spot and set up chairs in the bed of the truck to view the movie. There was also an area set aside near the concession stand where chairs were set up and you could sit out and enjoy the show. There was a fireworks show before and after the movie on the Fourth of July holiday. They offered Veterans Day specials and most all holidays had a special show of some kind that was featured.

Then there were us "poor" boys looking for some excitement. We'd pile as many guys as possible into the trunk and when one boy in the car drove up to the gate, most of the time, you were busted. No one comes to the drive-in by themselves and you'd be asked to open the trunk.

Hot, sweaty boys would crawl out and if you had no money, you were escorted out. Sometimes the management waved you in and then they'd send someone over to where you parked. They'd stand by the car pretending to pick up trash or work on a speaker. After a while, whoever was policing things would hear noise and laughter coming from the trunk. That's when the driver would get a flashlight shown in his face and would be forced to open the trunk. When this happened, all in attendance were booted from the property. Anytime we were successful and got in free, you felt like you'd really gotten away with something!

Some nights my buddies and I would get liquored up and would be raising hell. After other patrons would complain, we'd eventually be asked to leave and would be escorted from the premises.

One thing I think just about everyone did at least once is, you'd forget to remove the speaker hanging from your window. When you drove off, the speaker would break, or your window would—sometimes both. If you got caught, you had to pay for the speaker, and then you had to pay again when you got home and your parents saw the broken window.

Other times when the weather was cold, there was nothing better than to take a date to the drive-in. It was usually a double-date and the driver was obviously relegated to staying in the front seat while your buddy was the lucky one; he had the back seat to himself and his girl. On date nights, you always enjoyed some kissing and staying warm and close. Sometimes the passion got so hot it was nothing to melt the vinyl on the car seat or dash. Lucky we never caught the car on fire!

On really cold nights when you didn't have a date, the management would sometimes give you a small portable heater that would plug into the speaker stand.

Sodas, candy, hotdogs, beer, wine, whiskey, kissing, hugging, trying to grow up, and making memories … all of this was part of the drive-in scene. It was *no-holds-barred, anything goes* at the drive-in. The millennials don't have a clue, and never will, about what a great generation it was, and what a wonderful, innocent and opportunistic time it was growing up in that era. I consider any of us who grew up at that time as being privileged.

The area drive-in favorites for the locals were the New Albany, Clarksville, Georgetown and Kenwood theaters. The Oldham County, Kentucky, drive-in was the hot spot to enjoy the outside movies as well as the local females looking for some bodacious Saturday night fun—think Daisy Duke and let your imagination carry you away on that! Oldham County, just this year, built and opened a brand new facility.

The Georgetown is still, to this day, open for business. Back when my wife and I were dating, a cheap night out, but an enjoyable one and one that we looked forward to, was a trip to the Georgetown. She would pop the corn and I would ice some Cokes in the Coleman cooler.

We'd take my company Chevy truck (free gas) and let her run all night, AC or heat, whatever the occasion demanded. In the truck, we had plenty of room to enjoy the movie. My dear friend drove a Honda Accord with bucket seats—definitely not the drive-in vehicle of choice.

On one occasion we were parked back on the next to the last row. Nature called and down to the concession stand my lady went. The Georgetown was in a cow field. There was grass but no stone or gravel to stumble on, on your way to the potty. After a while, I heard my lady crying out for help.

"Over here," I called back.

"There's a cow chasing me," she screamed. "He's going to kill me—I'm scared. Open the door and I'll dive in!"

I watched all of this play out and man, what a funny sight and show it was—for me anyway. MJ escaped the friendly cow and the bovine grazed around the truck most of the show. Knowing the cows were usually present, I came prepared with a large carrot. I stood by the side of the truck and the old cow ate from my hand. When she finished, she tongue-wiped her nose, let out a bellow and then slowly walked off down the row and joined up with the other cows who were going to each car looking for a handout.

Man—what a time! These were memories that would last a lifetime. My city girl, wife-to-be, was mad and upset at the time, and couldn't believe what had just happened. Weeks later on our next drive-in date, she brought the carrots and a camera. I'm sure this experience strengthened our bonds which have now lasted over 37 years, and it brings back many good memories.

Now that we're talking about making memories at drive-in theaters, I'd be remiss if I didn't mention the old Theatair X in Clarksville, and boy were there some fond memories made in conjunction with this adult entertainment venue.

At GA, we had "Old Blue," which was the hot mix asphalt batch plant. It stood some three stories high and was made of steel. It was strong and sturdy. On the top deck of Old Blue was the shaker screen. There was a landing and an open area with a safety railing around to protect you from falling. The backside of Old Blue faced the larger-than-life outdoor movie screen which was about a hundred yards away, more or less.

Carloads of my high school buddies would gather around at the plant after dark. We'd pack coolers and lawn chairs to the top deck and prepare for the super-hot and erotic, and often downright nasty—but educational I might add!—color movie shows of how and what goes on between a man and a woman, and even what happens with animals and other gadgets.

We learned a lot from the top deck and had many a good time. Now that I think about it, there was no sound system or speakers up there. Amazingly, none of my buddies ever mentioned this or complained about the lack of sound or even the need for sound *at all* as far as that goes.

I could have made some good money if I had charged an admission fee, but we were all friends trying to grow up and spread our wings. We were learning and growing!

43

~ Body Hair ~

Hair plays a very important role in regulating body temperature. When it's cold outside, tiny muscles surrounding the hair follicle cause the hairs to stand up to trap more heat near the body. This is what happens when you get goosebumps.

Nostril hairs and eyelashes help to keep dirt out of our bodies. But what about things like chest hair, pubic hair, and eyebrows? Why do they grow so much longer than the hair on our arms and what's the point of them? Scientists still aren't entirely sure. Body hair doesn't last as long as the hair on your head. The reason body hair doesn't get longer than a few inches is because it only has a lifespan of about six months.

Your body hair has muscles. Believe it or not, your body hair has muscle cells; it's what makes them stand on end. Body hair is tied to intelligence. According to a 1996 study, the more body hair you have, the more intelligent you are. It's a tenuous connection at best, but researchers found that the majority of male Mensa members had more body hair compared to the average population. It's not a bad trade-off for all the extra shaving you have to do.

We have two different kinds of body hair—well, technically three. Terminal hair is long and thick, like beard hair, pubic hair, and armpit hair. Let that sink in for a moment—face hair and penis hair are the same thing!

Vellus hair is finer, like wispy arm hair. Infant hair is also a totally different kind of body hair called lanugo. But you lose all of your lanugo hair pretty much right after you're born.

Pubic hair is basically responsible for you smelling weird. Every terminal hair has its own sebaceous glad. The glands are responsible for producing sweat and protecting against germs and they also create body odor. But pubic hair is also responsible for sending out hormones that attract the opposite sex. There's a lot of ways our body produces

150

hormones, but our body hair can actually wick away hormones and send them toward potential mates.

Your body hair is basically the ultimate wingman. Body hair regulates your temperature. It can retain heat when we're cold and wick away sweat when we're hot. So before you consider laser hair removal, remember that's like shooting a laser into your central air conditioning unit.

Your hair color can actually be indicative of genetic disorders. Blonde women tend to have more estrogen; blondes also tend to have a higher percentage of learning disabilities and macular degeneration. Redheads are more susceptible to pain, brunettes are more likely to get addicted to smoking, and bald people might die earlier.

There are tiny creatures that live in your eyelashes. They're mites called Demodex and about half of all people have them. They're usually harmless, but in extreme cases, they can cause itching and inflammation.

Your hair can contain gold, but don't go carrying a bag of hair into your nearest pawn shop though. It only contains trace amounts..

Split ends are known as *trichoptilosis*. So now you know the scientific term of that thing most women hate.

Almost everyone trims. A recent study found that 90 percent of people have trimmed or shaved their pubes in the last four weeks. The study also found that 60 percent of guys prefer a partner with no pubic hair. A surprisingly high 19 percent of guys are pubic-hair-free. And if it makes you feel any better, 80 percent of those people who shaved their genitals also reported itchiness.

The above facts about hair are available to anyone who wants to check them.

Hair is something that, even at an early age, I always wanted. I never wanted to wait for it to grow and prayed hard to get some, but even prayer will not bring on a hair growth spurt.

At age ten, playing grade school basketball, some of the other players had hair on their legs and arms and thick locks on their heads. I was in envy of them. All I wanted was body hair. But the days and years passed and nothing seemed to sprout on my body. Maybe it was my Italian genes or my blond hair or the foods I ate? By my junior year in high school, fuzz sprouted on my legs and arms. I never had my first shave until I was a senior in school.

During my induction physical into the US military, the doctor in charge commented, "Where did your body hair go?"

"Sir," I said … "Yes sir, I don't have any, Sir."

At the age of 19 as an Airman in the USAF, I shaved every other day just to say I did. By the next year, at the age of twenty, something gave way. Armpit hair had developed, pubic hair was in full bloom and shaving became a daily affair. My head hair flourished but the hair on my legs, arms and chest was nowhere to be found.

At age 23, my facial hair was thin and of various colors, but it was long and healthy. By 30, my hair was thick. My ears were full of it, my nose hair was wild, but the chest hair was still nonexistent.

By age 50, thinning began and sprouts of gray appeared. By age 60, my head hair was thin and graying; my eyebrows were also thin but had wild hairs everywhere. At age 66, when I had a heart attack, I was lying on the operating table I was shaved closely. When the nurse lathered up my chest, I begged her to spare the ten long and light chest hairs that I had groomed and cultivated all those long years, but she replied that rules are rules and all of your body hair must come off—and off it came.

At age 69, my hair is all thin and departing. The ten chest hairs never returned; the ear hair stopped growing; the nose hair has flourished and the hair on my legs and arms is blond and fuzzy. The facial hair is still a daily chore and haircuts come once a month. The once-brown hair is all faded to white and the drapes no longer match the carpet!

My desire for thick body hair has withered and gone and is no longer a concern. Actually, just the opposite feeling has taken hold. Shaving is a bother, haircuts are a pain, nose, ear and eyebrow trims are a bore and the lack of arm and leg hair is a joy. The suntan lotion goes on rather easy these days.

Having a wax job is totally out of the question. I value more than ever the remaining hair that has decided to homestead on my body. The sun will come up in the morning and hair will continue to grow. Life is too short to be worrying about events and happenings that one can't control.

It's funny how our priorities change. In 1964 when the Beatles first appeared on the Ed Sullivan Show, every guy in the world wanted to have long hair. Then about the time when just about every guy in the world had grown their hair long, the Beatles cut their hair short.

What I've learned is, we always seem to want what we don't have. But then, down the road, we reach a point where we realize that those things we can't have really aren't all that important. If you have family and friends, and you're not six feet under, life is actually pretty good.

44

~ Ballyhoo Showers ~

Ballyhoo usually begin to infest the Key's waters during the fall, and the predators are close behind. Ballyhoo are excellent baitfish and also serve as a huge part of the diets for everything from Mahi-Mahi to sailfish.

When ballyhoo get really thick from Islamorada to Marathon, game fish will sometimes follow them into the shallows in their gluttonous pursuit. Sailfish and even dolphins will come in as shallow as 15 feet chasing the schools of fish.

An adventure that not all anglers—or just a lucky few—get to experience are known as ballyhoo showers. A ballyhoo shower is a not-too-common sight when massive schools of the fish erupt out of the water with predatory fish in hot pursuit. Ballyhoo showers make a compelling case for the old phrase that there are "no fences" on the water.

On the special occasion when I got to witness this event, the schools of baitfish were all over the reef and the frigate birds were diving out of the blue sky after them. The ballyhoo were jumping so much, they looked more like flying fish.

Ballyhoo can often be seen above the waters skimming the surface to escape from their predators. The appearance is similar to skipping stones on the water. The ballyhoo has a thin, bright and elongated beak with an orange spot at the end.

The ballyhoo (Hemiramphus brasiliensis) belongs to the family Hemiramphidae, and yes, they are good to eat. But their bodies are very thin making them hard to filet. I have never tasted one, but it's my guess that fried ballyhoo is probably excellent fare. Any fish that's fried is excellent eating in my opinion.

Two weeks ago, I and my fishing buddy were out some five miles from shore and about a half-mile from the reef line. We were fishing in

45 feet of water, anchored up and had a great chum line working. The current was swift and the yellowtails were hitting the silversides and cut strips of ballyhoo we had on our lines for bait. The seas were just about flat and the weather was warm. We were filling the cooler and talking about all the birds and frigates flying overhead and close around.

In the not too distant waters were boats—the larger sportfishing ones, as well as smaller ones and most all of them had tuna towers. They would run from one spot to another where the birds were circling and what looked to be like rain showers in small areas of the open water.

We were discussing what was going on and why all the commotion? We tuned in to Channel 65 and found out the showers on the water were large swarms of ballyhoo, and the predator fish were in hot pursuit. When the hungry predator fish were closing in on the school of ballyhoo, the small fish would take to jumping in and out of the water while swimming as fast as they could in order to escape the hungry mahi-mahi, sailfish, tuna and other fish from the offshore deep waters.

While we were fighting a double hook up of yellowtail snappers, off to the port side of the boat we saw the water surface and what looked and sounded like rain falling. The sound is unbelievably like rain but with a clear sky. It was a ballyhoo shower and the birds were all over the place diving hard and fast to make their catch.

We put our rods in holders on the stern of the boat and were watching the shower. Suddenly, the water went smooth and flat; then about fifty yards from the boat, there was an area some one hundred yards long by fifty yards wide. Again, there was the sound of rain and fish diving in and out just at the water's surface. A ballyhoo shower was coming straight at my boat and it was coming fast! The birds were diving and the action was intense.

As the ballyhoo got closer and closer to the boat, I leaned over the gunnel with my hands at the water's surface, and as the fish were near, the sound grew louder and the fish started bouncing off the side of the boat. I actually caught one of the escaping ballyhoos in my hands.

The shower of fish slamming into the boat was unbelievable. We were smack in the middle of the school of ballyhoo and, as I said, it was some 50 yards by 100 yards wide. As the school passed by we moved to the other side of the boat and watched in excitement as the school ran for another fifty yards and then disappeared into the water. The surface went flat calm again as if nothing had happened.

We then retrieved our rods from the holders and proceeded to crank in two 18-inch yellow tails even though our lines were twisted up with each other. We re-jigged, kept fishing and loading up the fish box. Come four p.m., we called it a day.

The ride back to the dock was an enjoyable one, but telling the story of the ballyhoo showers was the best as we sat under the dock tree with the other fishing fools, enjoying a cold Bud and each other's company and laughter. You just never know what a day on the water will bring. Tight lines and sunshine tomorrow for sure!

45

~ Europe ~

Somewhere around 2004, our daughter, who was 20 and a junior in college, chose to spend a semester abroad at the University of Saint Andrews in Saint Andrews, Scotland.

Off we went … Delta to Chicago and from there, non-stop to Heathrow Airport in a hazy, misty and interesting England. The black cab was a hoot. All of the cabs in England were black with four doors and looked like they should have been in grainy, black and white, 1940s movies.

I won't even talk about the currency we used. European money is a story in itself. The accommodations were very nice. I don't recall much about them, but I hear they were outstanding per my wife.

We visited many places and attended a few events, but about the only ones I remember were viewing the Royal Jewels and the guillotine where Marie Antoinette lost her head. I couldn't get out of bloody old England fast enough.

After a time, we purchased train tickets to Scotland by way of a stop in Ireland. The train station we were to depart from was Kings Cross Station in London. This is the same station used in the Harry Potter film where Harry and the rest of the students board a train to take them to "Hogsmeade" station. The students have to run through a wall to "Platform 9 3/4" which takes them onto an old steam train. The train we were going to be on was actually the one used in the movie as the Hogwarts Express! Our daughter, being a big Harry Potter fan, was extremely excited about this—and I have to admit, my wife and I were pretty excited about it too!

There were three classes of train cars and seats. We opted for the first-class car and diner. This was my first train ride ever, and being in a foreign country, I wanted to see the sights, enjoy the ride and escape from the place we were leaving.

The train car was very nice. We had a not-too-small table with a white tablecloth and captains' chairs facing one another. Another of the captain chairs faced straight out the window. This window covered most of the side of our compartment and afforded a perfect view of the countryside the whole trip.

The trip was some eight hours long and there were a few stops along the way. Time seemed to pass rather quickly, though. Breakfast, lunch and dinner were served along the way with drinks and snacks, and the service was wonderful. The bathrooms were neat and clean in the car we were riding in.

As we progressed on our journey, we crossed the border into Ireland. The landscape and the deep shades of green varied from the valleys to the hills and the mountain tops. It's easy to see why it's called "The Emerald Isle." Unlike here in the states where wire fences are built along property lines, the fields in Ireland and the ownership thereof were defined by stone walls/fences that were hundreds of years old. Most all of the walls were around four or five feet high and about four feet wide or so. All of the stones for the wall had been, at one time, hand-picked when the farmers and landowners were clearing the fields for pasture land.

I was surprised that there were no beef cattle or horses that grazed or roamed around. What we saw were mostly sheep, and there were plenty of them. There were very few homes along the rail tracks. We'd see a barn now and then, a small pond of water here and there and a lake now and then, but none were very large in size. Most of the sheep grazing on the hillsides had a bright paint mark on their sides. When I inquired why, I was told that this way, the owner could tell at a glance from a distance which sheep were his and which were his neighbors' when the herds merged. It was Ireland's simple, but effective form of branding.

The views were outstanding—picture book quality for sure. There were very few trees and if there were most were rather short and bushy. The trip was interesting. We left the gloom and doom of foggy England to be followed by the splendid beauty of Ireland, its various shades of green, the beautiful old stone fences, thatched-roof cottages and picturesque barns and pastures.

As we entered Scotland, the scenery became even more beautiful.

There was not so much the many shades of green; it was more a palette of grays, blues, and various other colors. The fields were smaller and there were a few more trees. The barns were of a different type of construction than those we'd seen in Ireland, but still beautiful. There were more hills and valleys and knobs like we have back home in southern Indiana.

The ponds were larger and we saw a few fast-moving, shallow streams. By far the most beautiful part of our journey was through Scotland.

On one part of the trip, as I recall, we approached the slope of a rather steep hill with lush green grass. There were quite a few large, dark-gray, brown and black boulders that had slid down the hill many years ago. There was a short stretch of old fencing and there, on a small mound in the center, flanked by a green velvet patch of grass, stood the most magnificent red stag buck I'd ever seen. There was no doubt—he owned that piece of ground! He was majestically strong and solid with a powerfully muscled body. He was some seventy yards or so from the passing train.

In just a matter of a few seconds, the godly creature was staring eye to eye with me. That eye contact would forever be an everlasting memory for me. It was a connection to a magnificent beast from another era that could have easily been a thousand years earlier. I have relived that moment over and over in my dreams and it will forever be burned into my soul.

We finally rolled into Saint Andrews. We checked into our room which overlooked the 17th hole of the world-famous Saint Andrews golf course. I had my clubs along with my signed letter from our hometown golf pro and Masters Champion, Fuzzy Zoeller, stating that I knew the rules of the game.

I was assigned a tee time. I showed up at seven a.m., and after I witnessed my three fellow golfers' pro skills—which they'd demonstrated on the practice tee—I decided to not embarrass myself. I bowed out claiming an arm injury and was immediately replaced with another willing golfer.

I walked along the 18th fairway as it was over by the viewing platform from our hotel. I had breakfast with the family and took in the sights of Saint Andrews. The next day, Sunday, the public is allowed to walk the course, observe the local farmers standing watch over their

John R. Gohmann

flocks of sheep grazing on the back nine. It was quite a sight to see. That was as close I came to playing the famous golf course.

I did purchase a box of golf balls that I had acquired from the nearby pro shop and rolled them over the 18th green. I proudly gave them to my golfing employees upon my return home.

The next day we drove up to Inverness and explored, visited and shopped. We returned the next day to try and see the Loch Ness Monster. I was told that the lake is the deepest in the world. It was very cold to the touch and is fed from the melting snow from the many mountains surrounding the area. Even though we never spotted the famous lake monster, it was still very beautiful indeed.

The girls took the ferry back to town and I walked along the steep, rocky shore a few hundred yards to an area of large chunks of stone and took a seat. Staring out across the north end of the lake, I quietly sat alone. After a while, there, some distance out in the lake, I spotted a slight riffle in the water. There was a rather loud slapping sound on the water, and out over the dark cold lake, I saw what looked like the tail of giant, black armadillo. After the slap on the water, it slowly sank away.

In disbelief I sat and thought, *Did this just really happen?* I took an oath to myself to keep the sighting of what I believe was the Loch Ness Monster a secret. And it's a secret I have honored to this day and until this moment in my story.

Back to town I drove and spent the day sight-seeing. We had dinner and drove back to Saint Andrews. Two days later we attended Parents' Day at the University. We enrolled our daughter and two days later, we were back home in the Knobs.

Eventually, the time came for us to journey back across the big waters and escort our daughter back home to reality. We attended the awards and graduating dinner there at Saint Andrews College, and we were very proud of our daughter's accomplishments and for me especially, her report or grade slip.

There on the report, was a list of her studies and grades, all of which were of high standards. At the bottom of the page was an elective class called "Scotch Tasting." I questioned it.

"Oh, Dad," our daughter said in an excited voice. "It was so much fun and I even aced it!"

She explained that once a week the class met and walked through the downtown streets of Saint Andrews. It's a small town, but there are some twenty bars and pubs. The class and the professor would stop at each pub and have a shot of scotch whiskey and discuss its merits.

She offered, "We would then proceed from one to the next until one of the students would get a little tipsy." They'd then walk back to the campus which was there in the middle of town, only to start up the next week's class at the next pub on the street where they'd left off.

"Oh," I said. "What a fun class. You're only 20 years old and hitting the pubs. What a fine memory—not … and at your parents' expense."

Needless to say, two days later we were home and our daughter was back at Kenyon College in Ohio. As parents, we were left wondering what the hell had just happened at our expense? Our daughter had matured some, but we felt as though our pockets had been picked somewhat, and the class of "Scotch Tasting 101" is history. I have to admit though, that I wish I'd had this kind of class when I was in college and what better place to sample Scotch Whiskey than in Scotland!

46

~ Interesting Facts ~

The following list is something that's been on the internet numerous times over the years, but I found the facts stated were so interesting, that I felt they were worth repeating. If you haven't seen this before, I think you'll be amazed!

SO YOU THINK YOU KNOW EVERYTHING???

A dime has 118 ridges around the edge.

A cat has 32 muscles in each ear.

A crocodile cannot stick out its tongue.

A dragonfly has a life span of 24 hours.

A goldfish has a memory span of three seconds.

A "jiffy" is an actual unit of time for 1/100th of a second.

A shark is the only fish that can blink with both eyes.

A snail can sleep for three years.

Al Capone's business card said he was a used furniture dealer.

All 50 states are listed across the top of the Lincoln Memorial on the back of the $5 bill.

Almonds are a member of the peach family.

An ostrich's eye is bigger than its brain.

Babies are born without kneecaps. They don't appear until the child reaches 2 to 6 years of age.

Butterflies taste with their feet.

Cats have over one hundred vocal sounds. Dogs only have about 10.

"Dreamt" is the only English word that ends in the letters "mt".

February 1865 is the only month in recorded history not to have a full moon.

In the last 4,000 years, no new animals have been domesticated.

If the population of China walked past you, in single file, the line would never end because of the rate of reproduction.

If you are an average American, in your whole life, you will spend an average of 6 months waiting at red lights (unless you live in Florida, then it's more likely a year).

It's impossible to sneeze with your eyes open.

Leonardo Da Vinci invented the scissors.

Maine is the only state whose name is just one syllable.

No word in the English language rhymes with month, orange, silver, or purple.

Our eyes are always the same size from birth, but our nose and ears never stop growing.

Peanuts are one of the ingredients of dynamite.

Rubber bands last longer when refrigerated.

"Stewardesses" is the longest word typed with only the left hand and "lollipop" with your right.

The average person's left hand does 56% of the typing.

The cruise liner, QE2, moves only six inches for each gallon of diesel fuel that it burns.

The microwave was invented after a researcher walked by a radar tube and a chocolate bar melted in his pocket

The sentence: "The quick brown fox jumps over the lazy dog" uses every letter of the alphabet.

The winter of 1932 was so cold that Niagara Falls froze completely solid.

The words 'racecar,' 'kayak' and 'level' are the same whether they are read left to right or right to left (palindromes).

There are 293 ways to make change for a dollar.

There are more chickens than people in the world.

There are only four words in the English language which end in "dous": tremendous, horrendous, stupendous, and hazardous.

There are two words in the English language that have all five vowels in order: "abstemious" and "facetious."

There's no Betty Rubble in the Flintstones Chewables Vitamins.

Tigers have striped skin, not just striped fur.

TYPEWRITER is the longest word that can be made using the letters only on one row of the keyboard.

Winston Churchill was born in a ladies' room during a dance.

Women blink nearly twice as much as men.

Your stomach has to produce a new layer of mucus every two weeks; otherwise, it will digest itself.

Now you know just about everything!

47

~ Shoe Shine Box ~

Whatever happened to the family "shoe shine box?"

As a kid growing up back in the 50s and 60s, just about every relative and most of your friends had a family household shoe shine box.

At our home with my grandparents, there was a hand-made box crafted by my Grandfather Gohmann that was most likely made of pine wood. It was about two feet long by twelve inches wide and maybe ten inches high. It was stained with a red mahogany and sealed with a coat or two of oil-based varnish.

It had two metal hinges, probably off of a packing crate of some kind, and a long metal handle centered on the top. It looked something like a barn door and a hasp-like attachment that folded over on a ring so you could put a lock on it if desired.

This was our shoe shine box and was locked with an old brass clasp off of a worn-out dog leash. The box shined. The metal was polished and the corners were neat and square. There were a lot of scratches and dings on the box, and it had marks of various shoe polish colors streaked across it.

Its place was there on the floor of the back porch, just down from the low, long, white, steam-heat radiator. It was just out of sight from anywhere you sat in the enclosed back porch room.

Here's a summary of *my* shine boxes through the years . . .

1968 – drafted by Uncle Sam; basic training; kept my can of polish and an old sock for buffing in a white tube sock.

Tech school – found a canvas money bag from the Bank of Biloxi—it even had a drawstring—and that became my shoe shine kit!

While in Oklahoma stationed at Altus AFB, I gave a nickel for an M16 green metal shell box. It worked great as a shoeshine box. Then in 1973 while chipping and sealing crushed stone roads in the Charleston

Powder Plant, I found a few of the M16 green metal shell boxes, only these were double the size of my shoe shine box at the time.

In 1982 after I was married, the wife had trouble opening the metal box, so I moved the shine supplies to an old black, cushioned 8-track tape box with the inside liner removed. As the shine supplies started to multiply, much like the suitcases in our side attic, I constructed a box from two discarded orange or strawberry crates. It had an open top and a rope handle.

Finally, about twenty years ago, over at the Mount Saint Francis yearly picnic at the down-in-the-basement flea market, I found my dream shoe shine box. For two dollars I came home with quite a prize! It was full of polishes, brushes, cloths, etc. and was truly a found treasure.

It was a dark, hardwood box, some 18 inches or so square. It has a hinged-lid top with a foam cushion. It's covered with a hunter-green, heavy vinyl covering that's held in place with fancy decorative tacks. It also has brass handles on two sides. The box also serves as a seat that I use most days when I go to put on my shoes. It has a prominent spot there against the wall in my closet.

My first shoe shine sock only had one color of polish … black. I only had black USAF issued shoes, boots and sneakers.

While in Oklahoma, I still only had black military shoes. My civilian shoes were suede leather boots. Then came my snakeskin boots (made of the back skin of boas) and also my lizard skin boots. My polish supplies now consisted of a can of black and a can of leather wax.

On my many trips to the Mexico border towns, while in stationed in Oklahoma and Texas, there were always shoeshine men, women, boys and girls, wanting to give you a shine for just a few cents or so.

They always gave me a dirty look because, you see, you can't shine suede leather cowboy boots. But the boots came in handy in the Mexican cantinas. With the pointy-toed boots, I was able to kill the large, nasty bugs in the corner with the toe of my boot. It always drew cheers and free shots of tequila. If you were lucky enough to get the worm in the bottle when you knocked back a big gulp of the juice, you got more cheers and this time *you* had to buy the bar a round.

When I finally arrived back home, my shoe polish color grew. I now had black, brown, oxblood, clear, saddle soap as well as other accessories and paraphernalia. As married life set in and the family grew, so did the shine supplies—from black, white, red and brown and most all other colors in between. It seemed that the women in my life collected (and still do to this day) shoes of many colors.

My collection of shoe shine supplies grew even larger over the years. I now had electric polishers with cloth wheels; I also had battery-powered polishers, a shoe wax brush to apply the polish, buffing brushes made with hog hair, rags and towels—cloth baby diapers are super for buffing although I now use micro-fiber towels. Those old white tube socks worked well in the past with the round cans of polish that came with a key to open them.

Today you have a large choice of liquid polishes of all shades. You even have spray-on shines, silicone, wax and all sorts of other materials to bring your shoes to a high shine, but back in the day, it was one can of wax, an old sock and lots of elbow grease!

48

~ Fish Club ~

The sportfishing capital of the world is Islamorada, "The Purple Island," located down in the Florida Keys just a short two-hour drive south of the Miami, Florida airport. After one hour of traffic congestion and frustration, you're on US #1 at the top of the Keys in Homestead, Florida. Then the enjoyable ride south truly begins.

Originally, the main road was just a two-lane affair lined with mom and pop stores, restaurants, small, locally-owned food markets and a gas station or two. The norm for most of the structures was one floor, but you'd see an occasional two-story job every now and then. It's approximately 100 miles from the start at the north end down to Key West, the southernmost point. From Key West, it's a mere 90 miles of open water to the shores of Cuba.

This is how I remember the atmosphere when I first began to visit the Keys starting back in the early 1960s. That was over 50 years ago. It's unbelievable how quickly time has passed and how the Keys have changed—some for the better and some not.

Today there is a four-lane asphalt road with a marked-off paved bike lane that runs from the top of the keys to Key Largo and all the way down to Key West. In place of the small establishments that once lined the road, there are now high rise condos, grocery and drug store chains and major brand gas stations.

Times have changed and change can be good, for the most part, but a few things in the Keys have not changed with the times. The atmosphere, the warm winter weather, the food and drink, the sunsets and the sunrises, the rising and falling of the daily tides, the laid-back feeling one gets there and some of the customs and ways of the years gone by are still preserved here.

For me, I still enjoy the wildlife, birds, Key deer, lizards and peacocks. And being a lover of fishing and crabbing, the Keys, the shallow reefs, the drop off at the reef's edge, the deep blue waters of the sea to the backwaters of the Gulf of Florida Bay, the fantastic and nearby fishing opportunities have remained the same for the most part.

Today, there have been some very much needed rules enacted on fishing, boating, catch limits, pollution, human waste management and environmentally friendly actions. These rules and regulations are closely monitored in order to maintain the importance of what makes the Keys special. This includes the islands themselves and the great fishing so that future generations can enjoy them to the fullest, much the same as my father's generation and even my own generation, have.

The World Famous Islamorada Fishing Club

This club has a wonderful website (www.theislamoradafishingclub. com) which goes into detail on the ins and outs of the club and its history. With permission from the club manager, who encouraged me to please write about and get the word out to the public about how great the fishing club surely is, the following, for the most part, is taken from the Club's website.

* * *

The Islamorada Fishing Club (IFC) was founded in 1950 by a group of avid fishermen, fishing guides, charter boat captains and their peers. With a distinguished and rich history of promoting conservation and responsible fishing traditions, as well as practices for future generations, the IFC became instrumental in the formation of the rules and regulations for the Everglades National Park, a true national treasure.

Now, more than ever, while celebrating our 60th Anniversary, we are still acutely aware that environmental concerns are equally as important today as they were at our genesis.

Our over 450 members, many of whom are multigenerational family members, are determined to continue on with the preservation and conservation of our natural resources so important to our local community, and are committed to preserving the island lifestyle we enjoy here in the Florida Keys.

In a clubhouse boasting of an understated past steeped in the rich history of sport fishing, the IFC offers a way of life forgotten by so much of today's fast-paced society. In the true spirit of a private club, the Club hosts a variety of events for our members and community:
  - *youth fishing tournaments, social events*
  - *family fishing tournaments*
  - *member-guest invitational tournaments*

The Islamorada Fishing Club enhances a feeling of belonging amongst our diverse membership that hails from around the world.

Nestled in the fishing capital of the world, the IFC offers novice and expert fishermen alike a place to experience camaraderie like no other. Whether you are enjoying a drink at the bar with one of the pioneers of fly fishing, or relaxing on the patio overlooking the water with the newest world record holder, or simply attending one of our fishing seminars led by the experts in their field, you are bound to meet like-minded people from all walks of life brought together by their passion for fishing and conservation.

* * *

One custom the fish club has is to hold its annual board meeting on the last Thursday in the month of March. The meeting is open to all the members, followed by a seafood and beef dinner feast. The cost of the event is covered by the club. It's essentially a free dinner of tasty delights and for most who attend, it's a night of eating, drinking and getting to know the board members and directors and other club members.

I personally have been a member for over 15 years and have only attended the event for the last three years since the time I retired from work. The last board meeting I attended opened with a members' Happy Hour. Then there was a closed-door business board meeting, followed by an open-door meeting for all of the members, where their input, questions and suggestions were heard and welcomed.

The manager blew his own horn a bit and enlightened the members on the improvements to the club after Hurricane Irma. He mentioned things like the freshly painted building, inside and out, new stone in the parking lot, new live hedge bushes planted where the wood privacy fences once stood, window repairs, new sound system inside, new sunshades on the back canal side porch, a second part-time bartender, a soda dispensing machine, new coolers in the kitchen and the purchase of a nearby vacant lot for additional parking. One such improvement that totally blew me away was the installation of a sink and hot water heater so the help can wash their hands.

Then came the financial report; all reported good health and all endeavors made a profit. The bank account was positive and the club would be able to cover the cost of the upcoming feast with ease. There were a few speakers who discussed the changes in some fishing rules along with the Everglades National Park's new requirements.

When that was all said and done, the floor was opened up to questions and comments from the members. Items discussed were leveling up the stone walk into the building, converting a few parking spaces to be dedicated to the physically-challenged members with walkers and canes, and other needed improvements. All were voted on and confirmed to have done ASAP.

One member suggested board member term limits and/or the rotating of members in and out. Another member commented that she stopped bringing guests for lunch because of the stink and unpleasant odors in front of and around the club.

A month or so ago I reported the foul smell and various other unsatisfactory items that were served me and my guests. I received a prompt reply from the club manager, Mr. V, and I was assumed the problems were being looked into.

I mentioned this, and to my surprise, the manager looked at me and asked, "John, can you describe the unpleasant odors that you experienced?"

I paused and gathered myself, not a happy camper for being called out. I immediately and politely responded with, "Mr. V, it smelled like a five-day-old pile of shit!" The room erupted into laughter and disbelief.

I later received a thank-you note which read, John, we will definitely look into this issue and come up with a solution.

The meeting adjourned and the feast was about to begin. The long, non-rotating hog trough ran one-third of the length of the dining room. Artistically arranged were a stack of square eight-inch plates, followed by bowls of different greens and salad offerings, trays of grilled chicken and chunks of juicy prime beef, an array of pulled-pork, fried, grilled and blackened locally caught-fish, clams, mussels in red wine sauce, tons of shrimp, piles of king crab legs, and a huge stack of grilled lobsters. There were also large bowls of baked potatoes, steamed carrots, zucchini and onions.

Drinks of your choice were served to your table. Alcohol was half-price while water, pop, tea and coffee were free.

When the signal to begin was given, for all who know a few things about saltwater fishing for yellowtail snappers, you drop anchor then throw, toss or place your chum bag off the gunnel and hope there's current so as to have the chum line moving away from the boat.

The members going to the chow line was much like a swarm of ballyhoo going to the chum bag. Then you had the "seagulls" darting in from the sides stealing a shrimp or fish from the food tables, and there were also the "barracudas" cutting line.

The mad dash for first-in-line began. Our table leader sprung up and declared in an urgent tone, "Let's go before all the lobsters are eaten!"

All rose and rushed to the food table. I stayed seated and watched the feeding frenzy. There were plates full of fish and meats, people chomping, eating and chewing with their mouths open and talking about what a great free meal it was. I heard one member tell another, "A free meal and a half-priced drink will bring out most all of the snowbirds, healthy or otherwise."

I noticed that the potato bowl, the veggies and salads were almost full and untouched while the meat and fish platters were scraping the bottom. The faces of those standing in line showed great disappointment. Then the trays were replenished and all were happy campers. This scene played out for hours and was entertaining for sure. It was amazing to see how a group of grown-ups could act and behave like starving wolves around a downed animal when the feast was free!

Like the chum bag draws in the ballyhoo, and the tossed-out oats draws in the runners and the prized yellowtails, the well-stocked dessert tables drew in the "fast swimmers" in the crowd. There was Key lime pie, apple pie, apple fritters, cakes, more chocolate then I have ever seen, and my favorite, good old cheesecake. No coffee was requested by the crowd—just more wine and spirits.

By the looks and sounds from the tables, a great time was had by all!

On the way out, I made a "pit stop" and there in the men's room was toilet paper and hand towels stacked high, just like at a Sam's discount store. The trash can was overflowing and the soap dispenser was producing a steady *drip, drip, drip* on the counter.

Upon leaving, by the front door we grabbed a handful of green, foil-wrapped mints and a stout- pointed toothpick and we were on our way home. The final comments from our party were, *It sure was good; Man, what a feed; Can't wait till next year's Islamorada Fishing Club Board of Directors Annual Meeting and Seafood feast.*

The next day, it was back to life as normal. Oatmeal, yogurt, peanut butter and jelly sandwiches for lunch, seafood soup and salad for dinner along with iced tea and a movie on TV. This retirement life is really good!

49

~ Deer Hunting Adventures ~

It was 1990, plus or minus a few years, when four of my friends and I were planning another deer hunt down at our farm in Harrison County. Our backgrounds were quite varied. One was a banker in southern Indiana, one was a high-roller nephew up in New York City, one owned his own pole barn business in Kentucky, and one was my father-in-law. He made four trips with us until his health failed and he retired from our yearly deer hunting trip.

Come opening day (a Thursday morning) we'd planned to meet up down in Corydon, have a big breakfast at Jock's Diner there on the corner. The meeting time was three a.m. sharp. If you were late, we left without you.

All knew where the farm was and that the gate would be locked, but the key was hidden under a big rock on the drive just inside the gate. I left the key there as encouragement to be on time at *Jock's*. Why, you ask? Because the gate is seven feet high and hard to climb over. In addition to this, on the fence rows next to the gate, the wire was strung tight and the blackberry vines there grew thick and tall. Anyone who's ever been around them will tell you, blackberry vines are full of thorns and will cut you like tiny razors. So it paid to be prompt and on time at *Jock's*.

In ten years, only the big-shot banker was late one time and was going to have to scale the fence. Instead, he chose to walk down the fence row about a quarter-mile and slip through a section of an old rusty, sagging, barbed-wire fence.

Now back to us gathering at *Jock's*. Each year we took turns buying breakfast. The early morning feast was three sunny-side-up eggs on top of a mound of corn beef hash, hash browns, a big slice of Vidalia onion covered with some kind of spicy thin gravy, orange juice out of a large Delmonte can—which had a thick crud around the triangle opening on top which was made with a beer can opener—and plenty of *Jock's* strong black coffee.

This country breakfast would hold you over till your return to the cabin at the farm at 12:30 p.m. sharp. One never used the toilet facilities at *Jock's*. For a #2, there was a bucket with a portable camp seat on top over a hole in the floor. For a #1, there was a waste-high green urinal on the wall. We always joked that from that urinal, there was a rubber hose line that took the warm liquid down around, over and directly into the coffee maker there in the kitchen, which explained why the uglier-than-homemade-sin waitress always had to go through the swinging door to the kitchen to fetch the coffee pot.

The unspoken goal among all of us was to hold any bowel movement until we'd arrive at the cabin. On most mornings, due to the excitement of the hunt, the readying of your gear and the desire to be in your tree stand 30 minutes before dawn, most of us passed on the trip to the cabin pot.

Two of us drove our pickup trucks through the fields and to within a 100-yard walk to our stands. The New York City boy was let out by the pole barn business owner, and he proceeded to walk to his designated stand, while old Pole-Barn Nate walked with his self-climber tree stand to the most remote and rugged spot on the farm.

Come daylight, all hunters were up in their stands and waiting on old Mr. Buck. I was cold, shivering, hunkered down and waiting when my worst fear hit me—I found out later, it hit the others as well.

I broke out in a cold sweat, my guts started to rumble, growl and cramp up, my throat was dry, my vision was a bit blurred, I was a little light-headed and my bowels were screaming that they needed some relief and fast!

Flashing through my mind were the runny eggs and gravy, the corn beef hash and the strong black battery-acid coffee which we all had enjoyed a few hours earlier at good old *Jock's Diner*. In addition to this, there was the liquor and other things we consumed the night before the hunt while at home gathering our equipment and supplies.

Deer hunting and Mr. Buck both took a back seat at that moment. All of my attention and focus was on the three choices I had to resolve my dilemma. One: I could drop my shorts from 12 feet up the tree, risk frostbite and whatever else may come of it, to relieve myself; Two: I could lower myself down to the ground, follow the same dropping of the trousers and unload there in the briar thicket; Three: decide which might be the best way to get myself quickly back to the cabin … walk the shortcut through the woods, or hike back to the truck and speed my way down the logging road through the field and down the steep hill to the cabin.

In fear of getting mistaken for a two-legged buck and shot at if I walked, I chose the fast trot to the truck. One must remember that it's super-cold out, very windy, cloudy and just after dawn. Frostbite was almost a sure thing if I exposed any bodyparts.

My old truck was like a cow headed to the barn after you've waved an ear of corn in the air in its direction. I was going as fast as I could go while still trying to keep her under control.

I burst through the cabin door, butt cheeks clenched tight and doing the "I have to go NOW!" stiff-legged walk. I charged through the cabin, and with no boots on, my hunting pants down and a line of clothes marking my path to the cabin toilet, in I went and assumed my rightful place upon the throne like a king.

The electric heater was on and there on the back of the pot was a copy of a 1969 Playboy magazine. I perused the magazine reading the very insightful articles while ignoring the colorful and delightful pictures. I'm happy and relieved to report that everything came out okay.

I returned to my deer stand to hunt out till noon thirty and then met up again with my hunting friends back at the cabin.

Now comes another good one.

As was the custom, after the first day of the hunt, I was always the first one up, stoking the cabin fire and making the coffee. My goal was always thinking of what made life easy for the other hunters. I'd make a pot of coffee and while it was perking, I'd boil a pot of water to fill the others' thermoses to preheat them. This little trick would keep the coffee hot in their thermoses for a longer time.

We'd all have a cup of coffee or two, choke down some breakfast, and then we'd be dressed, out the door and off to our stands.

Much to the hunters' surprise, after getting settled in their stands and ready for a warm sip of coffee, they discovered the thermos was full of hot water!

I had good, hot coffee. My father-in-law, who always stayed back at the cabin and waited for our return, also had plenty of hot coffee. Come 12:30 and we were all back at the cabin, I was told, "By the way … thank you for that delicious coffee."

You see, when they'd grabbed their thermoses on the way out, they were heavy and so everyone had assumed that I had filled them with coffee.

"Well," I asked. "What did you do once you discovered this?"

"We all sipped on the hot water," they replied, then added, "And we were thankful for something warm on such a cold morning!"

A good laugh was had by all and by 1:15, we were all on our way back to the woods for the afternoon hunt. With a smirk on his face, Old Joe asked each one on the way out, "Did you check your thermos?"

Then there was the time … the first hunt for my New York City nephew-by-marriage.

We got to the cabin just as it got dark, the night before opening day of gun season. There was a lot of "cheer" enjoyed by all along with gun cleaning, last-minute prep, strategic planning, stands checked and goals for each for the coming morning.

The alarm came early. We feasted on black coffee, Dunkin Donuts, Little Debbie's, moon pies, hostess cupcakes and twinkles, and what a breakfast it was. We were all buzzed on the anticipation of the hunt as well as the sugar rush we had going.

An hour before sunup, out the door we went, one-by-one. Some were walking, some were riding, some were stumbling and staggering off into the dark in search of their designated stands.

Just as we were leaving, I made a comment to my nephew, "If you harvest a buck, the single-barrel, 12 gauge with the sling and scope are yours for the keeping."

Come 12:30, all but my nephew showed up back at the cabin for lunch. A search party was formed. I and my father-in-law, Joe, rode the John Deere Gator up on the hill and through the fields and down the logging road towards my nephew's stand. "The Shitter Stand" is what we called it on the wall map back at the cabin.

As we approached the deer stand, we could see the boy leaning against the big oak tree where his stand was. There he sat playing with his iPad and cell phone.

"What's up, Big Guy?" I asked. "You never showed as planned for lunch at 12:30."

"Over there," he pointed. About twenty yards off lay a nice buck with seven gnarled points.

I replied, "That dude needed to be cleaned out of the gene pool."

He said, "I knew you'd show up soon. I need help. I can't drag him out by myself."

The three of us loaded the buck into the Gator and off we went back down on the long ride to the cabin. After we hoisted the buck up on the tractor hook on the bucket, I zipped open his stomach and his innards hit the ground. I felt a hand on my shoulder and a slap on my back.

"Uncle," he said. "That shotgun is mine," and off he walked towards the cabin.

He spent the next three days on the couch, sipping Jack Daniels, watching TV and just kicking back. The rack hangs quite stately on the wall next to the fireplace in the cabin.

Another fine deer hunting adventure was New York City-boy and his good buddy, Kentucky. The three of us left the cabin around one p.m. for the afternoon hunt. Our bellies were full of Wolf Weenies, white bread and yellow, baby-poop mustard. It's amazing how many of these tasty delights a young man can consume.

I drove my truck to the top of Hayes Hill and into the woods I went. I stayed till dark and waited a few minutes for the other two. They were a no-show and there was no answer on their cell phones.

Thinking all was okay and they were just staying a little longer, I proceeded on back to the cabin to enjoy happy hour and supper with the other hunters—five in total. Dinner was a repeat and consisted of Wolf Weenies, white bread, baby-poop mustard, Budweiser and venison chili that Paul had made from the deer he had harvested earlier in the day. With the fire going, bellies full and the cabin warm, one was cleaning his gun, one was reading a book, one was sharpening his knife, and here I was, worried about my nephew and his friend. It was long past dark and getting late. What had happened to them, I wondered?

PB and I drove back up the hill, across the field and proceeded to enter the woods in the last place I saw them. With flashlights in hand and a boat whistle, we searched the woods for an hour and finally, old PB called out, "Over here."

When I got to where he was, there was PB shining his light at the base of a giant, majestic white oak tree. There was an empty deer stand, two deer rifles, backpacks and all of their gear, but no nephew and friend.

Thinking they were maybe trailing a wounded deer, but uncertain, we headed back to the cabin and the "what if's" began to flow.

Back at the cabin about an hour later, we decided to call the Harrison County Sheriff's office. The sheriff advised us that if we didn't see them in another hour or so, to call back and they would send a search party out to help locate the boys.

It was 10:45 and approaching bedtime. Upset and worried, I decided to call the sheriff back. Before I got the last number dialed, old PB calls out, "Hold up, John. There are lights coming up the road towards the cabin."

An old, beat-up Willy's Jeep came to a stop ten feet from the cabin porch and out jumped two big fat, ugly as sin women and from the back seat, out crawled my nephew and his friend.

"Where the hell were you two?" I asked, relieved to see them, but feeling my anger rise. "We were worried sick and even called the sheriff."

"No worries, Uncle," my nephew said. "We're good. We were just tracking a deer, got turned around and kind of lost. We kept walking and saw a light off in the distance. We decided to walk to the light." This light was over three miles from their stands and gear.

The two females lived at the old farmhouse they'd found. Once they called off the dogs, they invited them up on the porch for a beer. One thing led to another and a few beers later, they told their story of being lost. One of the ladies asked where they'd come from and were told, "Over at Gohmann's Hayes Hill Farm."

After a good laugh, the two ladies told them to climb in the Jeep and they'd give the boys a ride back to the farm. Fortunately, it all worked out. They were safe and sound and both a little wiser. They were both very tired and hungry. After consuming a dozen or so Wolf Weenies, a little whiskey and beer, the two were happy as could be.

Out of nowhere, my nephew says, "Hey JR, those women were mighty friendly and kind. I tipped them $100.00 each."

"You did what?" I asked. "Tipped them … for what? You damned fools," I said. "Those ladies never expected a tip. Down here neighbors are friendly and happy to lend a helping hand. Well, Mr. New York City Boy, you just managed to ruin life here in the country!"

We all had a good hearty laugh, a round of drinks and turned in around midnight. Come morning we had breakfast and were off to the woods for another day of hunting. Not a word was said of last night or the tip. We accused them of letting the women have their way with them. They were just good old boys having a great hunt and making memories.

We all agreed to meet up again next year for opening day and our four-day deer hunt. On the fifth day after the hunt, we were all back at work and were already looking forward to the event next November.

50

~ Kenny and WWII ~

This short story is about a fine gentleman named Kenny who worked for Gohmann Asphalt & Paving for many years. Kenny was a good friend of my father's and one of his first job-boss superintendents on all dirt-moving jobs. I was on Kenny's crew out in the field in my early days with the company. Everyone was very fond of Kenny, respected him and his construction wisdom.

Kenny's right arm was very messed up from the elbow down. Half of the meat was missing from his arm and his fingers were permanently curled up as a result. His number two son, Donnie, worked for us for over 40 years and was the longest-lasting employee in the history of GA, Inc. In all the years Kenny worked for the company, he never mentioned his service in WWII

After Kenny's passing, his wife showed me the medals he'd received in WWII. There was a Purple Heart, a Rifleman's Badge, an Efficiency Honor Fidelity Badge, along with numerous insignia patches.

After his time in the service, Kenny came home and raised four children. Not only was he a loyal, trusted and respected employee of GA, he was, more importantly, a great father and husband. Kenny died unexpectedly and his passing left all of us stunned.

Two weeks after his passing, Kenny's wife called and asked me to stop by the house. She said that Kenny had told her that when he passed away, to give me his pearl-handled, Smith & Wesson .38 Special. I was honored, to say the least. She also gave me his large key chain with all his work and other keys on it, and a dog tag of his. I'm sorry to say I misplaced the dog tag but still have the keys.

Just last year, twenty years after Kenny's passing, I was having lunch with Donnie at the Cracker Barrel and our conversation turned to his father. I asked Donnie about Kenny's arm. Donnie told me all he knew of the story—which wasn't much because Kenny had never discussed it in detail—was about how Kenny had been shot in the arm and stomach while storming the beach in France.

At that lunch, I returned Kenny's Smith & Wesson to Donnie, who I felt should be its rightful owner.

I look back now on all the time I'd spent with Kenny talking about my military experiences, and I recall old Kenny just listened and never said a word or let on that he was in the Army. The time I served was nothing compared to his and not a day goes by that I don't think of my friend, Kenny.

I asked my friend, Patrick Naville, who assisted me in the writing of these short stories, to share the story of his own father, who served in WWII. Here's what he had to say.

John,

Thanks for asking me to share my dad's story of his service in WWII. He was a colonel in the Army. He enlisted when WWII broke out. I remember asking him why he did this and he said, "Because I felt it was not only my duty, but it was an honor to serve a great country that had given me, and so many others, such wonderful opportunities."

Dad never talked about his time in the service aside from mentioning the great bunch of men who were in his battalion. He always commented on what wonderful guys they were, and how they were like family to him. When it came to the actual war and the fighting, Dad was very closed-mouthed about it. I later came to realize that many of those brave souls who served in WWII were also the same way. Maybe it was their way of protecting themselves from the horrors they experienced. If you didn't talk about it, maybe you could somehow forget that it actually happened.

Dad brought back some souvenirs from the war, which the soldiers were allowed to do then. He brought back a Japanese 9mm Luger pistol and a 7.7mm Japanese infantry rifle, both of which he'd retrieved from the field after a battle he'd taken part in. He never discussed the battle that had taken place.

After many years of never hearing Dad discuss the war, I resigned myself to the fact that it was something he just didn't want to talk about.

In 1998, Steven Spielberg's, Saving Private Ryan *came out. I remember what an impact that movie had on me. It didn't glorify war or make heroes out of either side. It was a harsh representation of what the horrors of war really were, and how it messed up those who participated in it.*

I happened to be home visiting from Arizona not long after that movie came out. I knew Dad had seen the movie. I remember sitting at the kitchen table with Dad (it was just the two of us). I mentioned the movie. Dad said, "Yes, I saw it."

"That movie really moved me," I said. "I never realized what war was like until I watched it. What did you think about it?"

Dad stared out the window in silence for many long minutes as if composing his thoughts. I saw his jaw muscles clench, then a tear ran down his cheek. Without turning to me, he said in a very emotional tone, "We lost so many good boys in that damned war."

That was it. He never said another word about it and I respected his not wanting to talk about it.

Men like Kenny and Pat's dad, as well as my own father, my uncles and my great aunt, all of whom served in WWII, just drives home the point of a prayer I say daily, *Please, Lord—don't forget me and my family and friends.*

51

~ Crab Traps ~

Florida stone crab season is expected to take a hit this season from the red tide algae bloom that's been plaguing Florida's west coast for months. But the Keys, which accounts for 65 percent of the harvest of the sought-after claws, does not appear to be affected.

The crab season runs from October 15th through May 15th. Crabbers are limited to five traps per person. A recreational saltwater fishing license is required. The traps are about 20 inches square and are made of slotted plastic. The top has a lid that opens so you can add bait.

The crabs swim in through an oval opening in the lid, and there is an escape exit for the crustaceans should you not check the traps for an extended period of time—ten days for example.

Two inches of concrete is poured in the bottom of the cage to keep it soundly on the ocean floor. A line is tied to the trap and there's a Styrofoam ball on the end of the line which floats and makes it easy to find your traps. Your name and address are also affixed to the trap, and an "R" is painted on the ball, which designates that it's a recreational trap.

Legal-sized stone crab claws are 70 mm (2 3/4 inches) or greater in length. The measurement is taken from the base of the joint to the outer tip of the claw. The larger part of the claw (the immovable part) is what's measured.

Once a stone crab loses a claw it takes several molts to fully regenerate a new one. In adult crabs, it takes one year to re-grow a claw.

Stone crabs lose claws in several ways: the claw can be forcibly broken off when it is harvested by fishermen, it can also be lost in battle, or a crab can intentionally drop any of its legs or claws if they are damaged or sick. A stone crab can re-grow either of its claws only if the joint that linked the claw to the body is left intact.

A measuring stick, which is a notched piece of plastic, is used to check the length of the crab claw and it's required to be on your boat. The limit is … I don't really know. We never get that many at one time. For me, a good day is 10 to 15 crabs or so.

I usually bait the traps with pigs' feet, but I've also used deer feet that I sometimes brought from our home in Indiana. A friend of mine has a processing plant and he gave me the feet for free. Since I stopped driving down from Indiana a few years back, I now use the frozen carcasses of the fish we catch. I have a small chest freezer on the dock by my boat. We've also use roadkill but only when my New York City neighbor picks them up. Iguanas have been used as well when another neighbor, who happens to be the lizard exterminator on the condo grounds, saves them and puts them in the freezer.

Crabbing takes time, which is plentiful when you're retired. You obviously need a boat and you need to be able to catch fish for bait. After I run the boat slowly up to the trap, a friend on the bow takes a gaff, hooks the float and line, pulls the trap up and sets it on the deck. Then he opens the lid and, with gloves on and using BBQ grill tongs, removes the catch one by one.

If there's a question on a crab's size being legal, my friend will turn to me on the gunnel and we judge if it's a keeper or not. Wearing a pair of heavy leather welding gloves, I'll take the crab from the tongs and remove the claw with one quick twist.

Into the bucket of ice the claw goes, and over the side of the boat, the crab is returned to the water. By the way, by law, you can only take one claw.

Another technique I forgot about that we'll use is, we place the traps in a line in six feet of water about 50 yards apart. I use my Garmin to see the depth of water and to mark the location of the trap should another boater run over and cut the float loose. The man on the bow baits the trap and adds a small can of cat food with holes punched in the top with a screwdriver. This is also a good attractant for crabs.

The most exciting part of crabbing is when you first open the lid and view what you've just caught. It might be stone crabs, blue crabs, large, small and baby ones. Lobsters sometimes find their way into the trap and they also go into the ice bucket. You might catch fish of all kinds and one is more beautiful than the other. We even caught an eel one time.

Of course, then comes the steaming and eating them at supper time. They're obviously best if eaten fresh, but on occasion, we'll freeze them and they're still very tasty.

At the Key Largo fish market, the crab claws cost between $30 and $40 per pound. I once figured that after all the costs are added in (rent, fuel, boat cost, car cost, flight cost, etc.) to harvest a pound of crab runs me around $400 or more per pound.

Why not just buy them you might ask? Because it's the sport, the fun, and it's another reason to get out on the water because, as retirees, we have time to burn!

52

~ Four Friends ~

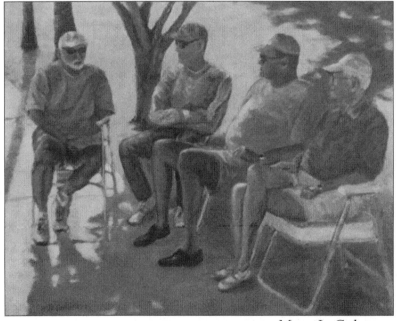

Mary Jo Gohmann

Four Friends

The painting you're looking at was done by my wife a few years ago. It depicts me and three of my friends who also reside in the condominium development in Islamorada, Florida. In the picture, we're doing what we do best when we're kicked back in our chairs - shooting the breeze and telling lies.

Following is a brief synopsis of each man.

John R. Gohmann

First man on left

Dr. Anthony (Tony). He's old ... 109. Actually, he's only 75, but we like to tease him about being an old fart! Tony can be a real smart-ass and he's full of shit, but he's a great friend.

He hails from Brooklyn, New York, where he was born and raised. He attended St. Savior Grade School in Brooklyn. He also attended Brooklyn Tech, Manual, John Jay High School, Long Island University and Hunter College in New York City. He's a graduate of New York College of Podiatric Medicine and Surgery and did his residency at Woodward General Hospital in Highland Park, Michigan.

He was a podiatric foot and ankle surgeon before he retired. He and his wife have three children. He loves to fish and play guitar. He's also a concierge doctor to yours truly.

When he's not staying at the condo, he lives in Grosse Pointe Farms, Michigan.

Second from left

John R. Gohmann—also known as JR, Sergeant and Boss Man.

USAF Veteran—3 years, 9 months, 7 days of honorable service.

Published Author—*Paving My Way Through Life*—on Amazon. com.

Born January 1950 in Georgetown, Scott County, Kentucky. 69 years old. Raised in New Albany, Indiana. Currently resides on Floyd's Knobs, Indiana.

Attended 12 years of Catholic schools—Our Lady of Perpetual Help grade school, Our Lady of Providence High School. Attended night classes and correspondence classes at Belleville Junior College in Belleville, Illinois. Attended night classes at Indiana University Southeast (IUS).

Master picture-framer. Certified bituminous hot mix plant operator. Other jobs include, worked at a gas station, a land surveyor for the Floyd County, Indiana Surveyor's Office, construction laborer, sergeant in the USAF, heavy equipment operator, truck driver, mechanic, asphalt paving superintendent, construction superintendent, Secretary, Vice-President, CEO, and Vice-chairman of one of the larger road and bridge construction companies in southern Indiana, Gohmann Asphalt and Construction, Inc.

Also managed and supervised two limestone quarries in southern

Indiana: Sellersburg Stone Company and Corydon Crushed Stone Company. Managed a fleet of tanker trucks, dump trucks and lowboys at Riverton Trucking in southern Indiana. Is a general partner in three LLCs.

John and his wife have one daughter who is a Ph.D.

John retired in 2014 from the family construction business.

His hobbies include a love of salt and freshwater fishing, deer and small game hunting, duck and geese hunting, frog and turtle hunting, pheasant, quail and turkey hunting. Other interests and hobbies he enjoys are lobstering and crabbing in the Florida Keys, collecting, woodworking, boating, drinking, cursing, country and western music and any and all college sports.

Third from left

Benny Ray Lowman (Buddy)

Benny didn't go to any trade school. He joined the Navy at age 17 and spent 4 years and 4 months in the service. He served on the USS Constellation and the USS Lexington.

He started a painting business with a school friend when he moved to Brooklyn. He specialized in sand-blasting, a profession that was self-taught.

He was a southern boy born in Columbia, SC. He started fishing with his uncle and got hooked on the sport. Then when he moved to Long Island, New York, it seemed he always caught a ton of bluefish. The next logical progression was acquiring the boats and fishing equipment, and after that, the condo in the Keys.

Buddy was born on October 15, 1944. He died on October 19, 2018. While half of his ashes are interred at Long Island National Cemetery, we scattered the other half of Buddy's ashes at sea. Here's my recollection of that event.

There was a five-boat flotilla. We left the marina at Coral Harbours following Captain Neail. He was on-board with Buddy's wife, Cathy, and friends. The other boats followed his lead. There was Captain Greg and friends, followed by Captain Mike and friends, then Captain Frank and friends, and me, Captain John, along with some friends, who brought up the rear.

We slowly motored out heading due east to a spot a mile or so off-shore. It was just before sunset and the seas were calm. We positioned our boats around Captain Neail's boat some thirty yards or so away. Neail keyed up his radio as we all went to channel 16 and listened with wet eyes to Buddy's farewell words from Captain Neail.

As Buddy's ashes slipped away, Cathy flung a bucket of rose petals into the water. After a few quiet minutes, Buddy was gone.

Neail's Yamaha came to life as well as the other boats and we proceeded back towards the marina and dock. As the others boats moved away, I held my boat, the *Joanna Marie,* out and off the port side some twenty yards away. The rose petals formed a perfect circle as a light westerly breeze pushed them out to sea. A few minutes later the petals dispersed, floated away and out of sight.

Buddy liked to make his own lead-head jigs and he even named his boat, *The Lead Head.* I and my two mates all tossed a Buddy-made jig into the drink and bid him farewell. We then departed and joined the others at the dock.

Cathy had arranged a party of sorts at the clubhouse and all joined in for a celebration of Buddy's life and his passing. To this day, every time I depart the dock on my way out to the reef or the hump, my dear friend Buddy comes to mind, and the memories of a true fisherman, husband, father and friend live on.

Buddy has two sons.

Fourth from left

Charles Simon (Charlie)

He was born in 1917 and is 102 years old. He attended Fordham University and is a US Army veteran of WWI.

He was a CFO of Eastern Airlines but retired many moons ago.

He was born and raised in the Bronx, New York, and has two sons a daughter.

He loves fishing and the Florida Keys, fine dining and red wine. But the Islamorada Fishing Club is just fine for dinner.

He skipped 2 grades in grade school (he attended P.S. 44), then Dewitt Clinton High School in the Bronx. He graduated from high school in three years. He went to Fordham University and graduated in three and a half years in a class of 1938.

The diversity in our four lives, our birthplaces, ages, homes, educations and careers has not diminished the friendship we have/had for one another. If anything, it only intensified it and made it stronger.

In the painting—the quality of which is excellent, by the way!—we're all sitting under the tree at the edge of the marina in our retirement community, the Atlantic Coral Harbours Association in Islamorada, Florida, in the Keys.

The great part of life in the Keys with retirement and the condo setting is that one makes a whole new set of friends from all walks of life of sometimes greatly differing ages. There are many who share my love for fishing and boating. If one chooses, you can attend the holiday events at the clubhouse, poker on Monday nights, bingo night, and for the ladies who are artist-types, there's oil painting. The ladies also enjoy the game, Mahjong, on their card night.

There's happy hour at the pool every Thursday, fishing tournaments, fishing, fishing, and more fishing. There's also biking, walking, tennis and pickleball just to name a few of the many activities that are offered.

When I'm away from my home in Floyd's Knobs, and I'm relaxing down at the condo, I have the opportunity to expand my friendship and acquaintances base. And with the variance of ages, jobs, hobbies, etc. it's easy to find like-minded people who you can choose to hang out with and do things.

After a five or six months' stay though, you look forward to your summers back home and doing other things you have on your plate. As nice as they are, you tire of all the people when you live in fairly close quarters.

There are many escapes where you can enjoy your peace and quiet and avoid others if you choose. It's just two different ways to spend your time—at home on the farm or in the woods, gardening and lake fishing, or during the fall and winter months you head down to the Keys to fish, interact with your other circle of friends doing various things like boating, happy hours, enjoying excellent fresh fish, crabs, eating delicious fresh-caught lobster, and of course Key Lime pie.

On the 14 private acres of land with eight buildings of condos, you'll find about 75% of the folks are retired and range in age from 55 years old, to my friend, Charlie, who's 102 years old. The other 25% are made up of younger couples (some with children, some not), singles, and a few families that live here year-round.

Back to my wife's painting at the beginning of this chapter—

we have the original hanging in the living room in our condo. We had three copies made and each of the other old boys in the picture has one hanging in their own condo and/or home. The kinship the four of us have felt for each other over the years is similar to what I've read about Doolittle's Raiders. We have bonds that will forever link our lives and we have friendships that can never be broken. No one would have ever guessed that as diverse as each of our lives were, that we'd ever become close friends. And, just like with Doolittle's boys, we wonder who will be the last man standing?

Live life to its fullest, my friends. You only get one shot at it!

53

~ What's in Your Pocket? ~

I will start this story with my grandparents. My grandfather on my mother's side was an Italian, legal immigrant, US Citizen. I only spent a limited time with Angelo when I was a young boy—maybe a week or two during the summer.

Most of the time he was either out working in his garden, sitting at the dinner table or relaxing in his easy chair in the living room watching the black and white TV. I would watch him very closely and listen intently just trying to understand what he was saying as he spoke mostly in Italian. I recall that he carried a handkerchief in his right front pocket that held an old, faded scapular.

The scapular is a Roman Catholic item usually worn suspended from the shoulders by a thin strap or cord. There are two types: the monastic and devotional scapular, although both forms may simply be referred to as "scapular". As an object of popular piety, it serves to remind the wearers of their commitment to live a Christian life.

The normal scapular has two pieces of wool inside a clear protective plastic sheath hanging from the strap that goes around the shoulders. One part goes in front of the wearer and the other part behind. The images on the wool can vary. Typically, one side will have an image of some religious significance, such as Christ or the Blessed Virgin Mary,. while the other side might have some very brief prayer or saying. Some scapulars have only one piece that hangs on the front side of the wearer.

My grandfather on my dad's side, Herbert Sr.—his nickname was Pam—was a very formal man who was always neatly dressed and well-mannered. Pam carried a handkerchief in his back right-hand side pocket and a small black, folding wallet in his back left pocket. He carried a money clip (silver with a flat blue stone on the top side) in his right front pocket and a flat book of matches in his front left pocket.

Somewhere along the line, after Pam's death, my Uncle Jimmy

gave me the money clip. I carried it for a while but now it's in my cuff link box—the one I had bought for a quarter from my Uncle Warren ("Big Warren") in a yard sale he had years ago. Big Warren gave me the quarter back after the sale.

My father, Herbert Jr., aka "Dad" or "the old man", I can remember while growing up, the various items he carried in his pockets. At a young age, he shared his bedroom with my two older brothers. The dresser was his, while the built-in drawers in the room were my brothers. On top of the dresser was a wooden tray and he would empty his pockets there every day. Dad always carried a brown folding leather wallet in his back right pocket and a handkerchief in the back left pocket.

He carried a crucifix about four inches long, brass with a black stone of some kind. It was very worn looking. He also carried a few coins, a short pocket knife (Schrade brand I believe), his Navy dog tag from WWII, and also a Zippo flip-top lighter. As time went on and the years passed, the dog tag went on his key chain and he gave the crucifix to my stepmother. When he stopped smoking his Camels and Roi Tan Cigars, the lighter disappeared.

Years later when my mother passed away, my aunt Marie who lived up in Manitowoc, Wisconsin, sent me two wicker baskets that were my mother's. In one of those baskets was a love letter and inside it was a very worn-down buffalo nickel (from the early 1940s is my guess; the year is worn off) and a note that said, "Herb carried this nickel all through WWII and he constantly was rubbing it when times aboard ship were trying."

I also have that nickel in Big Warren's old cuff link box at home on my dresser. It's one of my most cherished and loved possessions. Many times, I'll open the box and rub the nickel. It brings a lump in my throat and a tear to my eye as my thoughts go back in time to what I could have, or should have, done differently in order to tighten the bond between us.

And now for me ... what do I now, and what have I carried in my pockets? Officially, I'm John R. Gohmann, but I've also gone by Sergeant, Johnny Boy, Rumpter, Brother and Friend, but my favorite name of all was just, "Son."

As a young lad, I carried nothing. I never had anything to carry other than a pocket knife from my father.

In high school, I carried a handkerchief in my back right pocket. In the left, a brown tri-fold wallet with a few dollars, my hunting and fishing license, a picture or two, and later on, my driver's license.

After I got drafted, I still carried the handkerchief and the tri-fold wallet, but I also acquired a Zippo lighter with three stripes on it. It represented the rank of a buck sergeant. I knew that one day I'd be promoted to the rank of sergeant. I never smoked, but carried the lighter in case the TI, the Boss Man or a higher ranking SOB needed a light. This brought me many a brownie point. When I got out of basic training into my pocket went a pocket knife.

Today I carry my handkerchief and a brown wallet (a fold-over with a center flap)., I carried Grandpa Pam's money clip for years until my wife gave me a gold money clip with a file and a small knife on my 40th birthday. I had to retire this clip because the TSA at the airport threatened to take it away from me—I guess a one-inch blade can be considered deadly? Both clips are in my Uncle Warren's cuff link box.

I now carry a silver clip that my wife picked up in Ireland. It has a raised emblem that resembles the Toyota emblem on my Tundra pickup truck.

Most days, I carry a pocket knife in my other front pocket, along with two plastic toothpicks and every once in a while, a lucky buckeye or chestnut. I've also carried a pocket watch and fob for many years, too.

Take the time to think … What's in *your* pocket? It just may invoke some fond memories of the past!

54

~ Fishing Buddy and Friend ~

This man, my friend, Neail, knows just about everything—and at the age of 81, he probably does, especially when it comes to saltwater fishing and anything related to the garment industry. Neail fishes the summers up in Yankee-land, Long Island, New York, and the winter months here at Coral Harbours, Islamorada, in the Florida Keys ... the sportfishing capital of the world!

Certain adjectives come to mind when I describe Neail. The following are but a few examples:

- Arrogant
- Brash
- Certain
- Cocksure
- Conceited
- Confident
- Egotistical
- Hotshot
- Know-it-all
- Overconfident
- Overwhelming
- Positive
- Rocket engineer
- Aloof
- Bossy

- Cavalier
- Cocky
- Haughty
- Pompous
- Smug
- Presumptuous
- In-your-face

With all that being said—and said with tongue-in-cheek, I might add!—one could not ask for a more loyal friend or find a more honest and sincere man. Neail is dedicated to catching big fish and is more willingly open to teaching any young (or old) person how to fish than any man east of the Monongahela River.

He is truly dedicated to the sport, and I am most fortunate to be able to call him my good friend and fishing buddy!

55

~ Words of Wisdom ~

Growing up in the 1950s-1960s, there were many home-cooked remedies, sayings, how to do this and that and what was going to happen to you if you didn't walk the line—like the following lines that I can remember:

"Straighten up or your plate is going to be in the mailbox."
"I'll slap that smile off your face."
"You get nothing for nothing, and damn little for two cents."
"You'd best pray that comes out of the carpet!"
"If you don't behave, I'll knock you to Kingdom Come!"
"Why? … because I said so."
"If you fall out of that tree, you're going to break your neck and don't come running to me."
"If you don't straighten up and fly right, I'll knock your block off!"
"Do this—because I said so."
"Wear clean undershorts in case you're in an accident."
"You want something to cry about? Then keep on crying!"
"Shut your mouth and eat those peas."
"You're going to stay put until you eat all of that okra."
"Your room looks like a hurricane went through it."
"If I told you once, I've told you a thousand times …"
"Stop acting like . . ."
(Your father) – "Stop acting like your mother!"
(Your mother) – "Stop acting like your father!"
"You wait until your father (or mother) gets home."
"Don't come running to me when the lawnmower cuts your toes off."
"Shut the door … were you born in a barn?"
"The early bird gets the worm."
"No matter how bad it is, the sun is coming up in the morning."
"Let's rock 'n roll out of here!"

"You dance like you have two left feet."

"Stop it! You're going to put your eye out with that thing."

"Well, you broke it … are you happy now?"

"Hey boy—you got a Cajun in your pocket?"

"I'm going to stick that where the sun don't shine!"

"The carpet don't match the drapes."

"Sticks and stones will break my bones, but words will never hurt me."

"I'll buy you for a dollar and hope to sell you for what you think you're worth."

"When it rains, it pours."

"When you bend over, you'll crack a smile!"

"There are two givens in life - you'll pay taxes and you'll die!"

"Don't get dirt on your root … Do get honey on your stinger!"

"Blood is thicker than water."

"Turn off the lights—do you think we own stock in the electric company?"

"Don't eat crackers in bed."

"Don't take any wooden nickels."

"You reap what you sow"

"Come and get it!"

"Horse sense."

"Stump broken!"

"You play with fire and you're gonna get burned!"

"You're wrong-handed."

"Two rights don't make a wrong!"

"If you blink—it's over."

"The devil will get his due."

"You have no common sense."

"How low can you go?"

"Beware of Greeks bearing gifts."

"An apple a day keeps the doctor away."

"Drain the swamp."

"Time and tides wait for no man."

"Eat all of your carrots and you'll never go blind."

"The grass is always greener on the other side."

"If the shoe fits—wear it!"

"A bird in the hand is worth two in the bush."

"A penny saved a dollar earned."

"Don't put off for tomorrow, that which you can do today."

"Is a pig's ass pork?"

"Does the bear crap in the woods?"

"You truly can't judge a book by looking at its cover."

"Son … what were you thinking?"

"Son, if I was to lay a hand on you at this moment, I'd kill you."

"I'll hit you so hard your grandchildren will hurt!"

"Son, you'd better get your act together because the circus is coming to town."

"You can pick your nose, and you can pick your friends, but you can't pick your friends' nose."

"Good, Better, Best! Never let it rest, until Good is Better and Better is Best."

"If you can't outplay them—outwork them!"

"You drive that car like you stole it."

"If it feels good - do it."

"Happy as a lark."

"Knock, knock—Who's there?" jokes

"One and done."

"Do elephants fly?"

"Fast as a whistle."

"That's as clear as mud."

"Shaking like a dog."

"You've got a long row to hoe."

Dear readers–as you can tell, many words of wisdom were passed down through the ages. The 50s and 60s seemed to be the prime years (in my opinion) when the parents had control and influence over their children.

How many millennials are aware of, or can even recall, a single one of these phrases or words of wisdom, or more importantly, what each of them means? Why is it that they worked so well for us growing up in that era, but fall on deaf ears for many of today's kids?

I know a lot of youngsters look at us "Old Farts" and laugh at our values and beliefs, but those values and beliefs are the things that made our parents' generation great, and they made ours, the "Old Farts," great as well. Take heed!

56

~ Rank Has Its Privileges ~

Back in 1968 when Uncle Sam came a-calling (We want you!) I packed my bag and headed west to serve in the USAF. I made my progression through the ranks; Airman-no stripes, then, Airman (E 1)—one stripe—next it was Airman First Class (E 2), and then finally Buck Sergeant (E 4).

The first three grades, or ranks, you were at the bottom of the food chain and I mean *rock bottom*. You were catching hell from everyone and you were the grunt. If you were told to squat, you squatted or paid the price.

As an Airman, your main mode of transportation was to walk. As an Airman First Class, you walked, rode the base bus or managed to find the funds to drive a car, if you were fortunate enough to find one.

As an E4 Buck Sergeant, how you got around was pretty much your call. While on your original report for duty, the mode of transportation was by a Greyhound or a Continental Trailways bus. Then you walked, ran, rode the Base bus, rode the public bus, or rode in a car if you were lucky. Of course, you always had "Old reliable"—your thumb.

There were no commercial plane rides, no chauffeurs, no escorts, no USAF shuttles to and from the base. If you were lucky and there were seats available, you could hop a ride on a cargo or transport plane from one base to another, depending on their schedule.

And, if you were fortunate, the hops would go to a base near your home which, in my case, was Fort Knox. It was the base closest to my home on the few times I was able to catch a hopper. You still had to find your own ride home and back to your base, by any means available.

The seats on these hoppers were basically just wooden boards. There was one along each wall or side of the plane and more often than not, there was cargo tied down in the middle of the plane.

On each bench, you were assigned a parachute. There were

harness straps fastened against the sides of the plane and wearing them was mandatory. The noise level was high and no snacks were served. You basically just sat tight and hoped you'd reach your destination in one piece.

When it came to base auto parking, there were no assigned spots. It was park out by the base perimeter fence and walk over to your duty station, which could be a mile away. For your first few years, you moved around in a group, not much on your own. I think you get the picture—this was life in the enlisted ranks.

Now let me describe the officer pool. You were issued free flight tickets to your first base. There was also shuttle service, furnished drivers, pick up and drop off schedules, and it was all provided by the enlisted pool. It's no wonder the non-careers had a tendency to stick it to an officer now and then, especially the second lieutenants. I forgot to mention, the officers' pool had their own mess hall too, so it's no surprise that they were the targets whenever possible. But in reminiscing, it only took one good lieutenant-beating to catch up and even the score on all the behind chopping they thought was there rank-given right! (This could be another story all on its own.)

So where does rank have its privileges? Compare the above passage to the following and you'll see where and why.

Back in 1973 or so, my older brother was an officer in the U.S. Navy; possibly a first lieutenant, as I recall. He was flying most all of the planes docked on the USS Kennedy, an aircraft-carrier stationed in Norfolk, Virginia, the hometown of the famous downtown sign that read, *All sailors and dogs keep off the grass.* Some small things in a military town leave everlasting impressions.

This one particular weekend happened to be the celebration of "The Tall Ships" in Norfolk Bay. Large, old, sailing vessels from all over the world came to this event which was held every few years.

My brother was the Top Dog representing the Navy during this event. He wore a white dress uniform complete with a sword and really looked the part around the dock and ships. I will refer to him as "Captain."

He would be driven to and from various places around the event, and with me in tow, I was able to see firsthand the inside and workings of the sailing vessels. On each ship we entered, we walked the plank and all hands on deck stood at attention—it was real officer royalty.

Now, years later, looking back on it, Captain—me following with my long hair, a full beard, blue jeans and a long-sleeve wool plaid shirt—and I were 100% opposites. It was quite interesting for me as a USAF enlisted man, to see the workings of the Navy enlisted men and it brought back many good, and some not so good memories.

We later boarded the USS Kennedy and after a complete tour of the ship, had lunch in the officers' mess. Later, I got to sit in various planes and in general, had the time of my life. Captain was the *Big Man* on the ship and it was obvious he took that responsibility seriously. But it was also obvious that he enjoyed being at the top of the chain.

The next morning we were given the red carpet treatment with Captain in the lead. We spent most of the day on the Calypso, a floating underwater discovery and exploration ship. Its captain was the world-renowned explorer, Jacques Cousteau. The vessel was like a floating science lab and was quite interesting, to say the least.

The ship had a helicopter pad on the rear deck. We were introduced to the pilot and mechanic all rolled into one, a Mr. Bob Braunbeck. The Captain recognized him as a former classmate from Providence High School. We were then treated with even more royalty and respect than ever before.

It was a wonderful week. I saw many impressive sights, boarded numerous ships, toured the USS Kennedy and got to sit in the cockpits of all kinds of planes. What a week to remember. It goes to show you that it's *who* you know in the military that really pays dividends. Yes, rank does have its privileges!

Weeks later, Captain got an assignment and was shipping out overseas. Where to? I don't know. With him, everything was a classified secret.

After a long hard week at work, Dad stopped by and said, "Son, let's go pick up your brother." Into the Caddy I went and over to Bowman Field. Back then you could drive up close to the hanger and walk out to greet the planes. Well, here came a Navy plane—a two-seater, the make and model I don't remember. But I do recall him making two circles above, bringing her in for a landing and stopping about seventy-five yards from us.

Dad and I were escorted over to the plane where the glass canopy of the cockpit was shoved back and Captain gave us the thumbs-up. There in the back seat with a long scarf around his neck was Captain's dog, Rocky, a full-blooded Airedale.

As the story goes, Captain could not take his dog on assignment so he flew him home for Dad to care for. Rocky found a great home and never left Dad's backyard.

Three large waxy insulated cardboard boxes were unloaded off the plane, placed in the car and off we went. The next day Dad had a cookout at his home and all the family was invited. The boxes were full of fresh live raw oysters. The feast was about to begin.

When placed on a hot BBQ grill, an oyster will sizzle and the shell will slowly spread apart, just enough to run a fork in to pry it open. We'd dip the oyster in hot butter and chase it with a cold PBR. They were the most delicious oysters that anyone ever had.

Come Monday, Dad and I had Captain over at Bowman Field at seven a.m. sharp and again, in the same manner he'd arrived, Captain was in the air and gone in a flash.

I commented to Dad, "Can you believe what just happened and what a surprise weekend this was. How did he get to use a Navy plane to haul his dog home along with boxes of oysters?"

Dad didn't answer me immediately. Maybe he thought it was just a rhetorical question. He told me to get in the Caddy because it was time to head back to the office.

About halfway across the bridge, Dad looked over and gave me a knowing smile. "Son," he said. "In the military, Rank Has Its Privileges!"

57

~ Brandeis Fishing Trip - 1988 ~

February 1988, Islamorada, Florida, in the Florida Keys. This involves a third-generation heavy equipment supplier in Louisville, Kentucky. The best way to seal the deal and keep the customer coming back was, and still is, to treat the customer good, entertain them in ways they truly enjoy and show kindness and respect.

A fair deal is where both parties feel like winners. To achieve this is a sign of a great distributor, and extends even to the salesman. Brandeis Equipment and Supply had these qualities, plus many more.

This one particular trip was extra special and you, the reader, will see what was so special as we go forward.

Saturday, 23 January 1988, we departed Bowman Field in Louisville at nine a.m. sharp in the Brandeis Corporate King airplane. At one p.m., we were on the ground in Marathon, Florida, which was the closest airstrip to where we were going, and also one of the few in the Keys. We had an enjoyable lunch at Papa Joe's, and that evening at eight p.m., a wonderful dinner at the Quay restaurant.

Sunday, the 24th, time for fishing! There were eight of us. We left the dock aboard the charter boat, *The Carribsea*, with Captain David Day and his first mate, Dave, out of Bud and Mary's Marina at MM80 oceanside. Onboard with me was my brother, along with Tony, Joe, Greg and Steve. The sea was rough that day with waves three to four feet high. Back home that night we had dinner at seven p.m. at Ziggie's Conch.

Monday, the 25th, we went out for more fishing. The seas were rougher than the day before with waves in the range of eight to ten feet. Onboard with me were my dad, my brother, Joe, Greg and Steve. Tony stayed on the dock. He looked a little green and was very sick. It was a combination of the rough seas the day before, plus he had some bad grouper—hung-over. After a rough day on the water, we had dinner that evening at seven p.m. at Eric's Floating Restaurant.

Tuesday, the 26th, we spent the morning souvenir shopping in Islamorada and Marathon. We had lunch at the Seven Mile Grill followed by one p.m. flight on the King Air back to Louisville.

An accounting of the fish we caught and brought back home were: Kings, Cudas, Grunts, Spanish Mackerel, Cero Mackerel, yellowtails, Black Grouper, mutton snappers and porgies just to name a few. In addition to this great haul, I managed to catch the biggest fish on the trip, a 45-pound cobia. Greg caught the second biggest fish when he landed a 20-pounder of the same species. Ballyhoo, cigar minnows and pilchards were the bait of choice.

Then three weeks after the trip, I received a letter from Brandeis' Manager/Field Sales. It read:

Dear John,

I wanted to drop you a note and thank you very much for the order last week on the PC220LC-3. We very much appreciate the confidence you have shown in Brandeis and the manufacturers we represent. It is now our job to retain that confidence you have placed in us.

Again, thanks for the business and if I can be of any service, please do not hesitate to call.

Shortly thereafter, I received another letter from the sales representative. He again thanked me for the great time fishing and suggested that maybe we could make the fishing trip an annual event.

I might add, they've done this, but I heard they let the sales representative go. The replacement sales rep called on us for the next 25 years or so, and we continue to fish even to this day.

A sad day ... four weeks later on Sunday, 21 February 1988, at one p.m., we received a call from my stepmother that Dad had died of a massive heart attack there at the Palms condo. The last time I saw Dad, we'd fished together. He had driven us to Marathon airport and we shook hands as we said our goodbyes. Little did I know, it would be the last time we would share time together.

As a p.s. to this story, please share time with your parents. You never know when their time will be up.

58

~ State Penitentiary ~

The time was 1970. I was a young airman in the USAF stationed in Altus, Oklahoma. A sergeant friend of mine from Muskogee, Oklahoma, Old Ned, loved to hunt, fish and drink Lone Star beer. Ned was discharged before me and went home to own, run and operate his parents' gun and supply shop. Once a month or so I would ride up to visit him, do a little hunting or fishing and stock up on the great deals he had for me on ammo and supplies. Sometimes I'd just hang around his store to shoot the breeze.

Oklahoma State Police and other law enforcement officers and prison guards frequented Ned's store on a regular basis.

Along the way, I'd traded Ned for a sweet H&R, .22 western-style pistol. As time went on, I became a pretty good shot with it. I had it lying there on the counter display in the gun shop when two prison guards came in to browse and purchase a bucketful of reloads for their target practice.

The officer spotted the pistol and inquired about it. "No sir," I said. "It's not for sale. That's my varmint gun."

"How do you carry it?" one of the guards asked.

"Usually tucked in my front pants," I replied. "And at night, I keep it there on the stand next to my bed, wrapped in an old cloth, baby diaper."

One officer asked, "Are you interested in a leather holster for your pistol?"

"Sure," I said. "But I'm in the service and can't afford much in the way of unneeded extras."

The officer responded with, "Next Saturday at ten a.m., be up at the McAlester State Prison and we'll show you around and get you a deal on a holster."

The Oklahoma State Penitentiary, nicknamed "Big Mac", is a prison of the Oklahoma Department of Corrections located in McAlester,

Oklahoma, on 1,556 acres. The facility has five housing units, one for death-row inmates, two for medium security and two for general population.

Big Mac is the facility that carries out all of the executions in the state. The facility is secured by double-razor wire fences and several armed towers. Additional security is provided through a non-lethal stun fence and electronic intrusion detection systems. Oklahoma State Penitentiary has a maximum capacity of 1,241 adult male inmates.

Being 19-years old and having never set foot in a prison, I decided I'd take the officer up on his offer. I had plenty of time, so I figured I'd drive up there on the following Saturday and have a look-see around.

When Saturday rolled around, I got an early start and in two and a half hours, I was there at the first guard shack just off the state highway. I told them my story and presented the business card the one officer had given me.

A phone call was made; I was strip-searched (a first for me), and my Land Cruiser was searched and parked off to the side.

Ten minutes later, an old Willy's Jeep rolled up in a cloud of dust. Dressed in my pants, t-shirt, no belt, no hat, no socks and with a pair of prison-issue flip-flops, I climbed in the jeep and off we went.

Our next stop was in another holding area with a guard shack. There was another body-search, then into another Jeep where I was eventually delivered to the front gate. The building behind the gate was made of cold-looking stone. I was led through the gates—solid steel bars, with locks and guards everywhere—and into a small, holding room.

By this time, I was thinking, *This is not good.* There I sat holding a piece of cardboard with the outline of my pistol along with the make and model and a brief description of it. The reason for the drawing on cardboard was, back at the first gate, after declaring I had a pistol, knives and a shotgun in my Land Cruiser, a list of the weapons was recorded and a tracing of my pistol was done on the cardboard.

Eventually, the two guards I'd met at the gun shop the week before walked in. They brought a cup of coffee for me and I was instructed to stay between the two of them. Not a problem, I thought.

Don't fret or act nervous, I thought. *Just walk calmly.* This was easier said than done. I was a nervous wreck and was sweating a lot there in the Oklahoma sun.

We were in the center yard of the prison with multi-storied buildings on all four sides. My two escorts were armed with what looked like .357 magnums, western-style. One had a 30-30 Winchester in hand and the other carried a 12-gauge, short-barreled, pump shotgun.

The feeling of being a prisoner was overwhelming. The security was amazingly tight. The thought of being locked in a cell with taps being played just before *lights out* gave me the chills and shivers. And later, when I was home in my room at the barracks, I had nightmares for a week thinking about it. In spite of that, it was an experience of a lifetime.

In one corner of the square, there was a large steel door with a guard posted and in we went. There were two more guards inside overseeing a handful of inmates. This was the prison's leather workshop. There were no windows in the room.

There were benches, tables and a tool room. Each tool was signed and checked out. There were no power tools, only hand tools. There were no electrical outlets. Everything was made by hand.

"What you here for, son?" one of the prisoners asked.

I showed him my cardboard tracing and told him I'd like a holster made along with a belt and shell holders on the belt, just like you see in the western movies.

"No problem," he said, then asked, "What color? What kind of stitching do you want?"

I shrugged and said, "You be the judge of that."

He grumbled, "First time anyone ever told *me* to be the judge." He studied me a moment, then asked, "Anything else you need?"

"Sure," I said. "I could use a scabbard for my 30-30 Marlin with a sling on her."

"Is that all?" he asked.

"No," I said. "I really don't have much to spend." I told him about being in the Air Force, where I was stationed, etc. He was eager to talk, so we did. I eventually told him I could also use a new pair of leather boots, brown in color.

I explained that I usually got my boots down in Mexico. And when I wore them out, according to Oklahoma custom, you pull over to the side of the road, walk to the nearest fence and hang the boots over the fence posts. I never knew the history behind this, but did it anyway.

"How much money do you need?" I asked him. He never answered the question. The guards told me they'd figure up the costs back in the prison office.

When I was escorted back to the office, another guard put together an invoice for the leather goods. As I recall, the boots were $30, the holster was $25 and the shell belt was $20. Along with shipping and some additional costs, the total came to $100.

The guard gave me a word of advice. "Get the check mailed in. We won't start work until it's all paid in full."

I was checked out and escorted from the property and they returned my belongings. My pistol was in one bag, my shells in another and both were taped tight so as not to be able to reload quickly. I hopped in my Land Cruiser and was on my way back to the base.

Ten miles down the road, I pulled into the first bar I found and lunched on hot, spicy beans and some sort of mystery meat-filled chili. I also had a sweet onion sandwich on rye bread and a cold, Coors draft.

On the ride south, I kept rolling over in my mind what the old man said when I asked him when I might see my purchases.

"Son," he said. "I have all the time in the world. Don't expect it anytime soon."

I found out, he was serving a life sentence for murder. Two days later I was in the base Credit Union and had a money order for the $100 plus another $25 for the man in the leather shop.

Inmate Name and ID Number:
Joseph J. Jackson; 11745296
Inmate Mailing Address:
Oklahoma State Penitentiary
P.O. Box 97
McAlester, OK 74502-0097

Six months later, I received in the mail, the shell belt. One year later, the holster. Two years passed and the scabbard came. Three years later I was home and discharged from the service and the boots showed up.

I'll never forget this experience and the words of inmate Jackson: *I HAVE ALL THE TIME IN THE WORLD!*

59

~ Bikes ~

For as long as I can remember, bikes and biking seemed to be a part of my life, from my first all-metal tricycle, a family hand-me-down. It was rusty red with plenty of miles on her. She had hard rubber tires and looked like a trike you'd see in a Norman Rockwell painting.

Then came my first regular bike—another hand-me-down. It was a green Schwinn with larger diameter wheels. Then one Christmas I received my first new bike, a green one. It had a banana seat, rabbit ear handlebars and long strips of plastic streamers on the handle grips. For some reason, green seemed to be my color when it came to bikes. As the years went by I inherited a three-speed red Schwinn from my older brother. I rode this bike until I got drafted in 1968.

In 1970 at the base thrift store, for ten dollars I purchased a black Schwinn three-speed with skinny tires. I rode that bike all over western Illinois. When it was time to move on, I got transferred to Altus AFB in southwestern Oklahoma. My Toyota Land Cruiser was stuffed full and my trusty bike was given to PJ Wumble, my landlord and owner of the West Baden bakery—two of my service buddies and I rented the apartment upstairs over the bakery while stationed at Scott AFB near Belleville, Illinois.

Then around 1973 or so, I bought a new, orange Schwinn, ten-speed bike. What a cruising machine it was! Today this fine bicycle hangs from the ceiling in the garage at our home. I have not ridden that bike in some twenty years or so. I purchased it from Clarksville Schwinn (Mr. Bob P, a long-time friend and owner).

When our daughter came into the picture in 1983, I purchased from Mr. Bob a bicycle built for two. It was candy apple red, had ten-speeds, a child seat on the rear and a Howdy Doody horn. It also sported front and rear taillights and an oversized basket on the front. Boy, what a ride she was and many a fun trip was had with the family—me, wife and daughter in tow. In 2001 we hauled it to our place in the Florida Keys and there, enjoyed rides around Islamorada.

Last year (2018), I traded the tandem to another Mr. Bob, the owner Bob's Bikes in Tavernier, for a crossover bike with wide tires, motorcycle seat, and the oversized basket I had transferred from the tandem.

Going back a few years, I purchased a silver, three-speed Schwinn, again from Clarksville Schwinn Bike Shop. It was a basic model … no basket, no horn, just a comfortable seat and one that makes you sit up straight. It's parked in the garage and very seldom sees the pavement with me on it.

In 19-something (the exact year escapes me), my nephew introduced me to his favorite uncle who'd mastered the art of riding a unicycle. He sparked my interest in the one-wheel bike and after a year of practice, I managed to ride it up and down the drive and around. This fine bike is also retired to the garage ceiling, along with a collection of bikes my wife had and most all of the bikes our daughter had growing up.

My dream bike is one that I purchased just two months ago from an online bike shop in Washington State. It's a Rad, electric-powered bike; bright orange, basket on front, luggage rack on the back that holds two five-gallon Yeti buckets for hauling things in. It also has a three-speed front axle, seven-speed rear axle, disc brakes, lights, a bell horn, a squeeze bulb horn, and a horn that plays *Way down south in the land of cotton* from the song, *Dixie.*

She'll do 20 MPH in first gear with a normal cruising speed of about 10 MPH. There's a handlebar-mounted mini-computer that shows your speed, MPH, battery life (the fuel gauge), trip time, mileage and other useful information.

I've ridden her nine miles down the Keys and back and used two bars of the five-bar fuel gage. When the wife has the car, like most days in the Keys, and is away, the mouse plays (that's me!) riding the electric powered bike up and down the Keys. The average mileage to date is 80+ miles per month.

This may be my last bike, but then again, a Rad electric-powered bike is in the future when I return this month to Floyd's Knobs.

Biking has truly been a life-long pleasure. Always be sure to wear a helmet, my reader friends, and Happy Trails to You!

**My New Rad Electric-powered Bike
80+ Miles a Month!**

60

~ Lawnmowers ~

They go by various names, but a few of the more common ones are lawnmowers, grass cutting machines, Goats on Wheels, etc.

The first home I owned was back in 1975. I had a very small, fenced-in back yard with one very large oak tree. When the acorns matured, the squirrels moved in and stayed until all of the nuts were consumed or buried in the soil for the winter season.

The first mower I had hung out in the shed by its handle. It was what's called a push-mower. I inherited the machine from my Great Aunt Agnes. Growing up as a kid I still remember her mowing her lawn with it. I also remember the years she paid me to cut her yard with that machine.

The mower had gears attached to the wheels that caused a set of blades, set in a spiral-type arrangement mounted on a small drum, to rotate in a spinning motion when it was pushed forward.

The grass cutting process was one of pushing the mower forward through the grass, then you'd pull it back and push forward again repeating the process many times. Looking back on it, the mower was actually a pretty ingenious design for its time. The push mower was a Sears make. It had a T-shaped oak handle, was red in color, and had black, solid rubber wheels.

For small yards that were stick, twigs and acorn-free, the mower worked just fine. But in my small back yard, the nuts the squirrels buried were always coming to the surface and invariably the nut would become wedged in the blades and would stop their rotation. It seems like you'd just get a good forward momentum going when you'd hit one of the acorns and the mower would stop abruptly. The handle would be rammed into your stomach, midsection or crotch and you'd be thrown forward and over the handle. Many a time I was left doubled over gasping for air, or spread out on the lawn with my hands cupped over my man thing!

Having repeated this process many times, it became old, and at times, I came close to having severe injuries. I decided that it was time to find another way to keep the grass trimmed in the back yard. Then came the solution—a Black & Decker electric weed eater and a 100-foot extension cord.

This took care of my mowing needs until I moved on to another home with a good-sized front and back yard. I made a trip to Ace Hardware and after a discussion with Ben L, I was now the proud owner of my first new lawnmower. It was a Belknap brand with a five-horse Briggs & Stratton motor. It cut a 20-inch swatch and had a rope pull coil on top of the motor. This mower provided great service and ran for many a year. It now sits retired in the barn up at my Salem, Indiana, farm.

Then came another new home—the place where we still live after 35 years. A new mower was needed and we ended up with a Sears, 24 inch, self-propelled model, also equipped with a Briggs & Stratton engine. It provided many years of good service, and is still running strong, mowing grass up at the small rental house in Salem.

Next came the 12 HP, Cub Cadet mini-tractor with a 36-inch mowing deck. After years of trouble-free mowing, I traded it to a friend for a single-shot JC Higgins, .410 shotgun and a Ruger 45 automatic.

I hired out the mowing for some years, then, as retirement approached, and we hired a young man to manage and care for our properties, we purchased a Kubota 25 horse mini tractor with a 48-inch mowing deck. It has a front dump bucket and a three-point hitch for a roto-tiller that we use for the garden. This unit was necessary to keep up with the three acres we now have that need mowing.

Last summer, my longtime neighbor and friend, Bobby, retired from PSI. He had a yard sale to clear out his home as he was preparing to move to a retirement home down on the west coast of Florida. After a few sales, the only thing left was his Cub Cadet. (Bobby's home sold the day it was listed by his daughter's real estate firm).

A week later, Bob and Judy drove up with a U-Haul truck as well as his pickup truck loaded and ready to roll. They came by the house for one last farewell. As they were about to hit the road, I asked Bobby, "What did you do with your old Cub Cadet?"

He replied that no one had made an offer on it, so they decided to leave it in the garage for the new owner. I gave him a *go to hell* look.

Bobby said, "If you want it, hop in, I'll open the garage door and it's all yours."

So there I sat at the end of the driveway on his 30-year-old, still running, Cub tractor. Bobby turned left and was on his way to Florida while I turned right on my way home with my prize possession, the Cub Cadet. It was almost identical to the one Dad had out at the Big House where I mowed, mowed, and mowed some more until I was drafted by Uncle Sam.

A few weeks later I dropped a one-hundred-dollar bill, "Cousin Franklin," in the U.S. mail to my dear friend Bobby along with a note that read, *Hey, Bobby. This is for the Cub you gave me. Take Ms. Judy out for a nice shrimp dinner on me.*

Two years passed and the Cub was still purring like a kitten. She was all decaled up and looked fit for the John Deere showroom floor in Corydon.

This past winter we remodeled my woodworking shop, retired Dad's old power tools and bought new ones along with a dust abatement system. I called my electrician friend, Sean, to come to rewire the shop to power the new machines and dust system. All the while, I was down in the Keys, fishing.

Then one morning my cell phone rang. I was some ten miles out on the deep blue sea. It was my property manager and caretaker calling from Indiana. He tells me that Sean was there to do the wiring.

I tell him that's fine, just get it done. He tells me there's just one problem; Sean wants to know if I would be willing to swap the Cub Cadet for his labor and supplies. I replied, "10-4, I will." I instruct him to gas her up, give Sean a quart of oil and tell him to enjoy the Cub. She is one heck of a grass-mowing machine!

The zero-turn mower we currently have is showing its age and my caretaker is taking quotes for a new one. It seems that mowers have become a way of life for me. I've pretty much run the gamut on lawnmower types. I started with a push mower, went to a self-propelled mower, hired a lawn service to do the mowing and upkeep, to owning compact tractor mowers and finally—the latest zero-turn mower.

Homeownership and the chores that come with it makes old terra firma and having my roots planted my dream come true. Now that we have our fenced-in, six acres here on the Knobs, who knows? It may be the end of the mowers and tractors and time to invest in some goats to handle the grass mowing.

61

~ Urinal Pads ~

I remember the time we'd planned a trip around Halloween to go up in Floyd's Knobs over to Joe Huber's farm and pick some pumpkins, straight from the fields. We'd also planned to do some shopping at the General Store there afterwards, followed by a walk across the parking lot to the country kitchen on the premises where we'd chow down on some good fried chicken, collard greens, mashed potatoes, German potato salad, those famous biscuits with apple butter, hot chicken dumplings and a few cold Huber beers. All of it was to be topped off with a big slice of blackberry cobbler with two scoops of ice cream on top.

Total in our party were five or six kids, six or eight parents, myself, my wife and our daughter. We thought it would be good and a lot more fun if we all rode up together. The plan was that all of us would meet up at our house and I would borrow a van from my company's fleet of vehicles large enough to haul everyone.

As an aside, our company had expanded and business was good. We were fortunate enough to be the low bidder on a large construction project. It was one that had a short fuse and we were stuck with doing night and weekend work only. We invested a lot in our safety department and had an outstanding record. The safety director had requested a van to haul workers to and from the job site for safety reasons. There was nowhere to park on the job site. With the daily hauling of 12-plus men and women per trip to the job site, it didn't take long for the interior to begin smelling like road oils, lime dust, dirt, fuel, and other construction odors.

As the workweek was quickly coming to an end, I requested that Bobby, the lead mechanic in the shop, get the van gassed up and cleaned out. I needed it for the weekend to transport family and friends up to Huber's Farm.

Saturday morning rolled around and Bobby had the van in the

driveway at nine sharp and, per my request, it was all cleaned and gassed up and in safe mechanical order. By 12:30, all were assembled at the house, ready and excited to go and have a great afternoon at the farm picking out pumpkins, enjoying a great country meal and getting back home just before dark.

We all piled in and the van was full. There was too much noise to even hear the radio. With all of the windows rolled up and the air conditioning set on high, it was blowing lots of cool air in and around the cabin. There came a faint smell that quickly grew into a rather stronger smell. It was that of cherry—a fresh cherry scent.

Then the complaints started to flow and so did the laughter as I explained the weekly use of the van, Bobby cleaning her up and said I was sure that the smell was that of cherry auto air refresher.

About halfway up to the farm, I was asked to pull off the road, which I did. Everyone off-loaded and as we stood there joking and laughing, my nephew, Alfred, slowly and meticulously began his search of the vehicle for the air freshener in the van that had brought tears to our eyes.

Alfred looked like a cop searching for drugs or contraband. He looked under each seat, behind the spare tire, under the front floor mat, and just above the main blower vent in the back of the van; Alfred discovered some six or so of the red oval-shaped air freshener pads with small holes in them. Out on the pavement they went.

"Oh, my God!" exclaimed my wife. "Those are wild cherry urinal pads that John has in all the men's toilets up at the company's office."

Bobby, in his effort to try and mask the smell of oil, grease and fuel, had succeeded for a while until the cherry scent became overwhelming in the closed-up van.

The urinal pads were discarded there on the side of the road and off we went with all windows down ushering in the warm, humid air. The party went on as planned and all had a wonderful time. Pumpkins were loaded, shopping bags were full and most of my passengers were dozing off after a fine, country dinner.

I was carefully driving the van home when my wife, in a low tone, said, "John, you should be ashamed of yourself. I know it was your bright idea to hide those urinal pads. I just hope no one ends up getting sick from breathing that totally disgusting wild cherry odor."

I was also instructed that on all future family outings, we will all drive and meet up at our destination.

She admonished me, "No more of your brainy ideas of using the company van!"

62

~ Kettle & Bell ~

I recall the "Big House" on the hill. This was my grandfather and grandma's home. It sat on 86 acres, had a large red barn, a large red chicken house and a white, single-seat outhouse. I'll touch on the Big House briefly, and then will get back to my story.

For years, a Sears catalog sat next to the hole in the outhouse. This was the equivalent of our Charmin for quite a few years, but no one complained. You really didn't know any better. Yet we all survived, grew into strong and independent people who went on to make better lives for ourselves.

My grandparents bought the place back in 1937 when the Ohio River flooded and took their home, which was located in the west end of Louisville, Kentucky. They packed up what belongings they could salvage and moved north across the Ohio River. We were still close to Louisville, but we now lived in Floyd County, Indiana.

Grandpa continued working his job at Louisville Tent and Awning until his retirement. He commuted daily by car across the Second Street Bridge. When bridge work was taking place, he told us that he crossed over the river on the old K & I Railroad Bridge, or the "Singing Bridge" as the locals called it. A small toll was collected and you'd get off in the west end of Louisville. My grandpa—"Pam" was his nickname—drove to downtown Louisville every day of the week for work.

Now back to my story about the Kettle and Bell. At the Big House, we had a very large, old iron kettle. It looked like a big pot or a big bowl. It had two rounded bar hoops that extended out about five inches or so from the sides near the top of the kettle. These were for mounting the kettle on a stand that stood over an open fire of wood, coal and/or other burning materials.

Grandma would say that the kettle came with the farm and for a few years she used it for cooking things like blood pudding and the like.

220

She also used it for soaking soiled clothes, blankets, etc. as the story goes.

With the advancements in cookstoves and electric appliances, cooking, cleaning, and life in general, got to be more easy and rewarding and gave one more free time to enjoy it.

The usefulness of the old kettle had faded and she set on her hanger out back of the house for years over coals that had died out long, long ago.

Then Dad became a gentleman farmer. He worked long and hard at growing his construction business, but there in the field, eating and grazing on free grass, were two cows he'd purchased somewhere.

At the Big House, there was a very old hand-dug hole (the cistern) that was lined with red bricks from top to bottom. As the story goes, the bricks had been hand-fired on the property years ago as well as all the bricks that were used for the construction of the Big House. The well, or cistern, had a wood frame top supported with rusty old angle irons. It had a square opening for extracting water using a bucket attached to a rope.

The hole was covered with a chestnut-wood lid; this material resists rotting and hungry bugs. The number of Dad's cows was growing thanks to the neighbor's bull and an occasional visit from a man who would artificially inseminate the cows.

The large kettle was moved down by the well to be used as a container for the cows who required clean, fresh water. This required quite a bit of labor each day to fill the pot.

Since Dad was raising six children, he had cheap labor to help haul the water. For a few years, the kettle served the watering needs of the cattle very well. As things sometimes go, the kettle eventually sprung a leak and later, after a patch weld job, she grew a large crack and her usefulness came to an abrupt end.

The herd of cattle grew to some twenty head and water was a must. In addition to having fresh meat for the table, Dad would occasionally sell a cow to get money for clothes, shoes, and to send us kids to parochial schools. Dad's vision of raising cows for a purpose paid off over and over many times, much like his vision to start a construction business. The combination of his good, common sense coupled with his hard work ethic proved to be the one-two punch that made him successful.

Years later, the old kettle pot would find another resting spot at our home up in the Knobs and serves as a reminder of its past and the many good memories associated with it. To this day she sits in our back yard in sight from the house, filled with fertile soil from grandma's farm. It gets limed and fertilized every year or so and sports a large clump of beautiful, lush green ferns.

The large iron dinner bell we had at the Big House shared the same history as the kettle. She stood proudly between the Big House and the garage with a large stone step at the base. This helped raise you up so you could pull the rope attached to the bell. When you pulled on that rope, it made the bell swing back and forth with a heavenly, rhythmic sound.

The rope line was later replaced with a chain, and the pole was replaced a time or two with a tall, sturdy cedar pole. Originally the bell was used to warn of trouble. When rung, the distant neighbors would hear it and call for help if a fire or other emergency existed. When phones and automobiles became more standard, the old bell became an ornament of sorts. She became a signal for us kids that it was lunch or dinner time.

As the children grew and times changed, the bell became a way to ring in the New Year. In addition, it was also rung for special events.

The bell never made it to my home. She remained there at the Big House property with the new owner. Part of the sale deal was ... the bell stays!

Some 25 years ago I found a bell at an estate sale down in Danville, Kentucky. It was about a quarter of the size of the bell we had at the Big House on the hill. It's mounted out back of our house and serves as a reminder of the past, my love for the big iron bell and the chime she would sing when rung. To hear its beautiful sound brings back many fond memories of an innocent and wonderful time that has sadly passed.

63

~ Member Organizations ~

Throughout one's life, outside of what might be your normal, daily pattern, one needs to feel he or she fits into society; has a need for belonging or a sense of purpose. There are many outstanding organizations that one can join to fulfill some of those needs, organizations which can allow an individual the chance to share their knowledge and experiences, be it from life, work, entertainment, or just about anything else.

This sharing is a form of giving back or paying it forward. It can come in the way of financial donations, the sharing of knowledge or donating of one's free time, all of which supports the interests and beliefs in people, places and things that one holds dear to their hearts.

I challenge you, my fellow reader, to make your own list of organizations that you belong to, to reflect back on the contributions you've made, what you might be planning for the future for that special interest you hold dear, and where you can expand so as to feel more accomplished and at ease in your own life.

The following shortlist shows where my personal interests tend to lie, the causes I hold important and feel are worthy:

- The American Legion
- Ducks Unlimited
- Rocky Mountain Elk Foundation
- Bass Masters
- Wild Turkey Federation
- Grady White Boat Club
- NRA Lifetime Member
- Indiana Republicans and the Republican National Committee

In addition to these, there are many other medical, religious and other goodwill groups, clubs and organizations that I support which promote conservation, good health and the need for a good education.

During my 50 years of employment, my family's business always maintained active memberships in many different associations and non-profit organizations and strongly supported them over the years.

Our family business was sold and the former name of each company belongs to the new owners. Most were phased out, however, some were incorporated into the names of the purchasers' existing companies.

The following is a list of the memberships that Gohmann Asphalt & Construction, Inc. was active in and supported over the years. While our company name is gone, the memories and effects we had on the people of Indiana and Kentucky will live on forever. We touched many a family's life over the years through work, play and involvement in local, state and federal organizations and associations. I wish to thank the following for being supportive of my family business.

- American Concrete Pavement Association
- American Institute of Certified Public Accountants
- American Society of Safety Engineers
- American Traffic Safety Services Association
- Asphalt Pavement Association of Indiana
- Association of General Contractors of America
- Construction Financial Management Association
- Greater Louisville, Inc. and Indiana Chambers of Commerce
- Indiana Chapter of American Concrete Pavement Association
- Indiana Construction Association
- Indiana CPA Society
- Institute of Management Accountants, Inc.
- Kentucky Association of Highway Contractors, Inc.
- Kentucky Bar Association
- Kentucky Concrete Pavement Association
- Kentucky Society of Certified Public Accountants
- Louisville NAWIC
- Louisville Bar Association
- National Asphalt Pavement Association
- Actionable Association of Credit Management
- National Safety Council
- One Southern Indiana

- The Plant Mix Asphalt Industry of Kentucky, Inc.
- Indiana Association of County Commissioners
- Indiana Mineral Aggregates Association
- Kentucky Crushed Stone Association, Inc.
- National Stone, Sand, and Gravel Association
- Home Builders Association of Southern Indiana
- Harrison County Chamber of Commerce
- Kentucky Ready Mix Concrete Association
- Tennessee Concrete Association
- Accreditation's by American Association of State Highway Transportation Officials
- Approved by Federal Aviation Administration
- Indiana Department of Transportation
- Kentucky Department of Transportation
- Inspected by American Materials Reference Laboratory
- Indiana Motor Truck association

The above list is just a few of the many fine, materials, labors, equipment, haul, personnel, safety, financial, health, welfare and education associations and agencies of which we were active members for many years

The relationships I forged and the many fine people I met along the way will always be dear to my heart. I'm grateful that I was able to be active in so many wonderful and helpful organizations.

The moral of this story is, if you're lost and looking for your place—step out, join a club or trade organization, or volunteer your services. The groups are awaiting your involvement, but you must take the first step!

64

~ 24 Hours ~

Okay, this is not a day in *The Life and Times of Judge Roy Bean,* but a day in the life of John R. Gohmann (JRG) who, at the time of this writing, is currently living in Arlington, Virginia, in a condo on North Nash Street.

Today is Wednesday, 17 April 2019. Let me start with 10 p.m last night. We were watching a Netflix movie on TV titled "24." It's the fictional story of a Counter Terrorist Unit (CTU) and its key agent, Jack Bauer, brilliantly portrayed by Kiefer Sutherland. The story is devised into a 24-hour timeframe.

This is where I got the idea—would it not be interesting to track a day in my life? And you, the reader, might find that taking a look back at a 24 hour time period of your life may also be interesting.

So we start with and at the hour of 10 p.m. last night. The following events take place in the life of JRG during the following time frames.

10 - 11 p.m. – Watching an episode of "24" with Jack Bauer on TV. We have popcorn and Italian Pellegrino water with a large slice of lime.

11 - 11:30 p.m. – Shower, shave and dental care attended to.

11:45 p.m - 5:45 a.m. – Sleep and rest, some sound and some not so sound.

5:45 a.m. - 6:29 a.m. – I lay awake waiting for the alarm to sound at 6:30 a.m. I'm cursing my friend, Pat, for agreeing to help me write a book of short stories. There are many topics flowing through my head and I'm trying to decide where to start.

No longer being able to sleep and with *Reveille* playing on Alexa, I'm ready to bounce out of bed at 6:30 a.m. and face the new day.

6:30-7:30 a.m. – With two cups of decaf coffee, I'm sitting at our round dining room table. I'm peering out the very large picture window, facing east, overlooking Meade Street. There's a tall oak tree 50 feet away; a brick retaining wall with a stone cap. This wall, which separates the neighboring condo property from ours, runs downhill on a rather steep slope from the street in front to the street in the back of condo building.

As I sip my coffee, I see the sun rising in the east and people on both sides of Meade Street below. We're on the third floor of the Memorial Overlook Condominium, and from my perch, I can observe any person, animal or thing moving below me.

I see joggers, walkers, trotters, both men and women, boys, girls and army recruits from Fort Meyer Army Base. I see all types of attire—shorts, long pants, shoes of all colors, some clothing nice and clean, others dirty and ragged, people walking dogs of all breeds, sizes, colors, most picking up their dog waste, and some bums not. There's even one lady walking her cat on a leash.

My eyes go to the sky and my thoughts drift to the people on the one-after-another flights coming and going in and out of Reagan Airport and landing on the north-south runway.

I see a window washing crew suspended many stories above the ground at the Raytheon office building. My eyes and thoughts drift back to ground level and I observe cars, buses, bikes, motorcycles, scooters, trucks and vans of all makes and models. Also, I have a view of the monument to honor Iwo Jima.

The Battle of Iwo Jima was an epic military campaign between U.S. Marines and the Imperial Army of Japan in early 1945. Located 750 miles off the coast of Japan, the island of Iwo Jima had three airfields that could serve as a staging facility for a potential invasion of mainland Japan. American forces invaded the island on February 19, 1945, and the ensuing Battle of Iwo Jima lasted for five weeks. In some of the bloodiest fighting of World War II, it's believed that all but 200 or so of the 21,000 Japanese forces on the island were killed, as were almost 7,000 Marines.

7:30 - 8:30 a.m. – I move out to the small overlooking porch or balcony, from which I observe directly below me a large brown rabbit, a gray squirrel in the oak tree and a coal-black squirrel rooting in the ivy looking for a last year's buried nut.

Two large black crows are walking down the stone wall. There in the sycamore tree to my left and at eye level are two robins singing.

There's also a sparrow, a squeaking mocking bird, and over on the neighbor's property behind their dumpster is a big, fat, brown rat.

Spring has sprung and the smell of new buds and blossoms is in the air. I say to myself, what a lucky man I am. I'm free, healthy, financially set and eager to get the day moving. I see something dash across the yard down below. There goes a chipmunk!

8:30 - 8:45 a.m. – Breakfast consists of a toasted bagel, apricot jelly from France, a cup of cherry yogurt, three strips of turkey bacon and a glass of water.

8:45 - 9:00 a.m. – Shirt, shorts, shoes—I'm dressed, my face is washed, my teeth cared for, eye drops are in, my hair's brushed and my Old Spice deodorant has been applied.

9:00 - 9.02 a.m. – My daily pills are taken.

9:02 - 9:15 a.m. – Wife and I decide on what's the plan for today. Maybe a trip over to the Tomb of the Unknown Soldier, or a wagon tour of Arlington National Cemetery. Maybe we'll walk back to our condo and take a car ride to have lunch at a new place close by.

9:15 - 10:30 a.m. – Working on this story and waiting on the wife to get dressed so we can start our day. Departure time is 10:30 a.m. sharp.

10:30 a.m. - 1:00 p.m. – Walked to the main gate of Arlington Cemetery, caught the tour train and listened to the history of the cemetery, stones, grounds, monuments, graves, and viewed the changing of the guard at the Tomb of the Unknown Soldier.

1:00 p.m. - 1:45 p.m. – Lunch at Ireland's Four Courts Bar and Grill.

1:45 p.m. - 5:00 p.m. – Shopping at Home Depot and Michael's Craft Store.

5:00 p.m. - 7:00 p.m. – Decorated the outside porch of the condo with a rug and artificial tree, plants and vines we purchased earlier.

7:00 p.m. - 7:30 p.m. – Leftovers for dinner at home.

7:30 p.m. - 9:30 p.m. – Watched two one-hour episodes of the series "24."

9:00 p.m. sharp – Took my nighttime pills.

9:30 p.m. - 10:00 p.m. – Hot shower, shave and dental care.

10:00 p.m. - Lights out; Alexa playing "Taps."

This ends the 24-hour walk through my normal, daily life. As you might have gathered, my 24 Hours and Jack Bauer's 24 Hours are quite different. I managed to get eight hours of sleep while Jack had zero hours.

I was not involved in any shootings, killings, robberies, no death threats, no high-speed car chases, no love scenes—well, maybe, but I don't kiss and tell—and I managed to get three square meals for the day.

Jack's day was loaded with excitement, whereas my day was a day in the life and times of a retired, red neck, white, homophobe, etc. trying to take it one day at a time.

I may be in the fourth quarter of life, but many overtimes are still in the cards!

65

~ Veterans Day ~

My Veterans Day reflections for 2019.

The soldier, above all others, prays for peace, for it is the soldier who must suffer and bear the deepest wounds and scars of war.
–General Douglas MacArthur

Ways to Honor a Veteran

◊ Attend a Veterans Day event.

◊ Ask a Veteran about their time in the military, and really listen to the answer.

◊ Hang a flag in your yard.

◊ Visit the gravesite of a Veteran.

Ways to Express Appreciation on Veterans Day

◊ Show Up! Attend a Veterans Day event in your area, not just a picnic with friends but an honest-to-goodness parade or service for veterans.

◊ Donate.

◊ Fly a flag—correctly.

◊ Ask someone about their service.

◊ Visit a VA Hospital

Why do we honor the veterans?

This is why we should honor our veterans. They risked their lives so we, Americans, could live in a better country. For all our war troubles throughout history, we have depended on our soldiers to keep our country safe and free. They had to fight for their country, while also fighting for their lives.

Veteran's Day

While it's good to acknowledge a veteran anytime you see him or her, on Veterans Day it's appropriate to thank those who served by simply saying, "Thank You." They all know what you're thanking them for, so "Thank you for your service" can be excessive in some situations.

Veterans Day celebrates the service of all U.S. military veterans. Another military holiday, Armed Forces Day, a minor U.S. remembrance, also occurs in May, which honors those currently serving in the U.S. military.

I suggest, my dear readers, that you make an effort to visit yearly the following places that memorialize and honor those who've served this country:

• New Albany National Cemetery is a United States National Cemetery located in the City of New Albany, in Floyd County, Indiana. It's administered by the United States Department of Veterans Affairs. It encompasses 5.5 acres, and as of the end of 2005, it had 6,881 interments. It is managed by the Zachary Taylor National Cemetery.

• Arlington Nation Cemetery in Arlington, VA. Arlington National Cemetery is a United States military cemetery in Arlington County, Virginia, located across the Potomac River from Washington, D.C. In the 624 acres that comprise the cemetery, those who lost their lives in our nation's conflicts are buried here beginning with the Civil War but there are some who've been reinterred from earlier wars. More than 400,000 people are buried at Arlington National Cemetery including two U.S. Presidents, William Howard Taft and John F. Kennedy.

• The American Cemetery is located on a hill overlooking Normandy Beach, France. Over 425,000 Allied and German troops were killed, wounded or went missing during the Battle of Normandy. This figure includes over 209,000 Allied casualties, with nearly 37,000 dead amongst the ground forces and a further 16,714 deaths amongst the Allied air forces.

I'm proud to say that I visit the New Albany National Cemetery yearly and attend the local Veterans Day parade. I have visited the American Cemetery and walked the beaches of Normandy.

Today we own a condo in Arlington, Virginia, close to our grandson. From the small balcony porch at our condo, we're able to see the Iwo Jima monument and the north side of Arlington National Cemetery. I've attended the Changing of the Guard at the Tomb of the Unknown Soldier.

Also, when we're at our condo, I walk the cemetery daily. I've participated in the Veterans Day placing of the flag, and on Christmas, the placing of the wreaths—all solemn occasions and in honor of our veterans.

My most chilling memory of Veterans Day ceremonies is when I placed my hand on the Vietnam Memorial Wall and thanked the Lord I managed to avoid having my name placed there.

Good Lord, please don't forget all the men and women who gave it their all so we can live in freedom here in the USA—and in most of the world.

Again, I urge all to make a family event of participating in a Veterans Day affair and to visit the many military memorials throughout the country and in your local home towns.

66

~ Golden Ranch Farms ~

Back thru the years, the 70s, 80s and even later I believe, there were three major liquid asphalt suppliers for the southern Indiana/ Kentucky area and the asphalt paving markets there. Those companies were Chevron, Ashland and Marathon oil companies, all located in Louisville, Kentucky.

The competition was good for the consumer and pricing was very competitive during that time and for years to follow. I was responsible for all of the purchased liquid asphalt and road oils used in our construction and paving projects. We purchased oils from all three companies, but Ashland landed more sales than the other two combined. As you can surmise, there was more than the price that went into whom we purchased from.

Back then there were no traffic problems to speak of. All three company locations were easily accessible. Of course, to try and get your business, there was the back-patting, the hand-holding, and the giving of "gifts" for no apparent occasion, plus all of the extra perks and benefits thrown in. It was basically open season and the companies used whatever resources they had, or could think of, to get your business. It was definitely a "Good Ol' Boy" network, but we didn't mind. Road oil was road oil, regardless of who you bought it from, and as a result of the competitors wanting our business, we got the benefit of getting the best price.

In order to get business, Marathon was enticing their customers with freebie tickets to tennis tournaments, from high school to the professionals, to bowling events and tickets to venues that were geared more to spectator sports types of events. Not that there's anything wrong with it, but long before it became mainstream like it is today, the management at Marathon was of the gay persuasion. That lifestyle choice was pretty much kept under wraps back then, but as I said, oil was oil, and as long as we got the best price, we weren't particular about the lifestyle of the supplier.

With myself being somewhat—well, maybe a *lot*—of a redneck and a lover of all things outdoorsy, I was more comfortable with and preferred the more masculine, woodsy, water-related off-work-hours events.

In competition with Marathon Oil in volume sales to me, was Chevron Oil. For promotional events and to try and garner business, they were big on golfing, the arts and competitive basket weaving and knitting—I say with tongue in cheek, also not events I was particularly interested in or participating in.

Ashland Oil, on the other hand, were lovers of football, fine Kentucky whiskey, hunting, fishing and boating, all activities that appealed to me. Their marketing and promotional programs were geared around these events and it apparently paid off as their volume of sales increased steadily as the years rolled by. Many of Ashland's promotional events took place at the Golden Ranch Farms (GRF) in Gheens, Louisiana.

For those of you who aren't familiar with or have never heard of the Golden Ranch Farms, here are some things about the place you might be interested in.

Golden Ranch Farms sits on 52,000 acres of pristine Louisiana grown trees, marsh waters, distinctive Louisiana swamps, and almost 1000 acres of actively producing sugar cane fields.

Arlen, "Benny" Cenac, Jr., owner of this privately owned refuge in Louisiana, which happens to be the oldest of its kind, has made it his mission to preserve and cultivate this property so it remains immaculate and sustainable as it has been for over 200 years.

Mr. Cenac's mission knows no bounds as he has continued to invest his time and energy into the needs of keeping the land self-sustainable and thriving with numerous species of wildlife throughout the wooded areas and fresh water marshes.

The protection of Golden Ranch Farms begins with the fresh water marshland. Keeping the marshes healthy is vital to restoring and maintaining wildlife that calls the farm home–alligator, deer, fish, nutria and migrating birds to name a few.

Benny has invested in many floor control structures to help stop saltwater intrusion, which is vital to shield the marshes and the entire property. The trees that inhabit GRF are made up of Cypress, Tupelo Gum, Willow and Oak. They are unable to survive in even the smallest amount of saltwater. Between the flood control structures and extensive levee system, the heart of the farm has been set up to be greatly protected for many years to come.

The hunting and fishing trips sponsored by Ashland Oil were experiences that I'll never forget, and most likely, will never be able to repeat.

A party of six was the maximum number of guests that were allowed at the mansion house at GRF at any one time, and a maximum of four days was the limit a guest could stay.

We'd depart in Ashland's corporate jet from Bowman Field in Louisville and land in a matter of hours in Houma, Louisiana, the largest nearby town with an airstrip. We were picked up by a Cajun guide in a van and transported to the farm and mansion. We were assigned two to a room with single beds and showers upstairs for the six of us to share.

A typical long weekend was as follows:

Arrival, assignment of rooms, times for when the three meals a day would be served, cocktail hour when we returned from our day's adventure, and after a nice, hot shower, appetizers from heaven, dinner, then drinks in front part of the house, which was a large, stately living/ great room/den of sorts.

The mansion had a large, wrap-around porch. The doors, windows, flooring, etc. were from a time period of many years earlier and were preserved as if the clock had stopped forty years ago. There was a poker table in the game room and in the evenings after dinner, it was poker for money, reading, sipping cocktails or just turning in from a long day in the woods or on the water.

Mr. Elmo was the cook and chef who lived on the premises. The guides arrived at four a.m. each morning. It was up to us, the guests, to decide which adventure we wanted to participate in for the day.

One morning, I chose duck hunting and was assigned one of the guides. Mid-morning, it was squirrel hunting. After lunch and a short nap, I spent the afternoon dove hunting, and as the sun set, I was in a flats boat for some canal bass fishing. After that, I off in the Jeep for the mansion to enjoy cocktails, deep-fried chunks of alligator, shrimp, hot sausage and chips, cheese and crackers and deviled eggs just to name a few of the hors d'oeuvres that I recall.

When dinner time rolled around, we had the game or fish we'd harvested that day prepared by Chef Elmo along with all of the southernmost Cajun trimmings. After that, it was poker, drinks, reading the local newspaper (there was no TV at the mansion, just radio), shooting the breeze with the group or just off to bed early if that's what you felt like doing.

Day Two for me was deer hunting. I was dropped off early at my stand—all guns were furnished—and was told to take any buck or doe that presented itself. We were not allowed to harvest any animal that had a tag in its ear as these were the main, mature breeding does.

I took a nice ten-point buck which my guide skinned and dressed. The venison was the main course come supper time. After lunch, I finished out my day bass fishing out on the many canals that ran through the property. My fresh caught fish was also on the menu come supper time.

On Day Three, Sunday, come four a.m. and after listening to a half-hour of Billy Graham Sunday services on the radio, I was out the door for a half a day of fishing. We came across a steel-framed gate across a canal which we had to open to continue our journey up the canal. As we crossed through the gate into a private, secluded stretch of farm canal, I saw, within a few feet of me, the most beautiful bobcat standing on the bank just watching us.

The bobcat ran across the top of the gate we'd just crossed and disappeared into the swamp. As we continued up the canal, my guide said, "Let's have some fun." He shored the boat, jumped out and ran down an armadillo. He grabbed its tail and then climbed back into the boat. We drifted back out to the center of the bayou and Benoit, the guide, dropped the animal into the water. The water was as clear as looking through glass. We watched as the animal sank to the bottom and land on its feet. Then he started walking across the bottom in somewhat slow-motion like watching the astronauts walk on the moon. He walked along the bottom until he came to the shore, then climbed out and disappeared into the marsh on the other side like it was nothing.

We fished the rest of the morning and filled our cooler. We were to be back at the mansion at noon where we were each handed a box lunch to be enjoyed on the plane ride home. It seemed like one minute we were on the jet and in the air headed for Golden Ranch Farms, then the next minute we were back home in the Knobs.

Come five a.m. on Monday morning, I was off to work as usual and the Golden Ranch Farms was nothing more than a good memory. This scene played out for the next eight years or so. Ashland Oil became our primary supplier. Their construction company, APAC, later bought out our Texas asphalt operation. Years later, if I'm not mistaken, Ashland Oil sold their liquid asphalt division to Marathon Oil who then became our major supplier for many years to come. I forgot what happened to Chevron. They seemed to be here one day and gone the next.

The Golden Ranch Farms is a piece of my past and is a reflection of "The Good Old Days." All of the game harvested on the farm ... the deer, doves, ducks, squirrels, shrimp, gator and Canadian geese, were all professionally cleaned, processed and consumed by the guests of the farm, the guides, and the local soup kitchen in Gheens, Louisiana.

The place was, in my opinion, like a slice of heaven on earth!

67

~ Leavenworth, Indiana ~

This is another one of those good memories from an earlier chapter in my life from thereabouts-1970-something. I'd purchased my first real bass boat from old George, the owner of Sycamore Island where he sold live bait, tackle, boats and trailers. It was located across from the railroad tracks on Old Corydon Pike.

One warm Saturday morning when I was a single man, it was seven a.m. and I was headed for the water for a day of fishing. I was already dreaming of fresh fish for dinner when I got back to my shack on the tracks, bacon grease in my electric skillet, out in the back yard, just me and my old dog, Bearfoot. I'd get the fish and he'd get a loaf of Bunny Bread soaked in the twice-used bacon grease … it was truly a feast of sorts for both of us!

But back to my story; I had an early breakfast at Jock's in Corydon and then headed on down to Leavenworth, Indiana, a small flooded-out town on the banks of the Ohio River.

Once a thriving community, Leavenworth was now just a dilapidated old town with falling-down structures that were abandoned for the most part. Just a few people still lived there. There was a small general store which was also the home of the old Leavenworth Bar.

During the summertime, all of the patrons sat outside at picnic tables under the trees, just a stone's throw from the Ohio River's edge. The road through town came to a dead-end at the top of the river bank. The road went down the steep slope at this point and was known as the old Leavenworth boat ramp. It was just one of a few on this end of the river.

On this day, I backed my truck and boat trailer down the boat ramp; I chocked the truck wheels with large stones while I launched the boat. Once afloat, I tied it off to a fallen willow tree and drove back up the ramp to park the truck.

After a short boat ride up the river on the Indiana side, I was at the mouth of Blue River. There was a large sycamore stump and a wad of roots hung up over on the north side of the channel. I tied up to a long protruding root and lowered a big fat clump of freshly dug red worms over the boat edge. In no time, I had two of the largest black crappie I'd ever caught in my fish basket ... I'm talking pounds and umpteen inches long!

I pulled the tie line and proceeded up the river a ways and again anchored up. There, I caught a few nice bass, several big log perches, some rock bass and goggle-eyes and six of the largest redhearts one has ever seen. Redhearts are in the sunfish family, only stockier. Their color is similar to a sunfish but with a red belly.

Feeling good with my catch and having a good mess of fresh fish in my basket, I kicked back and took a break. I enjoyed a cold can of PBR, a small bag of Fritos, and a white-colored Zero candy bar.

As I enjoyed my late morning snack, I listened to the cacophony of the birds, squirrels and frogs. As I watched the turtles sunning on the driftwood, a large noisy ruckus broke out. From out of nowhere a large, light-colored owl flew low over my boat with a big, red fox squirrel in his claws.

The squirrel was going nuts but the owl had him tightly in his grasp and I'm sure, was already thinking of feeding him to his family. The squirrel eventually fought his way loose, fell and hit the water. In two seconds the owl's mate came in swiftly from across the creek and nailed the squirrel again. As it tried to gain altitude and had two dips of skimming the water, the bird rose high and peeled out of sight. This was something I have not seen again, nor heard of anyone else ever seeing such action.

A bit further on up the river, I was anchored up and used a dough ball my great aunt Aggie had made for me. With the ball stuck tight on the small treble hook, I was fishing it on the bottom and looking for a big, blue channel cat.

Catfishing is always a slow process, and it wasn't long before a short nap was in order. I was awoken by something thrashing in the water. There, a short distance from the boat, was a pair of dark-colored beavers dragging tree limbs across the river and building a dam up on the side where the river was lower and the water was about dried up. It was quite a sight to see. Having had enough excitement and luck for one day, it was time to head for home.

I stopped and fished a while at the mouth of Blue River and had no luck. With my boat again tied up to the root wad, along came my friend and his wife in their high-powered ski boat. He worked for our company and we were also good friends (and still are). He backed in close to my boat. We talked awhile, had a drink and then he handed me a wood handle attached to a long pull line.

Out came a pair of red water skis. I still had on my vest-type life jacket. I hopped into the water, slid my feet into the bindings and gripped the handles tightly. My friend slowly gave her the gas and the next thing I knew, I came out of the water and was erect on the skis. Down the river we went with me in tow. We made one big circle out and across the river. I made it back to my boat, alive and well and in one piece, and shortly thereafter, I was motoring back to the boat ramp.

I backed the truck down the steep ramp and loaded up my boat. As I tried to pull her out, my old truck sputtered and coughed while the clutch kept slipping. I was unable to pull up the steep ramp.

I sat there feeling pretty much hopeless when six big, burly, half-drunk dudes, who'd been drinking at the Old Leavenworth Tavern, came down the ramp. They got behind the truck and managed to push me to the top. Back at the tavern, I bought them a round of cold, Blatz beers while I consumed a thick juicy burger topped with a big slice of onion topped off with some paper-thin lettuce, all smothered in Tabasco-laden BBQ sauce. After an hour or so, and some good bull-shitting with my rescuers, I was on my way east towards home—a good one-hour drive.

Feeling tired and worn out, I managed to clean the fish and took a long, late afternoon nap. I called my father and not long after, was up at his home with the fresh fish. He fried them up and what a joyful weekend it turned out to be. I had a swim in his pool and, back at my place, I turned in early. I was up at five and on the job at six a.m. and the workweek was off and running.

All the while I was running that Cat 944 rubber-tire loader, I was thinking of the great fun and eats I'd enjoyed over the weekend, and was wondering what adventure the weekend ahead was holding for me.

Today the Leavenworth boat ramp is pot-holed and there are only a few who'll brave the steps and adverse conditions the ramp presented.

Up the river a short distance away, and just a short boat ride from the mouth of Blue River, the Army Corps of Engineers built a new, state of the art boat ramp along with a parking area, a few tables and trash bins. You pull down the circular concrete area with hardly any slope to speak of to launch your boat in the safest way. It's truly a huge improvement from days past!

68

~ Harrison County Fair ~

We begin this story back in the 1950s and 60s. There was a yearly event down in Corydon Indiana—the County Fair. Being a young person and following my dad around, we would attend the fair. It was a good time, and we kids got to run wild and witness some very unusual people, things and events.

Then in the 60s when I was in high school, my friends and I would attend the fair, sow a few wild oats and act up a bit, but never bad enough to be tossed out or have the sheriff called on us.

One year the events and shows were quite interesting, to say the least. There were freak shows, tents with body parts in large glass jars, tents with two-headed animals and critters with all kinds of deformities. There were tent shows featuring women of questionable character; shows with girls wrapping snakes around their bodies, carnival rides and games. Of course, there was all sorts of fair food like corn dogs, popcorn, tamales, hamburgers, hotdogs, fried fish and every other kind of carnival food imaginable.

I can't recall there being beer stands or liquor ever being sold (Corydon was a dry community back then), but behind the tents and rides, there were always plenty of half-pint whiskey and wine bottles littering the grounds and overflowing the trash barrels.

Every now and then a few fights would erupt and the county sheriff would step in and restore the peace while the fair went on. One year they even had a harness horse race and betting on the event. This was quite a big deal for a young lad who has never witnessed anything like it before.

But, come Monday, we were back in school or at play on the family farm, or were swimming or fishing. The County Fair was truly an event we looked forward to each year. It was a time when kids could run and jump, stay outdoors until after dark and no one ever worried about one's safety or threats from strangers or unknown people. It was

242

truly a unique and innocent time in life.

In 1968, Uncle Sam came a-courting. He decided he wanted me. There was a big disturbance in Southeast Asia in a little place called Viet Nam and he needed me to serve some time to help solve the problems, defend our freedoms and way of life. I went and did my duty. Time passed and in 1973 I decided it was time to start attending the Harrison County Fair again. It was a great place to take a date, or to go with a group of buddies. It was a cheap few days and nights of good honest fun and was close to home.

Back then, advertising for the fair was done with large posters hung in public places and also with announcements on the radio. A friend and I were at a tavern down in Lanesville, Indiana, and there on the wall by the pool table, was a very large color poster advertising the coming fair. The main attraction was going to be Miss Dolly Parton, and her singing partner, Mr. Porter "Porta-Can" Waggoner. This was a country-western singing duo that was hot on the charts and was rising in popularity at a rapid pace.

After sinking a perfectly-placed rail shot, I looked at my buddy, old Pat. He was standing there admiring the picture of Miss Dolly and her extremely ample pectorals.

"Hey man," he said. "Let's get tickets, head down to the fair and catch this show." We did and had the time of our lives! Dolly and Porter would go on to become a big music act. They even landed their own TV show. Dolly eventually went solo, had her own TV show, got into acting and is *still* selling out concerts and producing Number One Hits. She even started her very own—and quite successful—theme park, "Dollywood," down in Tennessee.

For our $1.75 ticket—the cost of admission for the show—and with no time limit on how long you could stay, we were entertained and even danced to Porter and Dolly's tunes. As times changed and stardom for the two took hold, they began playing bigger and bigger venues. In August of 2016, Dolly performed the Ravinia Music Festival in North Chicago. I didn't attend but was told by a friend that the place was sold out. There were thousands in attendance for the one hour show and if one was able to get a ticket, the cost was in the hundreds of dollars!

I have to smile at fate. To think … I was able to see Dolly perform when she was new to the stage with her partner. Who would have ever thought this singing pair would go on to be big stars and very famous. It was truly a Saturday night to remember, all those years ago.

The following is an accurate description and history of the Harrison County Fair. Times have changed and the fair goes on, but it's sure not like it used to be. Google it and see for yourself what a magnificent local event the fair was, and still is to a certain extent.

The Harrison County Fair is located in Corydon, Indiana.

The very first Harrison County Fair was held Sept. 11-14, 1860. It has been held in the same location for over 150 years, making it the oldest County Fair in the State of Indiana to be held continuously in the same location. Some interesting facts about the fair are:

1860: The 1st Harrison County Fair was held in September.

1863: The Battle of Corydon took place on July 9.

1866: Admission to the fair for a single person was 25 cents, two-horse vehicle, 25 cents; one-horse vehicle, 15 cents; single horse, 10 cents; season ticket, 75 cents.

1871: The Round Hall is built for exhibits.

1884: The 25th Harrison County Fair was held.

1896: A train wreck of two large, worn-out locomotives was staged as an added attraction.

1906: The first automobile, an air-cooled Richmond, was driven to the fair.

1909: The 50th Annual Harrison County Fair was held and the Homecomers Hall was erected.

1914: With the advent of electric lights the night horse show was held.

1916: A lunch stand sold fish sandwiches for 10 cents each.

1917: The Ferris Wheel arrived for the first time.

1921: Harrison County Agricultural Society purchases 13 additional acres.

1925: A new feature called the "Gosset's Bucking Ford" was presented by members of the Gosset Circus.

1927: A new grandstand is erected.

1929: The Queen Contest was added to the Harrison County Fair and the Stock Market crashed.

1932: George and Martha Washington were highlights of the Colonial Pageant.

1948: The Fair Board pays off debt.

1952: Wrestling matches drew a huge crowd as Friday's main event.

1955: 15,207 people were admitted to the fair during six days.

1957: The Grand Ole Opry was the largest grandstand feature for the week.

1959: 100th Annual Harrison County Fair was held in August.

1961: The grandstand burns and a new one was erected.

1963: The Re-enactment of the Battle of Corydon Centennial opens the fair.

1966: "Shindig-Record Review of Stars: A real Go-Go Show" was presented Thursday night. The public had the chance to meet and dance with the stars of the popular TV show.

1970: Roy Acuff and the Smokey Mountain Boys performed on Friday night.

1971: Jim Curry presented the big ADC Demolition Derby which drew a huge crowd.

1972: Dolly Parton and Porter Wagoner performed at the fair.

1976: The first tractor/truck pull was held at the fair.

1984: The 125th Annual Harrison County Fair was held and the Harrison County Fair Historical Marker was erected at the Fairgrounds.

1993: Premiums in Homecomers Hall were increased to: 1st -$3.00/Blue Ribbon, 2nd -$2.00/Red Ribbon, 3rd -White Ribbon.

1995: Monster Trucks were the grandstand show on Friday night.

1997: The Flood of '97 brought great distress to the Harrison County Fairgrounds.

1998: Gate Admission prices raised to $6.00

2001: Pay One Price Admission was raised to $7.00

2004: New seats were installed on the grandstand.

2008: Corydon and Harrison County celebrate their 200th birthday.

2009: The 150th Annual Harrison County Fair was held.

2013: The 155th Annual Harrison County Fair was held.

2015: The 4-H Livestock Show Pavilion was built.

2016: July 17 at 1:00 p.m. Grand Opening and Ribbon Cutting Ceremony for the Talmage Windell Memorial Agricultural Building

2018: November 13 at 7:00 p.m. annual meeting and elections of the Harrison County Agricultural Society (HCAS)

John R. Gohmann

2019: November 12 at 7:00 p.m. annual meeting and elections of the Harrison County Agricultural Society (HCAS)

Information for this timeline was prepared by the Historical Society of Harrison County and the *Corydon Democrat.*

I plan to attend the fair this year, walk the grounds, enjoy the smells and sights and reach back in my memory file and recall what a happy time it was in my life, memories cherished forever.

69

~ Remembering ~

Recently, my daughter shared the following quotations included at the beginning of a book, *The Library Book* (Susan Orlean, 2018)

- "Memory believes before knowing remembers." *Light In August* (William Faulkner, 1932).
- "And when they ask us what we're doing, you can say, 'We're remembering'." *Fahrenheit 451* (Ray Bradbury, 1953).
- "I have always imagined Paradise as a kind of library." *Dreamtigers* (Jorge Luis Borges, 1960).

"I have been reviewing the complete quotes of William Faulkner and I believe there's a subtle message here that I should be drawing ideas and thoughts from. But as of yet, the desired effect is still under consideration"

Susan Orlean

I believe my daughter's message here is to not forget one's family, friends and those you hold close and dear to you. They may be dead and gone, but their memories live on, and the circle you have formed of family and friends will never be forgotten.

My daughter is a Ph.D. I believe her message is sincere and everlasting.

70

~ Bird Likes ~

I have always been keenly aware, extremely focused and very interested in all forms of wildlife and I hold all in nature dear. I also have great respect for all animals, sea creatures, the land, air, rocks, and most all flora and fauna.

Let me be clear though—I am not a "tree hugger," a Green Peace supporter or a believer in global warming but rather, a man who respects all the world has to offer. My goal is to leave this world in some way, a little better than when I was old enough to start taking from her.

Yes, I'm a believer in PETA which, in my interpretation, means:

P - People
E - Eating
T - Tasty
A - Animals

With this being said, of all the earthly creatures to talk and write about, I chose birds. For the majority of birds, flight is the primary means of getting from one place to another. Flight also assists birds with feeding, breeding, avoiding predators, and migrating. Bird flight is one of the most complex forms of locomotion in the animal kingdom. For more on this, I used Wikipedia as my source of reference.

Birds have many physical features, besides wings, that work synergistically to enable flight. They need lightweight, streamlined yet rigid structures, for flight. Weight, lift, thrust and drag are the four forces of flight, and nature has provided all four of these to birds in a most perfect way. With this being said, it's apparent that birds are complicated in some ways and very easy to understand in others.

My two favorites of all birds are the hummingbird and the kingfisher. I believe these are the only two birds that can hover. While there are obvious differences in their habitats, in many of the places where I tend to spend time, they always seem to present themselves. Just yesterday while out back in my barn looking for a lost tool of some sort, there on the top shelf back in the corner, I discovered a perfectly preserved, dead hummingbird. It was way cool, very beautiful, yet also kind of sad. I placed the bird in small Mason jar to preserve it and the little lady sits on my desk where I can admire her beauty daily.

The kingfisher is an expert fisherman. He has the eyesight of an eagle; he hovers as he searches for prey and once he locates it, he dives into the water to snag it. He's nervous, curious and rather distant in some respects.

To keep my desire to see, feed, and observe the birds, I've had feeders of all sorts at every place we've called home over the years.

Today, here on the Knobs of Southern Indiana, I've finally perfected a squirrel-proof bird feeder. The "tree rats" now have to feast on the seeds that have fallen from the feeder instead of climbing up to raid the supply directly. They no longer have the run of scaring off most all of the songbirds. The feeder has a platform that's inviting to the larger birds as well as the smaller ones. The larger ones that we see daily come in the spring and then for the most part, disappear in the summer.

The larger birds observed here at our home on the Knobs are blue jays, doves, cardinals, thrushes, robins, orioles, blackbirds, cowbirds, starlings, goslings and four species of woodpeckers including the "Giant" of all peckers, the pleated woodpecker.

There are also the medium-sized birds that frequent the feeder, namely bluebirds, martins, jenny wrens, sparrows and finches of all kinds; the list goes on and on. I forget the names/species of most of the birds at this moment but remember each of them when they present themselves.

Then come the small ones, my hummingbirds, to my two red feeders. They supply the little hummers with an easy and convenient place for a liquid dinner that resembles the nectar of flowers.

From my window perch, sitting in my oak rocker, the chair we rocked our daughter in some thirty-plus years ago, that's where I watch what I call the "Big Birds" who come a-calling. The tom turkeys, the hens, the jakes, big black crows, and late in the evenings, two species of owls stop by. They perch on the swing's crossbar and quietly eye what the feeder has drawn in. The chipmunks are a favorite target; small squirrels also make a square meal.

John R. Gohmann

My walk, or sometimes a John Deere Gator ride, to the pond out back takes me to another beautiful location to observe yet another group of birds that avoid the feeders, like the martins, who skim the water surface for mosquitoes and insects.

From my swing in the screened-in dock house, I observe redwing blackbirds nesting in the cattails and also hummers hovering by the cattails as they pluck the fuzz from the aquatic plants to build their nests. Occasionally a family of ducks will take up residency on the pond, and every now and then, a Canadian goose will waddle along the dam.

Up from the Ohio River, we'll get visitors like the long-legged, long-beaked birds of various sizes and species, and of course, my favorite fish predator, the gray heron.

On trips to our farm down in Harrison County, the lake there attracts many of the same birds, but all are leery of humans and take to flight at any sign of movement of if they sense danger. One of my favorite things to do at the farm is sitting on the dock, sipping a cup of coffee from my old Stanley thermos-lid cup just before sunrise and listening to the flight of a teal. These ducks come in various colors depending on the species. What's the attraction you might ask? They sound like miniature aircraft flying overhead. They're fast as lightning and can land on the water's edge with barely a sound.

A mid-morning Gator ride presents an opportunity to flush a covey of quail, run up on a turkey or two and as you circle the barn, an owl might take flight. Years ago it was common to see a pheasant or two; nowadays the pheasants are gone it seems.

In late November, while sitting in my deer stand, I hear the music, the song and the sound of winter approaching way up in the cold blue sky. I might spot a flock of Sand Hill cranes on their winter flight north; what sound to remember. It'll bring goosebumps to all cold, hungry, lonely hunters awaiting the snort of a trophy buck deer.

While at our condo in Virginia, from our small, third-floor porch overlooking the Arlington National Cemetery, I'll see robins, mockingbirds, sparrows, and crows present themselves in the large oak tree that's just forty yards away and in direct view from the porch or picture window. Black, red and gray squirrels, chipmunks and a lone red fox might just happen by, and all demand a second look.

Moving on south to Islamorada in the Florida Keys, exotic birds are plentiful. By the marina, there are pelicans, gulls and ducks of all sorts. There are also songbirds, mockingbirds, smaller-bodied birds with long legs and beaks, a hummingbird or two, and for sure the kingfishers.

On backwater boat ride/fishing trips, I've spotted, egrets, white pelicans, bald eagles, ospreys, and miscellaneous other water birds, diver ducks, etc. While on one fishing trip out to the edge of the reef looking for some larger fish to catch, I spotted ducks, pelicans, flying fish and all kinds of white birds of various sizes. But of all of these, my favorite offshore bird is the man of war, also known as the frigate bird.

The frigate is any member of five species of large seabirds constituting the family *Fregatidae* (order *Pelecaniformes* or *Suliformes*). The frigate bird is perhaps the most aerial of all birds and alights only to sleep or to tend its nest (from Wikipedia).

As you can see, my opportunities to view the feeding habits and flight of so many birds that one can't help falling in love with them.

I most heartily recommend setting up a backyard feeder close by a window to observe birds and wildlife. What could be more satisfying than to hear your grandson say excitedly, "Papa John—look, there's a cardinal bird!"

Our daughter grew up helping me stock the feeders and to review and keep a record of the birds we were lucky enough to see. Bird watching has proven to be a very rewarding and worthwhile family event.

~ Rattlesnake Derby ~

The Mangum Rattlesnake Derby is an annual event featuring everything from carnival rides to live rattlesnake shows. Hunters register at the Rattlesnake Headquarters. A safety meeting is a requirement and if hunting rattlesnakes is not your idea of a good time, you might be better off to pass on this event.

The Rattlesnake Derby is a festival for the whole family and it sports one of the largest flea markets in Oklahoma and a visit to the Snake Pit is advised. The Snake Pit houses hundreds of rattlers as they roam about inside a glass enclosure. You can also have your picture taken with a live rattlesnake and family photos with live snakes were also offered. There's a pay-to-visit butcher's shop where you can see how the snake is processed. Close-by is the Bite-a-Snake Cafe where one can order fried snake meat.

A visit to the rattlesnake den site is recommended where picking up a live rattlesnake is also a possibility. Sunday is the "Longest Snake" Contest. To observe this, you go to the rattlesnake buying platform to see live snakes stretched and measured. The record was set back in 1971 and was close to 60 inches, plus.

The best part of the snake derby for me was when I managed to camp out under the Oklahoma stars for the weekend and was able to take part in and participate in all of the hunts, shows and lectures pertaining to the local rattlesnakes. I did this for two years in a row.

Had it not been for me being in the USAF and stationed at Altus AFB, in 1971 and 1972, I would've never had the opportunity to attend, or even know such an event was being held.

At the derby, we teamed up in pairs. I and my friend, Sergeant Jimmy, would take turns carrying the furnished burlap sack which was basically just old potato sack. One would operate the catch stick which was a three-foot-long rod with a squeeze lever on one end and a set of scissor-like fingers on the other end. It was similar to the kind of tool used to reach and grab canned goods off the top kitchen shelf.

The person carrying the sack was also the one who, bare-handed, would turn over the larger rocks so as to expose the rattlers. Sometimes when you'd get near a tumbleweed bush, you'd hear the snakes shake their rattlers.

You had to be alert and on your toes at all times. After a few cold beers, one would become brown-bottle brave and the threat of a bite was just another nuisance, a problem not to dwell on.

After gathering two or three snakes the bag got heavy and the thought of the snakes just inches from your hand and with only the bag material between them and you, it was time to go back to camp and have your catch recorded, graded, and your name placed on the judges' scoreboard. In 1971, the cost of admission was purely by donations. There was a large bucket on the judges' table where donations were accepted. Today the derby is advertised as "free." In the years I attended and participated in the events, there were maybe 300 to 400 in attendance. Today, however, the usual attendance is over 30,000. My how the times have changed!

Today, some 47 years later, I still have the poster advertising the derby—it's at the beginning of this story. The sign on the airbase bulletin board encouraged all airmen to attend. The framed poster is displayed in my man cave at home on Floyd's Knobs.

The following information is how the derby operated back in 1972. I'm sure the prices have changed and the awards have improved. The goal has never changed though. It's always been about the harvesting of rattlesnakes.

Rattlesnake Derby and Flea Market
April 16-17-18, 1971
Mangum, Oklahoma

Registration Friday, April 16
Hunting, Flea Market Opens, Dances

Saturday, April 17
Registration, hunting, snake pits, butcher shop, flea market, snake races, Queen Crowning,
Domino Tournament, country and western sing, banquet, dances

Sunday, April 18
Registration, snake pits, flea market, hunting, snake auction, awards.
AWARDS
Most pounds of snake caught
$50 first $25 second $20 third $15 fourth $10 fifth
LARGEST SNAKE
$50 first $20 second $10 third
Trophies
Most snakes trophy
Shortest snake trophy
$15 plus trophy-first
Trophy for 2nd and 3rd
MARKED SNAKE—— $25
Snakes will be bought from registered hunters as follows:
Friday - 15 cents/lb. Saturday - 10 cents/lb. Sunday - 5 cents/lb.

FEATURING

The Flea Market

Dealers from throughout the Southwest will be showing.

Come to browse or to buy.

SEE

Bob Jenni in the snake pit. Oklahoma's foremost Naturalist, Author and snake expert.

See him extract venom

See him with hundreds of snakes

Hear his interesting talk on snakes

BIG BARBEQUE AND GAB-FEST SATURDAY NIGHT

As you can see, the Rattlesnake Derby is an annual event that is family-friendly and for anyone looking for adventure. I encourage all to pay a visit if you're ever in or around the Great State of Oklahoma. I guarantee you will not be disappointed!

72

~ My Hero - Kenny ~

In this short story, I'd like to give thanks to Kenny Rush, a long-time employee of Gohmann Asphalt, Inc., for sharing his remembrances of a terrifying day in his life while serving in Vietnam back in 1969 at the young age of 19.

A New Albany High School graduate, and lifelong resident of Floyd County, Kenny was looking for something more exciting to do than spending his first summer out of high school partying and just hanging out doing basically nothing.

So, at the age of 17½, he joined the United States Marine Corps. One year later, he was doing his tour in a violent hotbed area of Southeast Asia called Vietnam. Young men of Kenny's age—many from his hometown of New Albany—as well as young men from every other city and town across the country, gave up everything and made the ultimate sacrifice in their service to the country during this bloody conflict.

Kenny definitely had some tense days in the jungles of 'Nam, as did all of the U.S. soldiers serving there, but he was one of the lucky ones who got to come home. While he put that episode from his past behind him, he never forgot the lessons he learned as a Marine—faith, dedication, the will to improve, and the determination to move ahead and succeed in life.

And improve his lot in life, he did! He went from being a truck driver for Gohmann Asphalt, Inc. to the vice-president of operations of its two limestone quarries. He was a loyal and dedicated employee and one that we were lucky to have.

Kenny never mentioned it, and I wasn't aware of this until recently, but he was a hero during his time in 'Nam. What defines a "hero?" If you ask those who've gotten medals and awards for what they did, they will, more often than not, tell you that they didn't do anything that anyone else in their company wouldn't have done. Most are humble and reticent about it. This was Kenny.

Here's a transcription of a commendation Kenny received for his actions during a firefight in 'Nam.

The Secretary of the Navy takes pleasure in presenting
the NAVY COMMENDATION MEDAL to:

Private First Class Kenneth B. Rush
United States Marine Corps
for service as set forth in the following
CITATION:

For heroic achievement while serving as a Tracked Vehicle Repairman with Company A, Third Amphibian Tractor Battalion, in connection with combat operations against the enemy in the Republic of Vietnam. On 13 May 1969, the Second Platoon of Company A was conducting a reconnaissance along the Cu De River in Quang Nam province. Suddenly, the lead vehicle came under a heavy volume of automatic weapons fire and hand grenades from a well-concealed North Vietnamese Army force occupying emplacements in a cave. When his platoon sergeant obtained his vehicle's machine gun and maneuvered forward to deliver suppressive fire at the enemy. Private First Class Rush, reacting instantly, secured all of the ammunition he could carry and followed his companion across fifty meters of fire-swept terrain to a tactically advantageous location. Resolutely maintaining his exposed position until ammunition was expended, Private First Class Rush unhesitatingly ran back to his position. His hold initiative and timely actions inspired all who observed him and contributed significantly to the defeat of the North Vietnamese Army force. By his courage, aggressive fighting spirit and steadfast devotion to duty in the face of great personal danger, Private First Class Rush upheld the finest traditions of the Marine Corps and of the United States Naval Service.

The Combat Distinguishing Device is authorized.

For the Secretary of the Navy.
H.W. Buse, Jr.
Lieutenant General, U.S. Marine Corps
Commanding General, Fleet Marine Force, Pacific

Kenny —you will forever be a hero to me. I thank you for your service and the heroism and courage you showed on behalf of this country's freedom.

Nothing in life is so exhilarating as to be shot at without result.

Winston Churchill

73

~ Last Story ~

This, being my last short story for the book, will actually encompass three short stories. The first takes place in the small town of Bucksnort, Tennessee.

Short Story #1

Bucksnort is a small, unincorporated community in Hickman County, Tennessee. It's located near Exit 152 on Interstate 40, just east of the Tennessee River. Back when I stopped there, there were no U.S. Census statistics for the location and there is no post office.

Bucksnort is also the hometown of wrestlers Bunkhouse Buck and "Dirty White Boy" Tony Anthony. Tony Anthony even had a signature move called *The Bucksnort Blaster*.

It was 1974, give or take a year, and I had just purchased my first new automobile, a blue Chevrolet pickup truck. It had a three on the column, air conditioning and sported a cab-high topper covering the truck bed. I had a week off from work and being single and free, I called my old USAF buddy, Jimmy Braxton to see if he wanted to hang out and have some fun.

"Sure," Jimmy said. "Come on down. We'll feed you, provide a warm place to sleep and you and I will fish the bayous around Bastrop, Louisiana till you have to head back home. I loaded the cooler with Coors beer, two pounds of thick-sliced bologna from the meat counter of Wolf Meat Market in New Albany, some sharp cheddar cheese, a loaf of white bread, my sleeping bag, some clean jeans, my toothbrush, my fishing gear and my nine-shot H&R .22 long rifle, western-style pistol.

I got on the road early and had my AAA TripTik and map on the dash. By mid-afternoon, I was growing tired and was ready to stop, take a rest, stretch my legs and maybe catch a fifteen-minute nap in the cab.

I pulled into a small backwoods, wide spot off the road in a place called Bucksnort. As I recall, there was an old store building that was falling in. It looked closed, uninhabited and need of a lot of repair including paint and just about every other kind of hardware supply that was available.

I spotted an old battered international pickup truck slowly pull away from the older-than-dirt gas pump—it was the kind where you could see the fuel going through a glass bulb. I fueled up, took a long look around the place, paid my bill and thought I had better get back on the road.

Across the road was another building, also falling down, but it had a small sign that read BAR OPEN. There were three steps up to the front porch. On the porch were three old rockers, a swing, and a few stools—most of which were occupied by some unfriendly looking fellas from the surrounding hills and hollers of Bucksnort.

To the far right of the porch, on a straight-back, handmade, hardwood chair sat a slim old man named "Buck." Along the wall were stools, like milking stools, step stools, etc. Most were made of red cedar. No one said a word and for a minute, I feared for my life!

"How much for that three-legged stool on the end?" I asked.

The old man said, "One dollar a leg-no tax. When I went to hand the man three, one-dollar bills, I noticed under his hat that his eyes were white with red marks.

He said, "Son, thank you. You can probably see that I'm blind."

"Yes sir," I answered.

Buck then went on to tell me how he makes the stools even though being blind. He told me how much he appreciated the sale. He must have heard my stomach growl because he suggested that if I was hungry, they served up some good food inside. "Enjoy," he said.

I entered the bar and saw the place was empty except for the barkeep leaning on the counter. His customers were broke and were sitting out on the porch until old Buck sold a stool. Then business would pick up.

"What are you having, young man?" the bartender asked.

"A glass of beer," I answered. Then added, "And what's for lunch today?"

"What would you like to eat?" he asked. "A burger and some fries?

How about the Day's Special?"

He tells me they're out of hamburger, so, in reference to the Day's Special, I said, "Sure, why not."

He goes out back and in a minute, returns with a large bowl of white bean soup. There was with a chunk of fat of some kind floating in it. There was also a four-inch-thick slice of cornbread, and a slice of onion some two inches thick.

"What's the matter?" he asks.

"Nothing, sir," I said. "Where's the pepper and hot sauce?"

He brought both to me and I dressed up the soup. When I finished eating it, I licked the bowl, ate every crumb of the bread, belched, blew my nose, paid the tab and was on my way.

After quite a few more hours of driving, I arrived safely at my friend's home. I enjoyed the company and ate the best Cajun food there is. I caught a lot of fish and slept very well. The week flew by. After some hugs and kisses, I was on my way north.

A long drive later I rolled into Bucksnort. I filled my truck with ethyl, walked over to the Bucksnort bar. There was no one on the porch; there were no stools and no old blind man. I walked into the bar and the bartender asked, "What do you want?"

I said, "I'll have the Special and a glass of beer." It was the same special and had the same good quality. I paid my tab and was on my way. That was 47 years ago and I've never been back.

Two years ago, my friend saw the three-legged stool hanging in my basement. "Hey," he said. "What's the story behind that stool?"

I told him how I came about owning it and asked if he'd like to have it?

"Yes, sir," he said. "I sure would."

The stool is now on display down at his home on the hearth of his family room fireplace in Orange County, Indiana.

Short-short story # 2

Changing the pace a little, a few years back, I got the brainy idea that I needed to remember the good times of my past and relive them over again in some way. I found a solution to this minor problem. Whenever the feeling strikes me, which is sometimes only once a month, I get on my iPad and type a list of persons, places, things, happenings, trips, food ... you name it. Whatever made me smile and brought happiness, or even sorrow, to me and jogged my memory of the times past would get typed in.

Here are ten items I came up with the last time I did this.

Diving into cold water
Ice skating on the pond in the winter at the Big House
My first car
My last dog
Our honeymoon at French Lick, Indiana
Our daughter's birth
Our daughter starts college
Bucksnort, Tennessee
The town of HELL, in the Cayman Islands
My friend, Jason, agreeing to manage my property

My dear readers, I post this new list on my refrigerator, and each morning as I grab the milk for my breakfast cereal, I take one item off the list and make a point to spend a few seconds or minutes on the topic. This has brought many a smile to my face and made the workday easier to deal with. You may want to try this yourself. It sure has improved my outlook!

This almost brings my book of short stories to a close. My friend, Pat, said I have enough pages to go to print with. He also said there comes a time when enough is enough. If you put too much material into the book, you'll lose the interest of your reader. It's a fine line though, between how much is enough, and how much is too much.

First, let me say that it's been my pleasure to share these true-to-life stories of my days past. I wouldn't change a thing. Life goes on and my list of memories with these stories has only been scratched. I hope you've enjoyed reading them as much I've enjoyed reliving them. And if you've invested by buying a copy of my book, thank you and may God Bless! I have one last story for you.

Short-short story #3

I thought it very interesting the other cool morning when I went to the closet in the front hall just to the right of the front door. This side is mine. The closet on the left side of the door is my wife's.

I store or hang my fall and winter coats and jackets on the clothes rod in my closet. The floor catches miscellaneous stuff in the form of footwear. There, on the large, high shelf, is where I keep my hat collection. When I receive or purchase a hat, it finds its place stacked rather haphazardly and high up on the top shelf in my closet.

My clever idea today was to reach into the stack of hats, not looking or sorting, but literally grabbing and tossing them on the floor. As I pick up each one, I record the make, model, size, and note where they were from. I also note the country it was manufactured in. Talk about memories and how fast time has passed. It was most interesting to me. I hope you try and do the same with one of your collections and you draw your own conclusion. I also hope the exercise will take you back in time and will bring some wonderful memories back!

Here's what I found:

My cook skin fur cap, with a long tail, 1961, USA
My green USAF issued fatigue hat from 1968, USA made
My Gohmann Asphalt & Construction hat, China made
My father's Grady White, Islamorada, fishing cap with his boat's name, *Rita-Sus-Ann*
Captain, Louisville USA
My Golden Ranch Hunting Farm, Gheens, LA., USA hat
My good friend's hat from Braxton's Hunting Camp, Ouachita River, LA, made in the USA (My friend has since passed on.)
ASTEC hat, maker of hot mix asphalt plants, China made
Laine hat, 100% wool, looks like a French countryside hunter's hat made in place unknown
Louisville Cards Hat, made in Vietnam
Hayes Hill Farm, toboggan, bright orange, made in the USA

I'd like to close out this book by saying:

Semper Fi ... for God and Country!

Acknowledgments

There are many people I'd like to acknowledge who, whether they know it or not, were my "partners in crime" for many of the stories in this book. At the time, none of us knew our stories would end up in a book, but they did. And without each and every one of you, the events described would have never happened.

The funny thing about stories like I've told is, at the time, you know you're experiencing something you'll likely never forget, but the power or significance of those stories doesn't become apparent until years later. A bond is formed and those memories are forever etched in our minds—or at least they were in mine.

There are obviously too many people to name individually, so rather than trying to cite everyone, and possibly missing some key players, let me just say a big "Thanks" to all who were kind enough to be there with me, and also for not killing me, which, I'm sure, some of you wanted to do at the time!

With that being said, there are a few individuals I'd like to personally acknowledge.

I'd be remiss not to mention my dad, Herbert R. Gohmann, Jr. Dad led by example and had more integrity than anyone I've known. He showed me how to treat people with respect, and always reminded me to be thankful to the Lord for all I had.

To my wife, Mary Jo Francis Banta Gohmann, who has been by my side for many of the stories in this book. I'm sure there were times when she just looked at me and shook her head in disbelief.

I'm happy to say that Mary Jo still loves me after 35 years of good times, and, through some rough times. She stuck with me through thick and thin. She painted the very fine picture used in the story, "Four Friends," and did an incredible job on the likenesses of her subject matter—she actually made us look good!

Thank you, Mary Jo. You are truly my best friend!

I also want to thank our incredible daughter, Joanna Marie. Joanna helped in clarifying some things in some of the stories. We are so proud of everything this amazing young lady has accomplished. Her mother and I couldn't have asked for a more perfect lady for our daughter.

I want to also thank Laura Ashton for the wonderful cover and interior she provided for this book, as well as for the great work she did on the editing. Laura is an incredible talent. I owe her for the nice book you are currently holding in your hands.

To my friend, Patrick "Pat" Naville—we worked together over 40 years ago and then, for only a year and a half, yet we formed a friendship that has remained strong to this day. It was Pat's own books that first got me interested in doing a book of my own. After he helped me on my first book, *Paving My Way Through Life*, I decided to do a second book—my short stories.

Pat made the telling of these short stories fun. He hung with me as I submitted my story ideas to him and always provided encouragement.

To my good friend, Kenny Rush. A story on Kenny is featured in this book, but I wanted to thank him again for his service in Vietnam and for risking his life. In all the years I've known Kenny, and worked side-by-side with him, he remained humbly quiet about his heroic actions during the war. It wasn't until fairly recently that I was made aware of his story.

I do believe that God has blessed me in life with a wonderful family, a successful career, a loving marriage, a beautiful daughter and an incredible grandson. I will always remain thankful for that blessing!

When the Almighty calls, I'll be ready, for life has been good to me.

Made in the USA
Columbia, SC
10 December 2019